Between
Freiburg
and
Frankfurt

For Robert, life-long friend

Omni tempore diligit amicus
et frater in angustiis . . .

Proverbs

Constant meeting and companionship are superfluous:
it is the union of hearts that sustains the bond of friendship.

Tirukkural

. . . einen Freund am Busen hält
und mit ihm geniesst,
was, von Menschen nicht gewusst
oder nicht bedacht,
durch das Labyrinth der Brust
wandelt in der Nacht.

Goethe

Between
Freiburg
and
Frankfurt

Toward a Critical Ontology

FRED DALLMAYR

The University of Massachusetts Press
Amherst

Copyright © 1991 by Fred Dallmayr
First published 1991 by Polity Press as *Life-world, Modernity
and Critique: Paths between Heidegger and the Frankfurt School*
First published in the United States in 1991 by the
University of Massachusetts Press
Box 429
Amherst, Ma 01004
Printed in Great Britain
ISBN 0–87023–764–0

Library of Congress Cataloging-in-Publication Data

Dallmayr, Fred R. (Fred Reinhard), 1928–
    [Life-world, modernity and critique]
    Between Freiburg and Frankfurt: toward a critical ontology / Fred
Dallmayr.
        p.   cm.
    British ed. published under title: Life-world, modernity and
critique.
    Includes bibliographical references and index.
    ISBN 0–87023–764–0
    1. Heidegger, Martin, 1889–1976.   2. Adorno, Theodor W.,
1903–1969.   3. Ontology.   4. Critical theory.   I. Title.
B3279.H49025   1991
142—dc20   91–15780
                                                      CIP

Printed on acid-free paper

Contents

Preface

There is a long way to go before I am where one begins . . .
                                                            Rilke

Authors, one says today, are not very relevant to the reading and
understanding of texts – which is plausible as far as it goes. This book
might also be read without considering its author, but at the risk of
missing its human engagement. What is academically, and perhaps
grandly, styled as the *agon* of "life-world and critique" (or "ontology
and critique") has been for me a matter of lived experience and
even prolonged agony. For the last two or three decades, that is,
throughout my professional life, I have been troubled or torn by
the tensional-transitional character of our time: its precarious location
between modernity – which is basically an age of "critique" (or critical reason) – and incipient modes of post-modernism centerstaging
language and (post-critical) ontology. A product of modern life, hence
afflicted with Cartesian doubt and Weberian disenchantment, I found
myself steadily challenged to question critical doubt and the lingering
peril of solipsism in favor of a renewed openness to worldliness or what
Merleau-Ponty called "perceptual faith." Looking back, this tension or
conflict has marked long stretches of my intellectual journey – although
for many years the struggle was mutely lived and did not, until recently,
yield to efforts at theoretical articulation. The present volume assembles glimpses of the journey, way stations along a complex, not always
well-demarcated road.

Although rooted in personal experience, the inquiries of this book (I
believe) are not purely idiosyncratic in character. Wittingly or unwittingly, members of my generation – and probably of the next few
generations – find themselves enmeshed in the transitional status of our
age and hence in the *agon* of ontology and critique, regardless of what

avenues are chosen to "resolve" the conflict. To this extent, the volume may claim to be representative or symptomatic for widely sensed and shared dilemmas. To be sure, not all facets of the book can aspire to be representative in this sense; some features, no doubt, derive also from contingencies of the author's life-story. As it happens, my own approach to ontology – as epitomized in Heidegger's opus – has been slow and halting. While always attracted to the phenomenological movement (anchored in the "Freiburg School"), my initial sympathies were with a non-ontological or "critical phenomenology" drawing its inspiration chiefly from a blending of French existentialism and Habermasian "critical theory." Only subsequently did the rationalist and Cartesian overtones of this blending sensitize me to a certain modernist bias; in the same measure, the "being-question" – bracketed by critical phenomenology – began to loom up on my horizon and to infiltrate my concerns. In light of contemporary discussions, I need to emphasize that what complicated or delayed my approach to Heidegger was chiefly his political reputation, resulting from his fascist leanings at the beginning of the Nazi regime. As an emigrant from Germany I consider fascism in any and all forms deeply unpalatable and offensive. Hence, what drew me to Heidegger, and what continues to draw me, are the non-ideological dimensions of his work – dimensions which include his ontology and his thoughts on language (and which, on my reading, elude fascism). Turning to ontology, in my case, did not in any event signify an abandonment of critique, but rather a reassessment of the latter's meaning and role. In large measure, this reassessment involved a move from Habermas's framework to the older generation of Frankfurt theorists: particularly to Adorno's "negative dialectics" with its openness to world and its "double gesture" of critique heralding a mediation of modern dilemmas.

The outlook animating these pages might be called "critical ontology" – which is only a slight amendment of a label I used previously: that of a practical (or transitive) ontology. Yet labels do not mean much in this context, and might actually be counter-productive if they impede attentive reading and exegesis. In any case, the meaning of the label emerges only from the discussion of the concrete issues arising at the intersection of ontology and critique or at the juncture of the Frankfurt and Freiburg Schools. These issues are examined, with a different focus each time, in the successive chapters or inquiries assembled in this volume. The reader, and especially the hurried reviewer, is advised to start with the Introduction to the book, which provides a kind of road map through the terrain or problem areas traversed in the various chapters; depending on interests or preferences, the reader may then select a point of entry and possibly follow a different route through the chapters than the one adopted in this study. Whatever route is chosen, the opening chapter on "Life-world and Critique" probably deserves attention early on, because of its broad scope and because of its attempt to articulate the general sense of a critical or critique-engendering ontology.

Needless to say, an intellectual journey is not an isolated or solitary venture. As on previous occasions, this is again the place to acknowledge debts, influences, and bonds of loyalty. In the present volume, the chief intellectual mentors are Heidegger and Adorno, the leading representatives of the two schools of thought interrogated in its pages. Alongside these primary figures, the study pays tribute repeatedly to Hans-Georg Gadamer and Merleau-Ponty (and, subsidiarily, to Nietzsche and Lacan). With some caveats, I might also invoke as mentor Jürgen Habermas. Although his framework is frequently taken to task in this book, I do not perceive my reservations as sign of a radical differentiation (or a *Differenz ums Ganze*); above all, the issues between us are emphatically not of a political but of a limited theoretical kind (although some people may not wish to grant me that distinction). Narrowing the gulf further, his militant rationalist stance has of late tended to mellow—as is evident, for example, in *Nachmetaphysisches Denken*, a work bypassed in the present study. Among professional colleagues and friends who have helped me along the way I should mention, without order of preference, William Connolly, James Glass, John O'Neill, Calvin Schrag, Bernhard Waldenfels, and Drucilla Cornell. A special debt of gratitude is due to Stephen White who, not long ago, undertook the labor of editing a volume dedicated to my (modest) endeavors and to which most of the mentioned colleagues graciously contributed an essay.

Professional contacts of this kind, of course, are secondary to and can only flourish on the background of closer personal relationships. It may seem trite but is none the less plainly true that this book could never have been undertaken and completed without the daily support of my wife Ilse who, for so many years now, has been a loyal companion—albeit a baffled one sometimes—of my intellectual peregrinations. During the time of the writing of the book, our children Dominique and Philip underwent the joys and tribulations of college life and began their own independent journeys. The book is dedicated to Robert Bernhardt, a friend whose unswerving loyalty has been and remains a cornerstone of my life. Since our childhood days in Augsburg, our friendship has continued and grown throughout the years: persisting through my emigration, through marriage and family life, entirely unaffected by geographical distance. Fortunate indeed is a person who is blessed with such a friendship. At a time when I was still innocent of philosophical vocabulary, Robert taught me experientially the sense of "ontological

Acknowledgments

Chapter 2 first appeared in *Diacritics*, vol. 19, fall/winter 1989. The original version of chapter 3 appeared in *Politics, Culture and Society*, vol. 2, no. 4, summer 1989 under the title 'Freud, Nietzsche, Lacan: A Discourse on Critical Theory'. Chapter 5 first appeared in *Political Theory*, vol. 16, 1988, pp. 553–79. Chapter 6 first appeared in *Praxis International*, vol. 7, no. 3/4, October 1987–January 1988.

Introduction

In both political and philosophical terms, our age is marked by profound rifts and unresolved, perhaps irresoluble, tensions. Politically, the traditional primacy or hegemony of Europe has been challenged first by the rise of superpowers and next, more importantly, by the emergence of continents and nations previously located at the periphery of world political events. Yet decentering or loss of hegemony is far from complete, as can be seen in the spread of European-style political institutions and ideologies – not to speak of Western technology – around the globe; in this sense, insurgency against traditional hegemony is curiously or paradoxically coupled with the growing Europeanization (or Westernization) of global life-forms. On the philosophical plane, rifts and dilemmas are no less pronounced. In this domain, the chief tensions are between traditional metaphysics and "post-metaphysics" or between European or Western modernity and "post-modernity." By traditional metaphysics I mean here a philosophical outlook anchored in the primacy of the *cogito* or the accomplishments of critical rationality and consciousness – accomplishments which form the backbone of modernity and cultural modernization. In our century, metaphysics of this kind has been challenged or called into question by several developments – particularly by the turn to language seen as the matrix of human reason and, more broadly, by renewed concerns with the situatedness of thought or its embeddedness in the "life-world." However, just as in the case of political center–periphery relations, philosophical insurgency has not yielded a simple exit from metaphysics – mainly because of the high stakes involved. To a large extent, critical reason or rationality is linked up with scientific and technological advances, while the primacy of the *cogito* gives sustenance to individual autonomy and moral responsibility. Wittingly or unwittingly, and whatever our preferences, all of us are caught up in dilemmas of this sort: in the agonism between reason and its submerged conditions, between individual freedom and its "worldly" context or ecology.

To the extent that modern reason is seen in Kantian terms and "worldliness" as an ontological or quasi-ontological concern, the intellectual dilemmas of our age can be highlighted or summarized under the labels of *"life-world and critique"* or "ontology and critique."[1] The present volume explores the constellation of these rubrics from a number of angles and in different topical settings; but it does not aim to be comprehensive – something precluded by the pervasiveness of the theme. Thus, to mention only some intellectual vistas, the fortunes (and misfortunes) of critical reason have been assessed in our century by neo-Kantianism, critical rationalism, and versions of the philosophy of science. On the other hand, the turn to language and worldliness is exemplified in the work of Wittgenstein and some of his followers as well as in new initiatives in semantic and semiotic analysis. To avoid excessive generality, a principle of selection had to be adopted – one which was dictated largely by the author's own background and formative experiences. For purposes of the present study, the terms ontology and critique are basically stand-ins for two prominent German schools of thought: namely, the "Freiburg School" inaugurated by Husserl and Martin Heidegger, and the "Frankfurt School" (or Institute of Social Research) founded by Horkheimer and Theodor Adorno. As regards the first school, the focus is placed chiefly on Heidegger's evolving opus – from his early project of a "fundamental ontology" to his later writings on language – and subsidiarily on some of Heidegger's students (like Gadamer) or broadly kindred phenomenologists (like Merleau-Ponty). In the case of the second school, attention is given to both the older and the younger generation of "critical theorists": mainly to Adorno's negative-dialectical formulation and to Habermas's rationalist-communicative program. Taken as a whole, the study probes the tensions operating between these prominent perspectives, thus seeking to steer a precarious path between Enlightenment and post-Enlightenment, critical autonomy and worldliness (or being-in-the-world).

The opening chapter delineates some of the major issues involved in the agonism of ontology and critique, as well as some avenues designed to mitigate or reconcile the conflict. The chapter takes its point of departure from one of the few instances in which the two schools of thought interacted in a serious manner: the debate between Habermas and Gadamer regarding the status and scope of hermeneutics. In this debate, Habermas resolutely took the side of critical rationality seen as part of the Enlightenment legacy; suspecting ontological arguments of complicity with pre-modern (or pre-critical) worldviews, his successive interventions strongly affirmed the autonomy of critical reason, that is, its possible aloofness from historical and cultural-interpretive contexts. On the other hand, taking his cues from Heideggerian insights, Gadamer stressed the "pre-understandings" undergirding critical inquiry and hence the historically and linguistically textured character of reason. In the estimate of most observers (myself included), the debate remained inconclusive and to some degree aporetic – mainly due to a certain unevenness of the respective positions. Thus, in vindicating Enlightenment rationalism, Habermas had to take refuge in part in quasi-objectivist structures and categories (like labor and domination), without showing the exemption of these categories from hermeneutical understanding. For his part, in extolling historicity, Gadamer did not always sufficiently differentiate the worldliness or concrete texture of reason from a compact traditionalism or the legacy of traditional metaphysics – options forestalled by Kantian and post-Kantian thought.

In an effort to move beyond the parameters of the debate, the chapter next outlines the contours of a critical ontology, bridging reason and world, as found in the work of both Heidegger and Adorno – a discussion which does not erase significant differences between the two thinkers. In seeking to revive the "question of being," Heidegger's *Being and Time* (*Sein und Zeit*) did not champion a substantive or objectifiable ontology but rather a mode of radical questioning unsettling received answers; to this extent, his "fundamental ontology" involved simultaneously a program of critical "deconstruction" (*Destruktion*) aimed at traditional philosophical doctrines and worldviews. This critical impulse was further buttressed by the being–nothingness nexus permanently jeopardizing established (ontic) arrangements as well as by the conception of language as medium of both the disclosure and concealment of meaning. While initially wedded to an Enlightenment project of critical-social praxis, Adorno subsequently came to favor a dual or double-barrelled critique: a critique addressed both at pre-modern worldviews and at the domineering thrust of modern rationalism (its bent toward instrumental control). This double gesture was reinforced in his later formulation of "negative dialectics," a formulation which acknowledged reason's teleology only in its absence or its absent presence in worldly finitude. Thus, in comparison with Heidegger's critique-engendering ontology, Adorno embraced a critical theory sensitive to ontological concerns, that is, to worldly otherness and "non-identity" as complements of reason.

The comparison between the two thinkers is pursued in greater detail in the following chapter. As its guidepost or Ariadne thread through their entangled works, the chapter chooses an instructive study published about a decade ago: Hermann Mörchen's *Adorno and Heidegger*, subtitled *Examination of a Refused Philosophical Communication*. A former student of Heidegger who lived for many decades in Frankfurt (and thus became closely acquainted with critical theorists), Mörchen was uniquely qualified to explore the complex differences, misunderstandings, and subterranean affinities operative between the two schools of thought, and especially between Adorno and Heidegger. Regarding differences or contrasts, the chapter discusses and compares respective life-styles or life-worlds: the divergence between rustic tranquillity and urban-industrial pace, between Heidegger's presumed "autochthony" and Adorno's cosmopolitan leanings – challenging the cogency of the alleged dichotomy. More pertinent are social-political tensions, where Adorno's Leftist position conflicts with Heidegger's (temporary) pro-Nazi stance and also with his later "apolitics" or aloofness from political affairs. On a philosophical plane, the most serious dispute concerns the meaning and status of ontology – with Adorno accusing Heidegger's perspective of complicity with pre-critical speculation or else with the "totalizing" ambitions of metaphysical systems. Closely connected with this accusation were the charges of naïve intuitionism, of the neglect of dialectics, and of a "cult of origins" bent on mystifying existing reality – points which are closely scrutinized and rebutted in the chapter (following Mörchen's lead).

In terms of submerged affinities, attention is given to the rootedness of the two thinkers in the dilemmas of late modernity, their joint departure (or turning away) from the metaphysics of subjectivity, their shared opposition to scientific objectivism and technological domination, and particularly their common turn to language seen as matrix of thought (irreducible to an instrument of communication). While Heidegger treated language as a site of ontological disclosure, Adorno referred to a "language of things" transcending subjective speech and the fetishizing jargon of contemporary culture. Summarizing the tangled agonism or tensional relationship, Mörchen acknowledges his teacher's relative distance from social-political concerns (an aloofness sometimes distending the nexus of being and time), while also questioning Adorno's incipient pessimism if not Manicheism, evident in his focus on the existing "wrong reality" (*falsche Welt*). What surfaces behind these conflicts, he surmises, are ultimately different modes of "reconciliation" or messianic hope: one in which this hope is incarnated in worldliness, and another in which it is infinitely delayed without in any way being abandoned.

In philosophical-historical terms, the last comments conjure up the legacy of Hegel – who has justly been desribed (by Gadamer and others) as the pre-eminent philosopher of reconciliation. The impact of that legacy on Freiburg and Frankfurt has been complex and varied. Heidegger's relation to Hegel has been deeply ambivalent, a mixture of approval and deconstruction. While applauding the focus on being and "absoluteness," Heidegger rejected the metaphysics of subjectivity, preferring to view spirit not as purposive teleology but as worldly ambiance in which human striving is "always already" enmeshed.[2] A similar ambivalence characterized the Frankfurt School. Starting from a Left-Hegelian concern with social praxis, the first generation of critical theorists cancelled the vision of a final synthesis (on the level of absolute ideas) – but without abandoning attachment to broad-scale reconciliation accomplished through dialectical "mediation" and determinate negation. Only the writings of the second generation heralded a definite eclipse of the Hegelian legacy, including its notion of reconciliation. The third chapter examines the story of that eclipse – with a critical edge in favor of the earlier conception.

The review begins with a discussion of some of Horkheimer's and Adorno's seminal works (especially *Eclipse of Reason* and *Dialectic of Enlightenment*) where the ascendancy of the modern *cogito* was held accountable for the progressive sway of instrumental reason and for the steadily deepening rifts between subject and object, man and nature. As an antidote to this trend, the authors invoked the reconciling power of Hegelian mediation, a power allowing ultimately a reciprocal "mirroring" of nature and spirit (or a "recollection of nature" in reason) – though without yielding final coincidence. In an emphatic manner, the same thrust was preserved in Adorno's *Negative Dialectics*. While shunning affirmative synthesis, the study upheld a chastised Hegelian outlook, by reinterpreting mediation (and determinate negation) in the sense of an openness of reason to its otherness or to the domain of non-identity. The chapter next traces the eclipse of Hegelian mediation in Habermas's evolving opus, by showing the progressive streamlining of reconciliation into communicative consensus, and of non-identity into rational-discursive categories. The chapter concludes by endorsing the non-orthodox Hegelianism of Horkheimer and Adorno (minus their incipient Manicheism). Reconciliation against this background means the insertion of human thought and action in the context of worldliness, and particularly in the matrix of a language capable of evoking or calling forth beings in the mode of (non-propositional) "naming."[3]

Unsurprisingly, the retreat of Hegelian impulses has been matched in recent critical theory by an upsurge or resurgence of Kantian motifs – although these motifs are recast under linguistic and communicative auspices. The fourth chapter, titled "Kant and Critical Theory", probes the changing fortunes of Kantian thought in the writings of Frankfurt theorists, with a main focus on recent developments. Kant's impact was evident already in the chosen label "critical theory," patterned on the former's critical philosophy. Both Horkheimer and Adorno were originally reared in a neo-Kantian framework – although the idealist notion of subjective constitution was quickly replaced in their work by a (loosely Marxist) stress on labor and social praxis. As previously indicated, the fascination with constitutive praxis subsequently succumbed to the indictment of instrumental mastery, making room for a broadly Hegelian concern with mediation involving the interplay of reason and otherness. In Habermas's work, by contrast, Hegel's thought was always subordinated to Kant whose teachings, over the years, steadily gained ascendancy over dialectics. His early treatise on *Knowledge and Human Interests* extolled Kant as the last great practitioner of critical epistemology, while denouncing Hegel and Marx for their epistemological deficiencies. Kant's influence was especially manifest in Habermas's formulation of a "universal pragmatics" of language and in his essays on cognitive and moral development (indebted to Kohlberg's neo-Kantianism). In recent years, the critical legacy has surfaced most prominently in the proposal of a "communicative" or "discursive" ethics guided by standards of an ideal speech community.[4]

Following Kantian preferences, discourse ethics is portrayed by Habermas as deontological (rather than ontological), cognitivist (rather than skeptical), formal (instead of material), and universalist (instead of particularist); in line with the "linguistic turn" of contemporary philosophy, Kant's categorical imperative is transcribed into a maxim (or maxims) which could obtain the consent of all participants in a properly organized discourse or communicative exchange. In fleshing out this program, Habermas has specifically asserted the primacy of Kant over Hegel, by seeking to rebut attacks leveled at Kantian morality from the vantage of Hegelian *Sittlichkeit*. Traditionally, these attacks have stressed four points: the empty formalism of moral maxims; their aloofness from concrete settings or problem contexts; the distance of theory from practical implementation; and the danger of puritanical coercion. The chapter discusses Habermas's defense of discourse ethics against these charges – finding his rejoinders largely problematical or unpersuasive. The conclusion of the chapter returns to the older Frankfurt School, particularly to *Negative Dialectics*, paying attention both to Adorno's critique of Kantian "noumenalism" and to his effort to formulate an unorthodox version of *Sittlichkeit* premised on the mediation of man and nature, reason and sensibility. From the latter perspective, ethics cannot simply be deontological but must involve care for human happiness or the "good life" – which in our time means chiefly avoidance of suffering and unhappiness.

Moving beyond the confines of discourse ethics, the fifth chapter scrutinizes in greater detail the quasi-Kantian and formalist features of

Habermas's communicative rationalism. The accent of the chapter is placed on Habermas's *magnum opus*, *The Theory of Communicative Action*, and particularly on the notion of reason or rationality operative in that work. As presented in the study, reason has basically an epistemic or epistemological status by being related to knowledge or validity claims; manifesting this cognitive status, rational arguments typically are couched in propositional form and are amenable to argumentative validation or disconfirmation. According to Habermas, validation procedures apply not only to empirical data (located in the external or "objective world"), but extend to moral or "norm-regulated" behavior and even to "expressive self-presentations" (in the "social" and "subjective" worlds, respectively). What his study calls "communicative rationality" is in essence a mode of argumentation encompassing the broad spectrum of validity claims – in contrast to "instrumental rationality" narrowly tailored to control of nature. As one should note, however, rationality in every instance pertains to the form or procedure of argumentation, as distinguished from the particular content (factual, normative, or expressive) of a given assertion. Broadly in line with Kantian teachings, the focus is placed on the formal-rational "conditions of possibility" rather than *a posteriori* modes of experience; in fact, philosophy itself is defined as a "metatheory" designed to analyze the "formal conditions" of cognition and behavior.

With this focus, rationality in the Habermasian sense gets embroiled in traditional Kantian dilemmas: the dilemmas of how to account "philosophically" for the nexus of form and content and for the relation between different modes of "critique" or different spheres of validity claims. Habermas's turn to language camouflages rather than resolves these problems; for the question remains whether the (formal) conditions of rationality antedate linguistic articulation or are themselves dependent on language and communication. A brief excursus in the chapter glances at an essay specifically dealing with the role of "philosophy" in our age (and dating roughly from the same time as the *magnum opus*). While distancing himself from Kantian "foundational" ambitions regarding *prima philosophia*, Habermas assigns to philosophy the dual roles of a "stand-in" or "place-keeper" for specialized cognitive inquiries and also of a mediating "interpreter" of validity spheres – two roles which are in open conflict since hermeneutical (language-dependent) mediation is irreducible to the analysis of formal conditions reserved for a "place-keeper." In an effort to move beyond formal rationality, the conclusion of the chapter alludes to substantive-experiential modes of reasoning as found in Adorno's turn to "*mimesis*" and non-identity and particularly in Merleau-Ponty's stress on "embodied" or "incarnate" reflection, that is, a thought closely intertwined with worldliness and language.[5]

Embodied reflection of this kind bears close affinity with Heidegger's notion of "recollective" or "commemorative" thinking (*Andenken*), a recollection attentive to the ontological matrix or world-context of human life. As mentioned before, attention to this world-context is the distinctive hallmark of Heidegger's opus in all its multiple dimensions – including the dimension of politics. As it happens, the latter domain is easily the most controverted and hotly debated aspect of his work; for many observers, in fact, this is the domain in which Heidegger's thought floundered or came radically to grief by abetting a pernicious political ideology and regime. Without excusing his blunder in 1933 or trying to belittle the gravity of his mistakes, I sense the need for a more nuanced assessment; the accent on ideology, in any case, seems to me lopsided and capable of telling at most half of the story. In another context I have attempted to probe Heidegger's work for its possible contributions to a (recollective) "rethinking of the political," in contradistinction from his embroilment in ideological partisanship. This attempt relied on the distinction – found in recent European and American literature – between "politics" seen as partisan-ideological policy-making and "the political" viewed as paradigmatic framework or ontological matrix (a distinction which, to be sure, must not be misconstrued as a rigid dichotomy). My thesis was, and continues to be, that Heidegger's promising teachings are found basically on the level of ontological framework, the level touching the very notion or meaning of political life.[6]

To some extent, the distinction between politics and the political, between ideological partisanship and ontological matrix, can also be transferred to the arena of Marxism (and its neo-Marxist offshoots). Implicitly or explicitly, Frankfurt theorists have always adhered to such a distinction – by severely criticizing existing communist or socialist regimes while, at the same time, freely reformulating the metaphysical parameters of Marx's teachings. While considerably more distant from Marxism and its practical political manifestations, Heidegger's work likewise contains strands pertinent to a metaphysical or rather postmetaphysical reading of Marx's legacy. Rather than discussing his overt statements on Marxism, the sixth chapter examines recessed clues for such a reading, concentrating for this purpose on four themes or topical strands: the status and meaning of "dialectical materialism" (often used as a synonym for Marxism in socialist countries); second, the role of "labor" and "production" as central determinants of social life-forms; third, the relationship between "base" and "superstructure" (especially the presumed derivation of the latter from the former); and lastly, the thesis of the "withering away" of the State and of class domination in favor of an impending "reign of freedom."

In the first domain, primary attention is given to the notion of "materialism" seen as a metaphysics grounded on matter or thingly objects (*res extensa*). As is well known, a crucial ingredient of Heidegger's opus is his endeavor to rethink the character of objects or thinghood. Instead of relying on empiricist epistemology or traditional form–matter (or mind–matter) dualisms, his writings portray thinghood as the site of an ontological "gathering," more specifically as occasion for the fourfold intersection of world-elements (termed *"Geviert"*). Allied with the rethinking of matter is the reassessment of "dialectics" – in the direction of an ontological intertwining in lieu of a logical-conceptual schema. Regarding labor and production, Heidegger's work resolutely shifts the accent from instrumental fabrication to a broader ontological type of agency or praxis – in his terms, to a praxis devoted to the aim of "bringing forth" or "putting to work" the disclosure of being. The aspect of intertwining surfaces again in the third domain where causal dependence (of superstructure on base) gives way to modes of agonal interplay or contest – such as the contest between "world" and "earth" or between "existence" and "ground." The Marxist goal-point of the "reign of freedom," finally, is recast not as simple termination of power (or the political) but as the unleashing of an enabling potency making room for difference and reciprocal "letting be."

The concluding chapters of the volume shift attention from the relation of human praxis and world (or worldliness) to the dimension of "inner" nature, in an effort to probe the connection between psychic dispositions and world (and specifically between *psyche* and *polis*). The focus of the inquiry is on Freudian psychoanalysis, particularly on the role of psychoanalysis in the confines of the Frankfurt and Freiburg Schools. The seventh chapter deals with the changing assessments of Freud's legacy by a succession of critical theorists, from Adorno and Marcuse to Habermas. Basically, the older generation of Frankfurt theorists clung to an orthodox Freudianism centered on the libidinal "id" or unconscious, finding (or hoping to find) in libidinal drives a counterpoint to growing societal constraints in late capitalism. Despite his concern with mediation, Adorno tended to construe the relation between libido and social rules (or inner nature and reason) in a strongly conflictual, if not antinomial vein. Adhering to the same Freudian model, Marcuse sought to resolve or mitigate this conflict by subjecting society to the sway of libidinal regeneration. Countering this instinctual paradigm, Habermas opted to give primacy to social norms or normatively regulated relations (in Freud's terms: to "ego" and "superego" components) – and finally to abandon Freud's legacy in favor of cognitive psychology. In an effort to

overcome the opposition of libido and norms, the chapter next turns to
the perspective of Jacques Lacan whose linguistic reinterpretation of Freudian theory undercuts both the privatization of the unconscious and the
streamlining effects of communicative rationality. Most importantly,
bypassing dualism as well as coincidence, Lacan's correlation of the
"Imaginary" and the "Symbolic" points in the direction of a complex
intertwining of nature and culture, psyche and society – in a manner akin
to Nietzsche's entwining of Dionysos and Apollo in *The Birth of Tragedy*
(a work given a psychoanalytic reading at this point.)

While greatly enriching Freudian theory, Lacan's outlook is marred (in
my view) not only by excessive obscurity but also by a lingering semiotic
nominalism which truncates his linguistic approach. The closing chapter
turns to Heidegger's views on psychoanalysis and psychotherapy – views
which reverberate distantly in Lacan's writings. The emphasis of the
chapter is on the so-called *Zollikon Seminars*, a publication recording
Heidegger's extensive interaction with a group of psychiatrists in and near
Zurich. As these seminars and discussions show, Heidegger was familiar
with Freudian theory, but objected strenuously to its indebtedness to
modern metaphysics with its bifurcation of inner and outer worlds, of
res cogitans and *res extensa*. Freud's notion of libido or the unconscious,
according to Heidegger, was actually an extension of natural science
canons to psychic life, by seeking to explain behavior causally via libidinal
impulses. The same scientific bias was operative in Freud's theoretical
formulations of repression, interjection, transference, and related processes. In rejecting libidinal causation, Heidegger was far removed from
embracing the alternative of ego or superego psychology (and even the
subjective-existentialist psychology promoted by Binswanger). Faithful
to the general direction of his work, he sought an exit from the consciousness–unconsciousness dichotomy, replacing the latter with the
more intimate entwining of reason and nature, revealment and concealment, presence and absence. In line with this theoretical shift, psychotherapy meant neither social adjustment nor instinctual euphoria but the
curing of a "lack" or "privation" – a cure restoring *Dasein*'s ontological
relation to world (and fellow beings). Drawing on expert testimony, the
chapter ponders the compatibility or incompatibility of Freudianism and
Heidegger's ontology – finding some helpful hints in William Richardson's invocation of Lacan's mediating role. Bridge-building of this kind,
perhaps on a philosophically more solid plane, was also the goal of one
of Merleau-Ponty's last writings which suggested a treatment of "nature"
not along physicalist lines but in terms of an unfolding potency – a view
restoring to the human body its "oneiric and poetic" quality.[7]

The volume does not end with a chapter offering final or definitive "conclusions" – which is entirely in keeping with its central theme. Given the tensional relation of ontology and critique, of worldliness and reason, the study cannot terminate in conceptual synthesis without jeopardizing the experiential and intellectual *agon* undergirding its inquiries. As it seems to me, the issues pending between Frankfurt and Freiburg are by no means settled and perhaps not amenable to settlement or resolution – at least at a time when the contest between modernity and post-modernity, metaphysics and post-metaphysics still hangs in the balance. In this situation, the wish for solutions must be jettisoned, in favor of a readiness to "undergo" the dilemmas of our age in a reflective manner. It is for this reason that the volume offers only some paths through complex and frequently uncharted terrain. These paths do not coalesce into a solid highway yielding a panoramic overview of the land-scape. The successive chapters in this volume provide only partial or fragmentary vistas: by exploring such topics as critical ontology, the legacies of Hegel and Kant, the respective merits of deontological and substantive ethics, the meaning of reason, the political implications of ontology (or the "ontic–ontological difference"), and finally the status of psychoanalysis as seen from the vantage of both Frankfurt and Freiburg. Other topics might have been added; but no collection of themes could be exhaustive. Jointly the chapters should at least convey a strong sense of what is at stake at the juncture of ontology and critique. Without granting the comfort of a safe abode, they mean to erect some guideposts or roadmarkers for the traveler willing to remain underway.

NOTES

1 For a discussion of "life-world" – and its changing status from Husserl over Heidegger to Derrida – see my "Life-World: Variations on a Theme", in Stephen K. White, ed., *Life-World and Politics: Between Modernity and Postmodernity; Essays in Honor of Fred Dallmayr* (Notre Dame: University of Notre Dame Press, 1989), pp. 25–65. As one should note, "ontology" in the present study does not designate a metaphysical doctrine, but only alludes to the worldliness or world-context of human thought and action.
2 For an instructive comparison of Heidegger and Hegel see Dennis J. Schmidt, *The Ubiquity of the Finite: Hegel, Heidegger and the Entitlements of Philosophy* (Cambridge, MA: MIT Press, 1988).
3 On "naming" and the importance of proper names see Walter Benjamin, "On the Mimetic Faculty", in *Reflections: Essays, Aphorisms, Autobiographical Writings*, ed. Peter Demetz, tr. Edmund Jephcott (New York: Schocken, 1978), pp. 333–6; and Emmanuel Levinas, *Noms propres* (Montpellier: Fata Morgans, 1976). The significance of names, incidentally, is not peculiar to

Western thought or the Judaeo-Christian heritage. As Nishitani writes with regard to Buddhist teachings: "In Buddhism, the name of Amida is taken to be the sign of the fulfillment of the Buddha's vow of compassion, and indeed is itself the name for the unity of the Buddha and all things." He also quotes this passage from a text of Pure Land Buddhism: "Without the practicing devotee who opens his heart to faith in the Name, Amida Buddha's vow to save all and forsake none would not be fulfilled." See Keiji Nishitani, *Religion and Nothingness*, tr. Jan Van Bragt (Berkeley: University of California Press, 1982), pp. 26–7.

4   For a broader discussion of this ethics see Seyla Benhabib and Fred Dallmayr, eds, *The Communicative Ethics Controversy* (Cambridge, MA: MIT Press, 1990).

5   To some extent, the chapter might also have turned at this point to hermeneutics, especially as outlined in the concluding part of Gadamer's *magnum opus*. See Hans-Georg Gadamer, *Truth and Method*, 2nd rev. edn, tr. and rev. Joel Weinsheimer and Donald G. Marshall (New York: Crossroad, 1989), pp. 381–491 (Part III). Compare also Jean Greisch, *L'Age herméneutique de la raison* (Paris: Editions du Cerf, 1985).

6   See my "Rethinking the Political; Some Heideggerian Contributions", *Review of Politics*, vol. 52 (1990).

7   In Rilke's words: "Poetic power is great, strong as a primitive instinct; it has its own unyielding rhythms in itself and breaks out as out of mountains." He also speaks of the prospect that sensual-bodily experience might some day be "lifted up into the god," into the protection of "a phallic deity who will perhaps have to be the *first* with which a troop of gods will again invade humanity, after so long an absence." See *Rilke on Love and Other Difficulties*, ed. and tr. John J. L. Mood (New York: Norton, 1975), pp. 36–7.

1

Life-world and Critique

The status and meaning of knowledge have fluctuated throughout history. Modernity has tended to underscore the limits and circumscribed functions of reason, in comparison with the broader latitude granted to knowledge in earlier periods. In classical and medieval times – or so it appears in retrospect – mind or reason was closely meshed with the universe, in a fashion allowing "ontological" knowledge of the world to emerge; critical self-reflection progressively undermined this confidence. Following the teachings of Descartes and Locke, and cancelling the classical correlation, knowledge was increasingly ascribed to "inner" faculties of reason or else to the lessons of sensory experience. With Kant's "Copernican Revolution," mind was entirely severed from nature and the cosmic order, with the result that cognition was now firmly rooted in the constructive or knowledge-constitutive capacities of rational consciousness. In the wake of the Kantian revolution, critique or critical analysis gained primacy in the domain of knowledge, while contemplative or "metaphysical" ontology was devalued to a pre-modern or pre-critical legacy. Since this legacy was closely tied up with many cultural and political traditions, critique inevitably became the antipode of tradition-bound beliefs and institutions; Kant's motto *sapere aude*, in fact, installed reason as the nemesis of historical customs and as pacemaker of modernization–a process which was only partially eclipsed by the later upsurge of scientific positivism. What rendered the eclipse partial was the rootedness of modern science itself in critical reason – a fact of which scientists were eloquently reminded by a number of philosophers, including Edmund Husserl.[1]

In our own century, the status of reason and knowledge was reassessed – against a backdrop which dramatically raised the stakes at issue. While modernity (in the Western sense) steadily moved to encircle the globe, modernization seen as linear progress became increasingly suspect or

dubious; in the same measure as science and technology reaped unprecedented triumphs, their benefits were found to be matched with unparal-
leled dangers. The reassessement was most acute in the humanities and
philosophy. While Freud uncovered the unconscious or preconscious
underpinnings of rational awareness, anthropologists and archae-
ologists probed the mythical and magical precursors of modern forms of
knowledge. On the philosophical plane, the primacy accorded to reason
and consciousness in modernity was progressively challenged in favor of
a contextualized and genealogical grasp of these premises; accordingly,
critical cognition gave way to a renewed ontological inquiry into the
meaning of "being" and the "world" – as exemplified in Heidegger's
turn to a "fundamental ontology." Ontological reflection was seconded
and reinforced by the upsurge of language in the thinking of our time,
an upsurge jeopardizing the "purity" of reason or the *a priori* character
of rational categories; closely intermeshed with diverse cultural settings,
language came to eclipse modern "subjectivity" in favor of complex conversational practices, historical narratives and, more generally, a renewed
esteem for tradition. Taken together, these developments signaled a shift
of attention from rational autonomy to the "life-world" or the "worldly"
underpinnings of critical reason as such. Small wonder that these changes
should have been greeted with alarm by defenders of modernity. The
turn to ontology – especially when coupled with a revalorization of
tradition – was perceived as an abandonment of rational critique and its
"emancipatory" potential, while the contextualization of meanings was
seen as a threat to individual autonomy and moral responsibility –
central postulates of the modern age.[2]

    In my own view, these dangers – while far from negligible – derive
mainly from a misconstrual of contemporary intellectual trends. Neither
reflection on "being" nor the upsurge of language, I believe, are meant
to herald a return to cosmic worldviews or to a "pre-critical" mode of
philosophy. In large measure, this move is blocked by the stress placed
by ontological (especially Heideggerian) thought on the "finitude" of
human *Dasein* or existence and thus on the limitations of reason or
rational cognition.[3] Cancelling these limitations, in our time, would
imply the possibility of erecting "being" and "world" into targets of
cognitive analysis – an assumption which inevitably entails their reification or objectification. Seen from a post-Kantian vantage, cosmic worldviews of the past appear not so much as outgrowth of rational knowledge but as products of "poetic wisdom" (in Vico's sense) – although a
wisdom not devoid of some rational insights. Contemporary ontological
reflection continues or recaptures this wisdom, but without cosmic-
metaphysical pretensions. In a post-Kantian or post-critical setting,

ontology can mean only the recollection of "always already" operative contexts or horizons of thought – contexts which are unavailable to direct inspection and which thus are recollected precisely in their unavailability and partial "absence" (or absent presence). In its unavailable absence, recollected being is not simply a nothingness or vacuum but rather itself a source of ferment and critique – namely, a critique of all positive-objective thought systems as well as social-political institutions. In the following I intend to explore the dilemmas and ambiguities besetting the contemporary relation between ontology and critique, by concentrating chiefly on "Freiburg" and "Frankfurt," that is, on Heideggerian philosophy (and its offshoots) and critical social theory. In a first step, I shall briefly review the well-known and instructive dispute between Habermas and Gadamer, the former acting as defender of critical rationality and the latter treated as spokesman of tradition. A second step shall turn from Gadamerian hermeneutics to Heidegger's evolving opus, in an effort to show the intimate linkage in that opus of (non-objectivist) ontology and critique. A concluding section shall trace incipient contours of a critical ontology in the early Frankfurt School, chiefly as reflected in Adorno's simultaneous endorsement of critical reason and of the need to breach reason's self-confinement in the direction of "non-identity."

I

The issues surrounding ontology and critique are often alluded to in contemporary literature, but commonly in an offhand fashion; only rarely have these issues figured as the central topic of sustained discussion or debate. Roughly two decades ago, such a debate actually took place between two prominent spokesmen of Continental thought: namely, between Heidegger's foremost student and associate, Hans-Georg Gadamer, and the leading younger representative of the Frankfurt School, Jürgen Habermas. In the course of this debate or rather series of exchanges, the basic problems or dilemmas besetting the topic were highlighted with unusual eloquence and poignancy – although the outcome can hardly be described as yielding a conclusive settlement of these problems. In large measure, the inconclusiveness of the outcome can be traced to a certain unevenness of the respective arguments. Taking the side of Enlightenment rationalism, and equating ontology with pre-critical metaphysics, Habermas resolutely vindicated the autonomy of critical reason – but at the price of having to take refuge occasionally in extra-linguistic and quasi-objectivist structures and categories. For his part, in articulating a "philosophical" or ontological hermeneutics, Gadamer was perhaps not always careful enough to screen ontology from earlier metaphysics and, more generally, to differentiate the "worldly" entanglements of reason from the solid pathways of tradition – pathways rendered fragile or dubious by post-Kantian thought. For present purposes I can only pinpoint or lift up certain crucial strands in this confrontation and in the sequence of critical rejoinders.[4]

Before entering the debate propoer, some comments seem advisable regarding the general background leading up to the exchange. As is well known, Gadamer's major work is *Truth and Method*, a volume which first appeared in 1960 (and later was revised in successive editions). In articulating a philosophical or ontological hermeneutics, *Truth and Method* vastly went beyond previous conceptions of hermeneutics as a mode of intellectual empathy or else as a narrow methodology for the "mental sciences" (*Geisteswissenschaften*). As Gadamer acknowledged, this innovative step was basically due to Heidegger's *Being and Time* (*Sein und Zeit*) in which "understanding" or interpreting had been grasped as a constitutive or ontological characteristic human *Dasein* seen as "being-in-the-world." "How is understanding possible?" Gadamer's Preface (to the second edition of 1965) asked, and continued:

> This is a question which antedates or precedes any interpretive act on the part of subjectivity, and also any methodical inquiry of the "interpretive sciences" with their norms and rules. Heidegger's temporal analytics of *Dasein* has, I believe, shown convincingly that understanding is not just one of the possible behaviors of a subject but rather the mode of being of *Dasein* itself. It is in this sense that the term "hermeneutics" is used here.[5]

The departure from earlier forms of hermeneutics was underscored and further elaborated in the body of the volume, particularly with reference to Dilthey's notion of empathy and Husserl's focus on intentionality. In the wake of *Being and Time*, we read there, "understanding is no longer, as with Dilthey, a resigned ideal of life-experience in the twilight years of spirit; nor is it, as with Husserl, a last methodological standard of philosophy vis-à-vis the naiveté of unreflective life; rather, it is the original operative mode of *Dasein* which is being-in-the-world" characterized by its "potentiality for being [*Seinkönnen*]." In inaugurating this change, Gadamer added, *Being and Time* broke decisively with traditional metaphysics and its speculative type of foundationalism: "Heidegger's thesis was that being itself is time. This notion burst asunder the whole subjectivism of modern philosophy – and in fact, as was soon to become evident, the whole horizon of questions asked by metaphysics, which tended to define being as what is present."[6]

Pursuing the temporal thrust of Heidegger's ontology, *Truth and Method* underscored the temporality of hermeneutics itself, in the sense that hermeneutical understanding is deeply embroiled in ongoing historical experience rather than being merely the distant witness or spectator of historical events. This insight stood at the heart of Gadamer's notion of "effective history" (*Wirkungsgeschichte*) which served as a leitmotiv throughout the volume.

> It is the thesis of my book that the element of effective history affects all understanding of tradition, even where (under the auspices of the methodology of modern historical science) everything historically grown or historically transmitted is turned into an "object" of analysis to be "determined" like an experimental finding – as if tradition were as alien and as unintelligible from a human vantage as an object of physics.[7]

In conformity with this thesis, the study turned against the modern divorce of reason from tradition and, more generally, against the Enlightenment "prejudice against prejudice" (or against historically grown prejudgments). Hermeneutical inquiry, we are told, cannot place itself "in a stark antithesis to the way in which we, as historical beings, relate to the past." The prominent issue in our relation to the past, in any case, is "not distancing and emancipation from tradition"; rather, we are "always situated in traditions – and this not in an objectifying manner which would present tradition as something other or alien." Accordingly, *Truth and Method* stipulated as starting point of hermeneutics, especially historical hermeneutics, the "cancelling of the abstract opposition between tradition and historical science, between history and the knowledge of it," and ultimately between tradition and rational critique. As Gadamer emphasized, asserting the temporality of hermeneutical understanding was not synonymous with endorsing an overall historical teleology in line with Hegelian "spiritualism" – mainly because the latter presupposes a superior standpoint beyond history, in violation of hermeneutical premises: "Understanding must be thought of not so much as an act of (transcendental) subjectivity, but rather as immersion and participation in the event of tradition where past and present are constantly mediated." Immersion in tradition, for Gadamer, was closely linked with the embeddedness of understanding in language – an insertion which again signals a concrete embroilment rather than a road to semantic transparency: "The phrase 'being that can be understood is language' must be taken in this sense. It does not herald the absolute mastery of intelligibility over being, but denotes on the contrary that being cannot be experienced as something produced or fabricated (and hence understood) by us but rather as a happening (accompanied by understanding)."[8]

Given the pervasiveness of language and tradition, Gadamer was led to champion the "universality" or universal status of hermeneutics – where "universal" does not imply an Archimedean vista but rather the embracive scope of the historical nexus: "It is not due to caprice or a one-sided over-accentuation of its role, but rather accords with its very nature if the movement of understanding is seen as comprehensive and universal." This claim was taken up and further developed a few years after *Truth and Method* in an essay specifically devoted to "The Universality of the Hermeneutical Problem" (1966). As the essay observed, hermeneutics has to do with human "world experience" (*Welterfahrung*) in its full breadth – where "world" denotes a context which is "always already" interpreted and organized and into which experience enters "as something new upsetting our expectations." Since interpreting and reinterpreting the world revolves around semantic meaning, world experience was said to be intimately tied up with language in a broad sense. "The claim to universality proper to hermeneutics means this," the essay stated: "understanding is language-bound" or closely enmeshed in linguistic contexts. Language at this point was not equivalent to an abstract "system of signals" or an anonymous rule structure amenable to computerization, but rather denoted a lived context or an experiential mode of being-in-the-world nurtured by historically grown judgments and prejudgments. As Gadamer added, however, contextualism of this kind did not entail or vindicate a "linguistic relativism" – because there "cannot be enclosure or captivity in a language, not even in one's mother tongue. This we all experience when we learn a foreign language and especially on journeys insofar as we somehow master a foreign idiom." To this extent, every living language had to be viewed as unlimited or "infinite" (that is, as a gateway to the universal), and it was "entirely erroneous" to infer from the diversity of languages a necessary fragmentation of understanding. "The opposite is true," the essay concluded: "Precisely the experience of the finitude and particularity of our being – a finitude manifest in the diversity of languages – opens the road to infinite dialogue in the direction of ontological truth" (or the truth "that we are").[9]

Shortly after publication of this essay, Habermas fired the opening salvo in the ensuing debate in the course of an extensive review critically assessing Gadamer's *Truth and Method*. A central target of the attack was the universality claim of Gadamerian hermeneutics – a claim which Habermas considered spurious or overextended in light of competing modes of cognition dealing with non-semantic or extra-linguistic reality domains. Closely tied up with this target was Gadamer's notion of "ontological truth," and particularly his privileging of such truth over "method" or scientific methodology – a privileging incompatible with the tasks and ambitions of modern science, including the human and social sciences. As it happens, at the time of writing this review, Habermas was in the process of composing his path-breaking epistemological study, titled *Knowledge and Human Interests*, a study which assigned to hermeneutics or interpretive understanding a prominent, but by no means a comprehensive or universal role. Following loosely in the footsteps of Kant's three *Critiques*, the study outlined a three-tiered or tripartite model of epistemology or human knowledge, a model differentiating between empirical science, hermeneutics and critical self-reflection and further anchoring these knowledge types in underlying motivations or "cognitive interests" (namely, the technical interest in control, the practical interest in understanding, and the "emancipatory" interest in self-realization). Only a recognition and correlation of all three types of cognition, the study asserted, could furnish the basis for a truly comprehensive or universal theory of knowledge. In abbreviated form, this epistemological scheme was already sketched in Habermas's inaugural lecture presented in Frankfurt under the same title (1965). "There are three categories of inquiry," the lecture stated, "for which a specific connection between logical-methodological rules and cognitive interests can be demonstrated": namely, empirical-analytical sciences, historical-hermeneutical sciences, and "critically oriented sciences" (concerned with self-knowledge and ideology critique). While the first type was geared toward "expanding our power of technical control," and while the second seeks to facilitate "action-orientation in the context of shared traditions," the last type pursued the goal of "freeing consciousness from its dependence on hypostatized powers." Ultimately, the three modes were said to originate "in the interest structure of a species which is tied essentially to distinct means of socialization: work, language, and power" (where work and power appeared as non- or extra-linguistic categories).[10]

Returning to the review of *Truth and Method*, Habermas considered Gadamer's approach valuable in the context of tradition-bound texts and actions, but of little or no help in the analysis of empirical data and even less in the generation of critical knowledge. Regarding empirical inquiry, Gadamer's downgrading of "method" in favor of truth-disclosure was found to be harmful not only to the natural sciences but to the social sciences as well. As Habermas affirmed, reservations raised by hermeneutics against a narrowly construed empiricism or positivism could not possibly "bring dispensation from the business of methodology as such"; even if some of the humanities might be so exempted, the social sciences (or "sciences of action" in Weber's sense) could not avoid supplementing understanding with "empirical-analytic" and thus rigorously methodological procedures. In terms of the review, what linked scientific methodology with critical-emancipatory knowledge was the distancing operative in both cases, that is, their critical removal from taken-for-granted beliefs or traditions. According to Habermas, this distancing had to be seen as a crucial corollary of the liberating aims of modern rationalism or rational critique, aims extolled by Enlightenment thinkers and celebrated in German classical philosophy. Challenging the "rehabilitation of prejudice" propounded in *Truth and Method*, the review suspected Gadamer's work of harboring a latent "conservatism" or traditionalism deeply at odds with emancipatory goals: "Gadamer's prejudice for the role of prejudices certified by tradition denies the potency of reflection, a potency which proves itself in its ability also to reject the claims of tradition." Vindicating the emancipatory thrust of critical reason, the review insisted on a self-restriction of hermeneutics and the formulation of a "reference system" exceeding the confines of tradition-bound actions and texts. Appealing to his own epistemological inquiries, Habermas at this point invoked the tripartite scheme of knowledge in which understanding occupied only a limited position. Contrary to strictly interpretive approaches, he affirmed, "the objective framework of social action is not exhausted by the dimension of intersubjectively intended and symbolically transmitted meaning . . . Social action can only be comprehended in an objective framework that is constituted *jointly by language, labor, and power* (or domination)."[11]

Habermas's review almost instantly elicited Gadamer's spirited response, in the form of a broad-ranging essay seeking to disentangle the relations between "Rhetoric, Hermeneutics, and Ideology-Critique." Tracing the development of the former back to its Aristotelian origins, Gadamer emphasized the interlocking "ubiquity" or universalism of rhetoric and hermeneutical understanding – an ubiquity deriving from their joint rootedness in ordinary, everyday discourse and common-sense experience. This common matrix also was said to elucidate the relevance of hermeneutics for social inquiry (including the endeavor of "ideology critique"). While welcoming and applauding Habermas's incorporation of hermeneutics into the "logic" of the social sciences, Gadamer objected to the narrow concentration on methodology. "The merit of Habermas's penetrating analysis," he wrote, "was to have shown the contribution of hermeneutics to social inquiry," particularly on the methodological plane; however, he added, the significance of hermeneutical reflection "is not exhausted by its role or usefulness in scientific research." Given its moorings in ordinary discourse and experience, hermeneutics for

Gadamer also was able to uncover the latent premises and "guiding pre-understandings" operative in scientific inquiry; in addition, hermeneutical reflection could serve as a touchstone or measuring rod indicating "the price paid by scientific methodology for its own progress" – that is, the multiple types of "bracketing and abstraction" required by this progress to the detriment of ordinary understanding. Most important from Gadamer's perspective was the mediating role performed by hermeneutics and particularly by "effective historical consciousness": the mediation between common-sense beliefs and distantiated reflection, between trans-mitted traditions and their rational critique or assessment. "My thesis here is (and I think it follows necessarily from recognizing the effective-ness of history in our situated finitude)," he stated, "that the thing which hermeneutics teaches us is to perceive as dogmatic and untenable the opposition or separation between ongoing, 'natural' traditions and their reflective appropriation." To accept this opposition meant to objectify historical traditions – and hence to treat reason as an agency of reifica-tion; yet, even in scientific inquiry, the researcher was not extricated from all contexts to the degree that "understanding no longer parti-cipated in history." The demonstration of the continuous mediation of tradition and reflection could be found in ordinary language or the "domain of linguisticality [*Sprachlichkeit*] which carries and sustains all understanding."[12]

Regarding the segregation of language and hermeneutical understand-ing from power and labor (seen as extra-linguistic spheres), Gadamer challenged the artificiality and basic elusiveness of the stipulated bound-ary. "The universality of the hermeneutical dimension is truncated," he asserted, "if a domain of understandable meaning (such as a 'cultural tradition') is demarcated against other determinants of social reality treated as 'real factors' [*Realfaktoren*]." Actually, the focus of ontological hermeneutics on common-sense experience and pre-judgments militated against its restriction to a sphere of clear or transparently intelligible meanings. From a hermeneutical vantage it was in fact "entirely absurd to regard the 'real factors' of labor and domination as lying outside the scope of hermeneutics"; for "what are the prejudices or pre-judgments with which hermeneutical reflection deals" and "where else are they sup-posed to originate?" The statement "being that can be understood is language," according to Gadamer, had to be read in an ontological rather than an idealist or rationalist sense. In the end, he noted, language is "not simply a transparent mirror" and what we perceive in it is "not merely a reflection" of ourselves but rather "the interpretation and instantiation of our way of being, in our concrete dependency on labor and domination as well as in all other spheres comprising our world."

Contrary to Habermas's imputation, the hermeneutical focus on language did not imply that linguistic awareness "determines material life-praxis" but only that "there is no social reality with all its factual constraints which does not in turn find expression" in linguistic awareness. Reality, in any event, does not happen "behind the back of language" but rather behind the backs of those "who subjectively assume to have understood the world." The latter assumption seemed to be shared by Habermas when he portrayed "emancipatory" critique as immune or aloof from hermeneutical contexts and as an avenue to rational insight beyond power and human finitude. From the vantage of effective history, this Habermasian notion of reflection or critique appeared "dogmatically encumbered" and indeed a "misinterpretation of reflection" – to the extent that reason was seen as an exit from or simple negation of being. This defect also carried political implications. As an unavoidable conse-quence, Gadamer concluded, emancipatory critique seems to aim at "the dissolution of all power and political constraints" and thus at "an anar-chistic utopia as its guiding telos" – an aim ultimately reflecting "a hermeneutically false consciousness."[13]

The first round of the debate, briefly sketched so far, was followed a few years later by a second round – initiated again by Habermas in an essay challenging "The Hermeneutic Claim to Universality" (1970). By that time, Habermas had further restricted the scope of hermeneutical understanding by a rearrangement of his epistemological scheme, a rear-rangement de-emphasizing hermeneutical self-reflection in favor of the endeavor of "rational reconstruction" geared toward the analysis of anonymous rule systems and universal competences. As should be evi-dent from the preceding, the essay – in opposing Gadamer – did not so much attack "universality" as such, but rather the lack or deficiency of genuine universality in the confines of hermeneutical understanding. Paralleling the critique of positivist scientism, the defect of hermeneutics was found to reside precisely in its limited standing if compared with the broader vistas opened up by critical epistemology in conjunction with "reconstructive science." Alluding again to his tripartite scheme, Habermas saw the scope of hermeneutics already delimited by the advances of modern science and the rise of formal-analytical frameworks no longer indebted to ordinary discourse or understanding. "Obviously," he wrote, "modern science can legitimately claim to capture the 'truth of things' by proceeding monologically rather than obeying the rules of ordinary speech: namely, by constructing monologically designed and empirically tested theories." Although obliquely linked with every-day communication, the intelligibility of such theories for scientists did not depend on this linkage. The same aloofness was characteristic of technological progress as well as of strategic or instrumental plans (or designs of "purposive-rational action"). At this point, Habermas appealed to the "genetic" epistemology of Piaget and its claim of speech- or language-independent roots of operational thought – that is, the thesis that language is only superimposed on pre-linguistic categories like space, time, and causality and on rules of formal logic. "If it is true," he observed, "that operational thought depends on pre-linguistic cognitive schemata and thus can utilize language instrumentally, then the hermeneutical claim to universality finds its limit in the frameworks of science and the theories of rational choice."[14]

More important than the advances of empirical science and technology, in Habermas's presentation, was the emergence of reconstructive science as a new kind of depth inquiry with potentially universal scope. Recapitu-ating arguments developed elsewhere, he portrayed hermeneutical insight as a mode of self-reflection tailored to the practical understanding of individual and group experiences or life-stories; by contrast, rational reconstruction held the promise of uncovering general rule systems gov-erning human behavior and speech performance, that is, of providing the key to "universal capabilities" like linguistic and communicative com-petence. As two possible avenues of reconstructive inquiry Habermas singled out generative linguistics (or generative grammar) and the explana-tory models employed in depth psychology. The program of generative grammar, he noted, was designed to furnish a "general theory of natural language" and thus to permit the reconstruction of a universal (culturally invariant) linguistic competence; on completion of this program, inter-pretive understanding could plausibly be replaced by structural descrip-tions stated in formal-analytical terms. In a different manner, depth psychology undercuts hermeneutics by focusing on – and offering expla-nations for – pathological or systematically deformed modes of sym-bolization. In this case, the prospect of a genuinely critical science emerges: a science no longer tied, like hermeneutics, to the domain of "natural" or ordinary-language communication and thus able to "repulse the hermeneutical claim to universality" by means of a theoretically grounded semantic analysis. In every instance, the move beyond hermeneutics was said to involve a strengthening of universal validity claims, especially the claim to truth. In Habermas's words: "Truth is the peculiar compulsion of unconstrained universal recognition; the latter, however, is tied to an ideal speech situation and thus to a form of life in which unconstrained universal communication is possible."[15]

Habermas's foray was followed again in quick succession by another Gadamerian rejoinder (1971) intent on sorting out the points at issue and at buttressing the broad scope of hermeneutics. Countering the restriction of hermeneutics to self-scrutiny or readily intelligible meanings – a restriction warranting resort to reconstructive science – Gadamer emphasized again its ontological character, that is, its ambivalent status between reason and unreason, between mind and reality. Hermeneutical experience, he observed, "cannot be subsumed under the idealistic scheme of self-recognition in otherness to the point where meaning would ever be fully grasped and transmitted. This idealist view of understanding, I believe, misleads most of my critics" (including Apel and Habermas). What the misconstrual ignored was the embeddedness of understanding in history and language, the refractedness of meaning in contingent contexts and events. As Gadamer added, historical experience was not the experience of transparent meaning or the discernment of a general "plan of reason" – an ambition plausible only *sub specie aeternitatis* ; by contrast, hermeneutical inquiry is an "ever renewed attempt to decode the meaning fragments of history, fragments limited by the opaque contingency of reality and especially by the twilight zone in which the future hovers from the vantage of the present." The notion of "universal hermeneutics" (or hermeneutical universality) had to be seen in the same subdued light: understanding was universal only in the sense of being an inescapable feature of the human mode of life, a mode articulating itself first and foremost in ordinary language and common-sense beliefs – into which even alien or abstracted idioms have ultimately to be translated. Recapitulating arguments advanced in *Truth and Method*, Gadamer presented hermeneutics not so much as a method or a methodologically trained exegesis but rather as "the medium of human social life which, in the last analysis, has the character of a linguistic or dialogical community" (though not one geared to uniform consensus in an ideal speech situation). In this sense, hermeneutics reflected not a universal reason but the plurality of modes of rational argumentation as well as "the pluralism which combines and connects mutually opposed or conflicting elements in society."[16]

II

Although conducted in a probing and spirited fashion, the reviewed debate did not manage to settle or even to sharply pinpoint disputed issues – mainly because of a lingering attachment on both sides to elements of traditional metaphysics. While vigorously asserting ontological claims (and even the primacy of "being over consciousness"), Gadamer's arguments were not free of idealist overtones reminiscent of a subjectivist hermeneutics (as well as the legacy of *Geisteswissenschaften*).

Idealist streaks were clearly present in the continued centerstaging of human consciousness – evident in such terms as hermeneutical consciousness or "effective historical consciousness"; at the same time, the portrayal of historical tradition sometimes intimated a solid framework or else the unfolding of a steady teleology – a process privileging continuity of meaning over discontinuity and rupture.[17] Accentuating these idealist strands, Habermas unsurprisingly narrowed the scope of hermeneutics in favor of non-interpretive "real factors" (like labor and power) – but at the risk of an incipient objectivism whose flaws can readily be detected. Basically, Habermas's "exit" from hermeneutics relied on epistemological premises of a dubious or at least contestable sort. Thus, regarding empirical science (and designs of technical control), recent epistemology has shown the dependence of scientific inquiry on historically grown "paradigms" whose ingredients continuously need interpretation; moreover, to avoid noxious political effects, scientific findings constantly have to be reintegrated into ordinary language and common-sense beliefs (a point repeatedly acknowledged by Habermas himself). Regarding rational reconstruction and generative inquiry, the presumed aloofness of operational thought or logic from language seems to pay tribute in turn to a metaphysical mentalism or idealism, in stark conflict with the "linguistic turn" extolled by Habermas in many of his writings. In view of the inherent quandaries besetting the debate, there has been no lack in recent times of attempts to overcome the respective one-sidedness of subjective hermeneutics and objective-universal knowledge; yet, in the absence of renewed ontological reflection, efforts of this kind hardly yield more than an artificial synthesis.[18]

Instead of recapitulating such attempts, I want to turn at this point to Gadamer's chief mentor, Martin Heidegger – with the intent of probing further the meaning and status of ontology and its relation to rational critique. As one may recall, Heidegger's *Being and Time* was meant to rekindle or inaugurate anew the "question of being" (*Seinsfrage*), a question largely abandoned by modern philosophy. As one must also realize, however, being for Heidegger was not simply an empirical target or "real factor" amenable to "objective" or representational analysis; at the same time, ontology – seen as the pursuit of the being-question – was not merely a synonym for speculative intuition or else for modern (subject-centered) metaphysics. Not unexpectedly, Kantian critical philosophy occupied a pivotal – though profoundly ambivalent – place in the arguments of *Being and Time*. On the one hand, by debunking the pretensions of substantive metaphysical knowledge (or a metaphysics of substances), Kant's "Copernican Revolution" had cleared a pathway to an "analytics of finitude" or mundane temporality; on the other hand, by anchoring rational critique in consciousness and internal categories of mind, Kant's innovation remained indebted to modern Cartesian metaphysics (with its distinction of mental and material substances). Pursuing the Kantian thrust but revoking the latter legacy, *Being and Time* elaborated an analytics of finitude construed as a "fundamental ontology" centered around human *Dasein*. In lieu of the earlier focus on the *cogito* (or critical reason), this analytics strongly contextualized human existence by presenting *Dasein* as intrinsically a "being-in-the-world" and also as a creature marked by "care" – where care included openness to the being-question or the "meaning of being." Enmeshed in the world and open to the being-question, *Dasein* was inevitably embroiled in the endeavor of understanding or interpretation – and insight which later furnished the inspiration for Gadamer's ontological hermeneutics. As Heidegger observed, in outlining the "method" of his inquiry: the analytics of *Dasein* "has the character of interpretation (*hermeneuein*), whereby the meaning of being and the basic structures of its own being are made manifest to the understanding capacity endemic to *Dasein*." Analytics of *Dasein* to this extent "is hermeneutics in the original sense of the term, namely, an enterprise of interpretation."[19]

The post-Kantian (or post-critical) character of the analytics of *Dasein* was clearly revealed in the domain of epistemology, particulary where the latter grapples with reality or the question of the "external world" (*Aussenwelt*). In Kant's *Critique of Pure Reason*, the absence of a conclusive proof of the existence of "things outside" had been termed "a scandal for philosophy and for general human reason"; to provide such a proof, Kant pointed to the flux of human temporal experience which required as condition of possibility a stable external world. According to *Being and Time*, however, this strategy miscarried: while seemingly invoking human finitude, it basically restated the Cartesian dualism of mind and matter, subject and world: "The fact that Kant demands a proof for the existence of 'things outside' demonstrates that he takes his departure from the subject, from the sphere 'within'." Starting from interiority or inner reason, "critical" epistemology necessarily distances and objectifies all phenomena or modes of being; having purged the *cogito* of all contexts, it inevitably faces the problem of the "external world" and of the "reconstitution of world" as such. In Heidegger's view, the "scandal for philosophy" resided not in the absence of epistemological proofs, but rather in the fact "that such proofs are time and again expected and attempted." Critiquing and further radicalizing critical epistemology, Heidegger shifted the accent from interiority to *Dasein* seen as being-in-the-world and thus as intimately enmeshed in reality: "From the vantage of *Dasein* as being-in-the-world, worldly beings are always already opened up and disclosed [*erschlossen*]." By stressing this disclosure, existential analytics concurs in a sense with epistemological "realism" – whose ontological naïveté or unreflectedness, however, it rejects. On the other hand, by refusing to reduce the being-question to empirical "real factors," the same analytics pays homage to epistemological "idealism" – whose focus on mind or consciousness threatens to displace ontology "into a vacuum."[20]

Construing *Dasein* as being-in-the-world (marked by care for being) did not signal a return to a pre-critical or substantive metaphysics – for the simple reason that neither world nor being as such were substances amenable to objectifying analysis. In terms of *Being and Time*, world was not simply an external appendage but rather a co-constitutive feature of human *Dasein* itself; instead of denoting an ontic (empirical) arena, world in this sense was "always already" present or operative as backdrop prior to any deliberate act of reflection or critical inquiry. One of the chief accusations leveled by Heidegger against traditional metaphysics was precisely its neglect or bypassing (*überspringen*) of the "world phenomenon," a neglect evident in the streamlining of this feature into an external complex of "extended matter" (*res extensa*). Countering this glaring omission, *Being and Time* thematized the "worldliness of world" as an ontological or "ontological-existential" category or notion – a notion presupposed, but persistently shunned by modern "critical" philosophy anchored in the *cogito*. Worldliness of this kind was actually shown to undergird and render possible critical epistemology, including the enterprise of modern science predicated on such epistemology: only "on the basis of the worldliness of world," we read, can inner-worldly phenomena be "discovered as substantive objects" accessible to scientific research. As in the case of worldliness and world, differentiation from substantive ontology was also the hallmark of "being" as employed in existential analytics; contrary to the traditional metaphysics of essences, being in Heidegger's usage signified a temporal happening pervading *Dasein* and the world – though a happening not reducible to "vulgar" or mechanical clock-time. *Being and Time* was forceful in stressing the non-substantive or anti-positivist status of fundamental ontology: "Being as the basic theme of philosophy is not a species of (ontic) beings, although it concerns all beings; its 'universality' resides on a higher level . . . Being is *transcendence as such*." Exceeding the confines of specialized disciplines, existential analytics had the character of a "universal phenomenological ontology."[21]

Given its basic anti-objectivism, fundamental ontology was not alien to, but rather a precondition of possible critique – though a critique cognizant of its underpinnings and limitations. The same relation to critique was also manifest in the study's attitude toward "tradition" which was far removed from any endorsement of a compact traditionalism. From the vantage of existential analytics, traditionalism appeared basically as a mode of ontological deficiency or negligence, that is, as a manifestation of *Dasein's* "fallenness" (*Verfallenheit*) into everyday-ness with its taken-for-granted beliefs. In accepting everyday beliefs, *Being and Time* stated, *Dasein* also tends to "succumb to tradition – which relieves it of its autonomy and its choices and questions," particularly the question of being. Understood in this manner, tradition was itself spurious or inauthentic and not conducive to a proper understanding: under its auspices, the heritage of the past was not so much rendered accessible as rather occluded or obstructed. Although seemingly wedded to history, traditionalism was said to "uproot the historicity of *Dasein*" and ultimately to prevent a "positive recovery of the past in the sense of a productive appropriation." In Heidegger's view, existential analytics demanded a deconstruction (*Destruktion*) of congealed traditions for the sake of ontological renewal. "If the history of the being-question is to be rendered intelligible," he wrote, "then we need a loosening up of hardened traditions and a removal of occlusions produced by them." This task had the character of a "*Destruktion* of the heritage of classical ontology" performed "under the auspices of the being-question." As Heidegger added emphatically, deconstruction or deconstructive critique did not have a purely "negative" or destructive aim, but rather served the goal of a critical renewal: "*Destruktion* does not carry the merely negative sense of an emancipation from the ontological tradition; instead, it seeks to pinpoint the positive potential and accordingly also the limits of that legacy."[22]

In Heidegger's subsequent writings, the linkage of ontology and critique was reinforced through a sharpening or deepening of the being-question itself – a move disclosing the intimate intertwining of being and nothingness, presence and absence. This intertwining was eloquently portrayed in "What is Metaphysics?", an essay written not long after *Being and Time*. As the essay indicated, metaphysics revolves around the question of being and nothingness – terms which lack a concrete empirical reference. In seeking to grasp the meaning of nothingness, Heidegger observed, we are tempted to offer a description or definition of the term, thereby treating it like a regular (ontic) being or entity; yet nothingness "is nothing of the sort." According to the essay, nothingnes was neither a positive entity nor was it simply the negation of such an entity – particularly not a merely semantic denial subsumable under traditional rules of logic. Nothingness, we read, "is more original than the 'not' and negation"; differently phrased: it is "the source of (logical) negation, not the other way around." This means that negation – as an exercise of critical reason – was not self-contained or self-generating but rather depended on a prior ontological access to nothingness (and being) – an access not unfamiliar to *Dasein* viewed as being-in-the-world. In Heidegger's portrayal, this access was provided by a peculiar slippage in the world-context of *Dasein*, namely, by a slippage affecting the entirety of beings (*Allheit des Seienden*) seen as a sustaining fabric. Although the totality of beings could never cognitively or substantively be grasped, its disintegration or absence was disclosed in a distinct existential "mood" or experience, particularly the experience of "dread" (*Angst*): "The slippage of beings-as-a-whole crowds in on us and torments us in dread. There is nothing to hold on to; in fact, the only thing remaining and overpowering us in the slippage is this 'nothing'. Thus, dread reveals nothingness." What is revealed at this point is not an entity nor a simple negation or negativity, but rather a hidden force – the potency of nothingness as a happening: "Nothingness nihilates [*nichtet*] of itself."[23]

For Heidegger, concern with dread and nothingness was by no means a sign of nihilism or pessimistic melancholy. On the contrary, the experience of nothingness was precisely a gateway to affirmation: a gateway to the disclosure of "being" – where the latter designates not merely ontic objects (subject to negation) but rather an ontological event. "Only in the clear night of dread's nothingness," the essay stated, "is being as such revealed in its original openness: namely, that there is being and not only nothingness"; thus, "the essence of nothingness as original nihilation lies in this: that it alone brings *Dasein* face to face with being as such." In encountering dread, *Dasein* finds itself dislodged from familiar moorings and radically "projected into nothingness"; in this manner, it is able to trangress or "transcend" the confines of ontic beings in their entirety and hence gain genuine autonomy and self-awareness. In Heidegger's words: "Were *Dasein* not basically transcendent, that is to say, were it not projected from the start into nothingness, it could never relate to being and thus could have no self-relationship. Without the original disclosure of nothingness there is no selfhood and no freedom."[24] Exposure to nothingness lies at the root not only of self-awareness but also of reflective or critical inquiry into the character of world and distinct phenomena, an inquiry proceeding from an initial puzzlement and unfamiliarity:

Only because nothingness is disclosed in the very core of *Dasein* can the utter strangeness of being dawn on us. Only when the strangeness of being forces itself upon us does it awaken and invite wonder. Only because of wonder – that is, the disclosure of nothingness – does the "why?" spring

to our lips, and only because of the possibility of this "why" are we able
to seek for definite reasons or proofs.[25]

Seen from this vantage, nothingness is neither an object nor a negation
of objects but an intimate corollary of being, relating to the latter in a
mode of close intertwining (though not fusion): "Nothingness is what
makes the disclosure of being as such possible for human existence"; it
is "in the being of beings that the nihilation of nothingness occurs."[26]
    The correlation of ontology and critique – or rather the derivation of
critique from the being–nothingness nexus – remained a persistent
theme in Heidegger's evolving opus, particularly in the writings during
and after his so-called *Kehre* or "turning" (which was also a turning away
from a systematic or formalizable ontology). A case in point is the treatise
titled *Beiträge zur Philosophie* written about a decade after *Being and
Time* (and only recently published). Trying to forge a path beyond
modern metaphysics in the direction of a more "originary thinking,"
Beiträge emphatically critiqued the notion of a self-contained rationalism
or critical philosophy anchored in the *cogito* or human consciousness.
While not inaugurating an "end of man," the departure from metaphysics
involved inevitably also a transgression of foundational (or subject-
centered) critique. "To the extent that history and historical awareness
sustain and govern human *Dasein*," Heidegger stated, "every reflection
is necessarily *also* self-reflection. Yet originally thought or reflection does
not take the selfhood or subjectivity of contemporary humans for granted
or as immediately accessible in the conception of the 'I' or the 'We' and
their situation." Instead, such reflection asks first of all "how selfhood
can at all be grounded," in a domain "where 'we' – you and I – are able
to find our *selves*." According to *Beiträge*, this domain is by no means
synonymous with subjectivity or the *cogito*, but can only be found
through a turn to *Dasein* in its openness to being and the "truth of
being." Being at this point, however, denotes not merely an ontic reality
nor a metaphysical "essence" of things, but rather a happening (*Ereignis*)
eluding human control or mastery and always hovering in the twilight
of nothingness. Being in this sense, we read, is the "ground" of all beings,
but simultaneously also the "abyss" (*Abgrund*) of beings, and even the
"un-ground" (*Ungrund*) where beings assert their "indifference and
taken-for-grantedness." This ambivalence derives from the linkage of
being and nothingness where the former does not designate an ontic
thing and where nothingness does not mean a total absence or vacuum
but rather "non-being as a mode of being": "Only because being happens
through nihilation does it have non-being as its corollary."[27]
    Beiträge also marked a resolute move in Heidegger's thought to

language seen as the articulation of *Dasein's* embroilment in being (and nothingness). Language, for Heidegger, did not denote a compact system or a closed set of syntactical or semantic rules (*langue*), nor a capacity for speech-performance or speech-acting (*parole*); rather it was part and parcel of the happening of being – which could never be grasped or stated *intentione recta* (without provoking reification). "Even when leaping into its domain," *Beiträge* affirmed, "we can never directly say or express being itself. For every saying arises and speaks out of being and its truth." The only possible way to adumbrate being was in a roundabout way by means of ordinary, particularly poetic, language. In this respect, *Beiträge* reflected Heidegger's growing preoccupation with Hölderlin, while also foreshadowing his later (postwar) explorations and tentative steps "on the way to language."[28]

Bypassing empirical and structural linguistics as well as speech-act theory, these later writings thematized language as an open-ended fabric or texture equivalent neither to intentional activity nor to a preordained structure or teleology. As Heidegger noted in an essay titled "Language" (1950): "If attention is fastened exclusively on human speech and if the latter is taken simply as articulation of human interiority," then "language can never appear as anything but as human activity and self-expresssion." Yet, he added, speaking is never in this sense self-contained or subject to control; rather, human speech always resonates (no matter how distantly) with the "speaking and saying of language itself" – a saying most fully manifest in poetry. This resonance, in turn, reflects language's complicity in the happening of being – that is, in the intertwining of being and non-being, speech and silence. As a later essay on the same topic succinctly formulated the issue: "The being of language – the language of being."[29]

III

In large measure, Heidegger's work can be seen as primary exemplar of a perspective combining ontological reflection with post-Kantian (not subject-centered) critique. Yet, depsite its prominence, this work did not emerge in isolation and cannot be segregated from broader intellectual trends pointing in a similar direction. Curiously, such a trend was operative – on a recessed level – during the first generation of the Frankfurt School, that is, in the early version of that project of "critical theory" which later was taken over and reformulated by Habermas. In a way, the move from Habermas to Adorno and Horkheimer parallels the turn from Gadamer to Heidegger: just as the latter's (ontological)

radicalism was to some extent subdued and confined in Gadamer's hermeneutics, so the tensions and predicaments besetting the early Frankfurt
School were streamlined and "smoothed out" in Habermasian epistemology. In my view, these tensions were a sign of productive ferment, of
an intensive struggle with the conflicting demands of (Kantian) metaphysics and post-metaphysics, of Enlightenment and post-Enlightenment
directions of thought. While often abandoning such conflicts on the level
of antinomies, early critical theory at least intimated or held open the
avenue of critical ontology by refusing to embrace a straightforward
Enlightenment rationalism (or else its simple negation).

No doubt, the initial beginning of critical theory was strongly indebted
to Enlightenment premises and critical-Kantian metaphysics; the choice
of the school's label itself reflected a rebellion against "tradition" and
against a contemplative acceptance of the world (or "the way things are").
Kantian criticism was buttressed and supplemented by resort to Marxist
(or Left-Hegelian) "praxis" philosophy with its focus on social critique
and real-life emancipation through collective action. The combined
strands formed the backbone of the school's endeavor of "ideology critique": an endeavor combining the critique of "false" or distorted forms
of consciousness with the removal of social repression or domination.
The confluence was clearly evident in Horkheimer's programmatic essay
titled "Traditional and Critical Theory" (1937). According to the essay,
Kant's philosophy signaled an insurgency against traditional metaphysics,
namely, by shifting the accent from passive contemplation to the productive or knowledge-constitutive functions of human reason. Despite his
idealistic construal of this productivity, Kant at least pinpointed crucial
cognitive ingredients of human agency or praxis. "In any case Kant
understood," we read, "that behind the discrepancy between fact and
theory (experienced by the scholar in his professional work) there lies a
deeper unity: namely, general subjectivity upon which individual inquiry
depends. Social praxis appears here then as a transcendental power, that
is, as the sum-total of spiritual factors." Critical social theory was bent
on expanding and concretizing this perspective – but without relinquishing the stress on agency and self-constitution. As Horkheimer
observed (in a Postscript to the essay): "In relating seemingly irreducible
facts (binding on the specialized scholar) to human production, critical
social theory concurs with the teachings of German idealism; ever since
Kant, the latter had marshalled this dynamic moment against the worship of facts and its concomitant social conformism." Moreover, in extolling critical reason and a rational telos of society, critical theory preserved
the heritage "not only of German idealism but of [Western] philosophy
as such."[30]

For Horkheimer and his associates, to be sure, critical theory could not remain content with the invoked legacy; as a dynamic social conception it necessarily had to link theoretical with practical critique and hence cognitive with social praxis – which required an extension of the notion of constitutive agency. While in German idealism agency had a purely intellectual or spiritual status – hovering on the level of a "transempirical consciousness as such," of an "absolute ego" or "spirit – Marxism from the beginning had stressed the "material" or concrete-social dimension of action or praxis. "In the materialist conception," Horkheimer observed, "the basic constitutive praxis is found in the domain of social labor whose class-divided structure puts its imprint on all modes of human behavior, including theoretical behavior." Accordingly, from this vantage, rational critique or the subordination of reality to conscious-rational control "does not occur in a purely mental sphere but rather coincides with the struggle revolving around distinct and concrete forms of (social) life." The continuity between idealism and Marxism resided in the joint focus on constitutive agency or production – whose character and scope, however, were radically transformed both in Marx's notion of social labor and in the program of critical theory guiding the work of the Frankfurt School. "Critical theory of society," we read, "has as its object human beings seen as producers of their entire historical way of life. Empirical conditions which are the starting-point of science are regarded here not simply as data to be verified and to be predicted according to probability calculations." Decisive was the insight that existing reality depends "not only on nature but also on the control human agents can exert over it" and that perceived conditions hence bear witness to "human praxis and the degree of human power." In the context of present-day capitalist society, genuine social praxis and critique were frustrated or stifled by the prevailing class structure and also by the atomistic character of social life – features which prevented rational planning and a coherent process of social rationalization. Only through persistent critique and transformative praxis was it possible to inaugurate the full reign of human freedom and rational control: "In recognizing the present economic mode and the entire culture built on it as the product of human labor" critical agents come to "identify themselves with this totality" and conceive it in terms of human "will and reason."[31]

Although strongly extolling constitutive human praxis, Horkheimer's essay did not completely or unequivocally subscribe to Enlightenment metaphysics or its Marxist variant. Deviations from Marxist doctrine were evident in a certain distrust of the proletariat seen as collective social agent and in the concomitant accentuation of the role of intellectuals and marginal social groups. At the same time, rationalist optimism or confidence in the benefits of rationalization was tempered by awareness of the intimate nexus of world and reason, that is, of the impact exerted by historical context on rational critique (restricting the latter's constitutive sovereignty). Most importantly, critical theory in Horkheimer's formulation was not wedded to a "positive" utopia, especially to the vision of an untrammeled self-production accomplished through rational planning and control. "For all the plausibility of particular steps and for all the concurrence of its tenets with the most advanced traditional theories," he wrote, "critical theory has no specific warrant on its side, except concern for the abolition of social injustice. Stated abstractly, this negative formulation is the materialist content of the idealist concept of reason."[32] In this manner, the Frankfurt School program was potentially critical in a dual sense: namely, critical of traditional (pre-modern) metaphysics and traditional forms of domination, and also self-critical in challenging the premises of a self-contained rationalism or rationalist critique aloof from historical contexts. As it happened, this dual thrust – and especially the aspect of self-criticism – was bound to be reinforced by events of the period, particularly the consolidation of the Nazi regime and the ensuing World War (events which forced the school's emigration from Europe). Under the impact of these developments, Frankfurt theorists steadily grew weary of Enlightenment optimism, while increasingly coming to suspect modern reason for its complicity in designs of global mastery and domination.

The most eloquent and dramatic outgrowth of this disillusionment (or rather: this deepening self-criticism) was *Dialectic of Enlightenment*, a study written jointly by Horkheimer and Adorno during the war years in exile. Without abandoning reason or rational insight, the study portrayed in stark terms the dark underside of modern rationalization and enlightenment: namely, its dogmatic self-sufficiency and resultant contribution to new forms of enslavement. As the Preface stated, the initial impulse of the study was the experience of a trauma or dilemma: the progressive "self-destruction of Enlightenment" – a trauma which did not warrant a retreat into traditionalism or irrationality.

We are wholly convinced (and therein lies our *petitio principii*) that social freedom is inseparable from enlightened thought. Yet, we believe to have just as clearly recognized that the notion of this very kind of thought – together with the concrete historical forms and social institutions in which it is enmeshed – already contains the seed of the regress or reversal universally apparent today. Unless enlightenment embraces reflection on this regressive element, it is bound to seal its own fate.[33]

According to Horkheimer and Adorno, evidence of the ongoing reversal was not so much provided by regressive worldviews or chauvinistic ideologies – whose effect was detrimental enough; rather, the central issue was the steady congealment of Enlightenment thought itself, manifest in the sway of scientism and the general addiction to technology or the rational mastery of the world. The prevailing worship of facts – ignorant of their cognitive and social-political underpinnings and prestructuration – went hand in glove with a social conformism dismissive of innovative social change. Inevitably, critical thinking or anti-positivist theorizing fell victim to this kind of "realism" or scientistic objectivism; the latter – by declaring all modes of non-affirmative reflection or analysis as "alien, outlandish and hence taboo" – in effect condemned enlightened thought to "increasing myopia and darkness."[34]

The opening chapter of the study provided a dramatic account of both the promises and the ensuing drawbacks of modern rationalization and elightenment. In Kantian language, enlightenment meant the stirring or awakening of mankind from the "slumber of immaturity" and the condition of external tutelage. To this extent, enlightenment signaled a process of human emancipation – a process extricating human reason from cosmic worldviews and mythological superstitions as well as liberating human praxis from illegitimate authority or domination. Yet, with the passage of time and especially with the rise of modern science, this emancipation exacted a price: the price of a growing anthropocentrism and rational self-sufficiency manifest in human mastery of the world – a mastery rebounding on society and human life in general. According to *Dialectic of Enlightenment*, this price was not fortuitous or accidental: with the extrication of reason from the world and nature, human beings were transformed into distilled "subjects" (an internal subjectivity) while the world and its phenomena were objectified as targets of human control. This transformation was endemic to modern science which recognizes things only as analyzable and "makable" and ultimately as products of fabrication; to this extent, scientific rationalization "behaves towards things like a dictator toward his subjects: he knows them only insofar as he can manipulate or control them." This effect, however, is not restricted to scientific inquiry but extends broadly to modern epistemology and its attendant metaphysics. As Horkheimer and Adorno pointed out, modern epistemology is wedded to discursive logic and to universal concepts or categories to which particularities are rigidly subsumed or subordinated; in this manner, the diversity and elusiveness of reality are sacrificed to the primacy of general rules. In their words: "The universality of concepts as developed by discursive logic – their supremacy in the conceptual sphere – is erected on the basis of actual supremacy or domination. The replacement of the magical-mythical heritage, of the old diffuse world-views, by conceptual unity reflects a hierarchical social constitution determined by freemen and implemented through chains of command."[35]

While yielding undeniable scientific and technological advances, the divorce of reason and world inevitably reified the latter into an arena of factually given and reproducible objects; more importantly, it generated the progressive self-objectification of reason and subjectivity under positivist-scientific auspices: "What appears as triumph of subjective rationality – the subjection of all phenomena to logical formulas – is purchased with the obedient submission of reason to factual reality." For Horkheimer and Adorno, however, the main corollary of self-objectification was a certain "loss of world" (or oblivion of being): namely, the loss of the qualitative richness of phenomena as well as of the resources of imagination and sensibility undergirding reason itself. "The unification of intellectual functions by means of which control over the senses is achieved," they wrote, means "the impoverishment of reason as well as of (sensuous) experience: the separation of the two domains leaves both impaired." The remedy for this loss or impoverishment, in terms of *Dialectic of Enlightenment*, had to be found in a renunciation of reason's domineering impulse, that is, in an opening of reason to the domain of "otherness" or non-identity – an opening or transgression which could not yield instant synthesis (a disguised form of reason's dominion). "Thought becomes illusionary," we read, "whenever it simply denies divisiveness, distantiation and objectification; every mystical union remains deceptive." This insight, however, did not preclude transgression – provided the latter signaled not mere mental acrobatics but the experience of a "wound" which solicited healing (while also needing to be undergone). Although precluding instant utopia, the experience of the "rupture of subject and object" at this point emerged as "an index of the untruth (of the rupture) and of truth." This means: enlightenment here becomes "more than enlightenment," – namely, "recollection of alienated nature" (or otherness). Although human thought cannot arise without extrication from nature, the result need not be blatant domination: "By recognizing and expiating its domineering impulse and reconnecting itself to nature, reason abandons its claim to mastery (which precisely enslaved it to reality)." According to Horkheimer and Adorno, this "recollection of nature in subjectivity" or reason was the potent though disguised "core of all culture," to the extent that culture intimates power (or empowerment) through non-dominion. As they concluded: "Enlightenment perfects and sublates itself when the nearest practical aims reveal themselves as attained far-off utopia, and when the lands of which reason's 'spials and intelligencers can give no news' – namely, the domain of nature bypassed by domineering science – are recollected as lands of origin."[36]

The double gesture or double critique initiated during the war years was continued and intensified in the later writings of both authors, particularly in Adorno's crowning opus titled *Negative Dialectics* (1966). The title of the study signaled a challenge to all forms of objectivism as well as all types of positive (or positivist) utopias; more specifically, it stood in opposition to an idealist-Hegelian dialectics guided by a telos imprinted in, and accomplished by, human reason or subjectivity. As used by Adorno, the term "negative" was not simply a synonym for pessimism or pure negativity; instead, the term pointed to the "always already" operative, but not directly available underpinnings of knowledge and action, that is, to the intertwining of reason and non-reason, presence and absence. To this extent, the study intimated contours of a critical ontology – a reflection critical also of the modern metaphysics of critique (anchored in the *cogito*). The doubly critical gesture was boldly announced already in the study's Preface. "Ever since he came to trust his own intellectual impulses," Adorno stated, "the author has considered it as his task to dismantle the fallacy of constitutive subjectivity, by relying on the strength of the subject (or reason)." Replicating arguments of *Dialectic of Enlightenment*, the study perceived in the triumphant ascendancy of modern subjectivity already the seeds of reversal – namely, toward self-objectification and self-congealment: "The dominant trend of modern epistemology was to reduce more and more of the objective world to subjectivity – a trend which needs to be reversed"; for, "the more autocratically the ego rises above the world, the more it encourages reification and recants ironically its constitutive role." In Adorno's presentation, modern epistemology basically paralleled and reinforced its apparent opposite, namely, naturalism or the naturalistic "survival of the fittest": "The primacy of subjectivity is a spiritualized continuation of the Darwinian struggle for survival"; in epistemological-metaphysical guise, the subject partakes in this struggle "by proclaiming itself as Baconian master and finally as idealistic creator of all things." By acknowledging and cancelling this complicity, critical enlightenment "transcends its traditional self-understanding.[37]

Against the backdrop of modern subjectivity, negative dialectics meant the disentanglement of reflection from subjective-rationalist enclosure – a disentanglement opening reflection up to otherness and non-identity. In contrast to Hegel's conceptualism (or purely conceptual dialectics), this opening up was designed to rescue or recover the non-conceptual hidden in the concept and the non-reason latent in reason. In Adorno's words: "To change the direction of conceptuality and turn it toward non-identity:

this is the emblem of negative dialectics. Insight into the constitutive role of the non-conceptual in the concept would end the identity-constraint which conceptualism entails unless impeded by such reflection." The turn to non-identiy heralded an effort to "save the appearances," that is, an attentiveness to the richness and diversity of phenomena not yet steamlined by rationalist constructs. Beyond its epistemological implications – the recovery of the life-world – this attentiveness harbored a larger promise: that of a "reconciliation" of the subject–object division (accomplished not merely on the conceptual level of ideas). Such reconciliation, the study noted, would "release the non-identical, ridding it of coercion, including spiritual coercion, and opening or disclosing the richness of difference"; differently phrased: reconciliation would mean "recollection of a no-longer-exorcised multiplicity (something which is anathema to subjective reason)." As Adorno added, attention to nonidentity required not only a cognitive change but a more profound human transformation: one enabling the individual to emancipate itself from self-enclosure and self-possession (without lapsing into objectivism). Liberated in this manner, the individual could also find a new relation to phenomena, namely, a "love to things" as they exist beyond reification and heteronomy, in a realm banished by the "endogamy of consciousness." Loving things in this way would not imply a desire for possession but rather a generous letting be: "Far from annexing the alien or other in an exercise of philosophical imperialism, the reconciled condition would have its happiness in letting close proximity remain farness and difference, beyond the bifurcation of mine and yours."[38]

NOTES

1 See particularly Edmund Husserl, *The Crisis of European Sciences and Transcendental Phenomenology*, tr. David Carr (Evanston: Northwestern University Press, 1970). In the progressive sway of critical rationality, Nietzsche occupied an ambivalent position – in that he both denounced a precritical metaphysics and the pretension of a self-grounding of critical reason.

2 The most elaborate and vivid depiction of these dangers can be found in Jürgen Habermas, *The Philosophical Discourse of Modernity: Twelve Lectures*, tr. Frederick Lawrence (Cambridge, MA: MIT Press, 1987).

3 For a perceptive account of this dimension see Dennis J. Schmidt, *The Ubiquity of the Finite: Hegel, Heidegger, and the Entitlements of Philosophy* (Cambridge, MA: MIT Press, 1988).

4 For well-informed discussions of the Gadamer–Habermas debate see Dieter Misgeld, "Critical Theory and Hermeneutics: The Debate between Habermas and Gadamer", in John O'Neill, ed., *On Critical Theory* (New York: Seabury

Press, 1976), pp. 164–83; Thomas McCarthy, "Rationality and Relativism: Habermas's 'Overcoming' of Hermeneutics", in John B. Thompson and David Held, eds, *Habermas: Critical Debates* (Cambridge, MA: MIT Press, 1982), pp. 57–78; and Jack Mendolson, "The Habermas–Gadamer Debate", *New German Critique*, vol. 18 (1979), pp. 44–73.

5 Hans-Georg Gadamer, *Truth and Method*, 2nd rev. edn, tr. and rev. Joel Weinsheimer and Donald G. Marshall (New York: Crossroad, 1989), pp. xxx (in this and subsequent citations the translation has been slightly altered for purposes of clarity). Compare also these comments (p. 270): "Heidegger's demonstration that the concept of consciousness in Descartes and of spirit in Hegel still pays tribute to the Greek ontology of 'substance' which sees being in terms of presence, undoubtedly surpasses the self-understanding of modern metaphysics, yet not in an arbitrary or willful way, but on the basis of a 'fore-having' [*Vorhabe*] that in fact makes this tradition intelligible by revealing the ontological premises of the concept of subjectivity. On the other hand, Heidegger discovers in Kant's critique of 'dogmatic' metaphysics the idea of a metaphysics of finitude which becomes the touchstone of his own ontological approach."

6 *Truth and Method*, pp. 257, 259.

7 *Truth and Method*, pp. xxxiii–xxxiv.

8 *Truth and Method*, pp. xxxv–xxxvi, 282, 290. Compare also the statement, directed both against Hegel and detached historical science (p. xxxv): "The wholeness of meaning which has to be understood in history or tradition is never the meaning of the whole history . . . The finite nature of our understanding surfaces in the manner in which reality, resistance, the absurd, and the unintelligible assert themselves. Whoever takes seriously this finitude must also take seriously the reality of history."

9 See *Truth and Method*, p. xxx; also Gadamer, "The Universality of the Hermeneutical Problem," in *Philosophical Hermeneutics*, tr. and ed. David E. Linge (Berkeley: University of California Press, 1976), pp. 15–16. For the German version of the essay see "Die Universalität des hermeneutischen Problems," in Gadamer, *Kleine Schriften I: Philosophie, Hermeneutik* (Tübingen: Mohr, 1967), pp. 110–11.

10 Jürgen Habermas, *Knowledge and Human Interests*, tr. Jeremy J. Shapiro (Boston: Beacon Press, 1971), pp. 308, 313 (Appendix). For the German version see Habermas, *Erkenntnis und Interesse* (Frankfurt-Main: Suhrkamp, 1968). The lecture appeared as "Erkenntnis und Interesse" in Habermas, *Technik und Wissenschaft als "Ideologie"* (Frankfurt-Main: Suhrkamp, 1968), pp. 155, 162.

11 Habermas, "A Review of Gadamer's *Truth and Method*," in Dallmayr and Thomas McCarthy, eds, *Understanding and Social Inquiry* (Notre Dame: University of Notre Dame Press, 1977), pp. 356, 358, 361. As he added (p. 361): "The happening of tradition – which seems to hold absolute sway only to a self-contained hermeneutics – is in fact relative to systems of labor and domination. Sociology cannot, therefore, be reduced to interpretive

sociology." First published in *Philosophische Rundschau* in 1967, the review was subsequently integrated into Habermas, *Zur Logik der Sozialwissenschaften* (Frankfurt-Main: Suhrkamp, 1970), pp. 251–90. For an English translation of the latter study see *On the Logic of the Social Sciences*, tr. Shierry Weber Nicholson and Jerry A. Stark (Cambridge, MA: MIT Press, 1989).

12 Gadamer, "Rhetorik, Hermeneutik und Ideologiekritik", in Karl-Otto Apel et al., *Hermeneutik und Ideologiekritik* (Frankfurt-Main: Suhrkamp, 1971), pp. 59–60, 63, 68–9, 79; also reprinted in *Kleine Schriften I*, pp. 115, 117, 121, 128. For an abbreviated translation see Gadamer, "On the Scope and Function of Hermeneutical Reflection", in *Philosophical Hermeneutics*, pp. 20, 24, 28–9, 39.

13 *Hermeneutik und Ideologiekritik*, pp. 71–2, 74–6, 82; *Philosophical Hermeneutics*, pp. 30–32, 34–5, 42. Opposing the rigid antithesis of traditional authority and reason as "inaugurated by the Enlightenment," Gadamer termed the dualism "a mistake fraught with grave consequences; for reflection is here granted a false potency, while the true contexts or dependencies (of reason) are *idealistically* ignored." As he added: "Effective historical consciousness is inescapably more *being* than consciousness – which does not mean that it could escape from ideological ossification in the absence of constantly renewed self-reflection." See *Hermeneutik und Ideologiekritik*, pp. 73, 78; *Philosophical Hermeneutics*, pp. 33, 38.

14 Habermas, "Der Universalitätsanspruch der Hermeneutik", in *Hermeneutik und Ideologiekritik*, pp. 129–31; for an English version see "The Hermeneutic Claim to Universality", in Michael T. Gibbons, ed., *Interpreting Politics* (New York: New York University Press, 1987), pp. 181–2. The English version appeared first in Josef Bleicher, ed., *Contemporary Hermeneutics: Hermeneutics as Method, Philosophy and Critique* (London: Routledge & Kegan Paul, 1980), pp. 181–211. For the turn to "rational reconstruction" compare Habermas, "A Postscript to *Knowledge and Human Interests*", *Philosophy of the Social Sciences*, vol. 3 (1975), pp. 157–89; also "What is Universal Pragmatics?" in *Communication and the Evolution of Society*, tr. Thomas McCarthy (Boston: Beacon Press, 1979), pp. 1–68.

15 *Hermeneutik und Ideologiekritik*, pp. 126–7, 131–2, 154; *Interpreting Politics*, pp. 179–82, 197–8.

16 Gadamer, "Replik", in *Hermeneutik und Ideologiekritik*, pp. 289, 301–2, 317. Taking the offensive, Gadamer questioned how Habermas's reliance on objective (empirical) knowledge and reconstructive science could yield the claimed practical or emancipatory effects (p. 305): "I do not see how communicative competence and its theoretical grasp should be able to remove the barriers between social groups which blame each other reciprocally for the deluded character of the other's understanding." What seemed imperative at this point was "recourse to a very different competence, namely, that of political action – with the goal of establishing the precondi-

tions of communication where they are lacking."

17 For a fuller discussion of the vacillation I find in Gadamer's perspective see
    my "Hermeneutics and Deconstruction: Gadamer and Derrida in Dialogue",
    in Dallmayr, *Critical Encounters* (Notre Dame: University of Notre Dame
    Press, 1987), pp. 130–58. An abbreviated version of this essay appeared in
    Diane P. Michelfelder and Richard E. Palmer, eds, *Dialogue and Decon-
    struction: The Gadamer–Derrida Encounter* (Albany, NY: SUNY Press,
    1989), pp. 75–92.

18 In my view, such an artificial eclecticism mars Paul Ricoeur's otherwise
    instructive attempt to synthesize Gadamerian hermeneutics and Habermasian
    critique under the rubrics of "recollection of tradition" and "anticipation
    of freedom"; see "Hermeneutics and the Critique of Ideology" (1973), in
    John B. Thompson, ed., *Hermeneutics and the Human Sciences* (Cam-
    bridge: Cambridge University Press, 1981), pp. 63–100. Another kind of
    synthesis can be found in Alasdair MacIntyre's *Whose Justice? Which Ratio-
    nality?* (Notre Dame: University of Notre Dame Press, 1988) where know-
    ledge is equated with a historical "tradition of enquiry" – a tradition
    endowed with strongly rationalist overtones (in a quasi-Habermasian vein).

19 Martin Heidegger, *Sein und Zeit* (11th edn; Tübingen: Niemeyer, 1967),
    paragraph 7, p. 37.

20 *Sein und Zeit*, par. 43, pp. 203–7.

21 *Sein und Zeit*, par. 7, p. 38, par. 14, pp. 64–5, par. 18, p. 88, par. 21,
    p. 95. On "world" and "worldliness" in Heidegger's opus compare my "Life-
    World: Variations on a Theme", in Stephen K. White, ed., *Life-World and
    Politics: Between Modernity and Postmodernity* (Notre Dame: University
    of Notre Dame Press, 1989), pp. 25–65.

22 Heidegger, *Sein und Zeit*, par. 6, pp. 21–22.

23 Heidegger, "What is Metaphysics?" (1929), in Walter Kaufmann, ed.,
    Existentialism: From Dostoevsky to Sartre (New York: Meridian, 1975),
    pp. 245–9, 251, 253 (translation slightly altered for purposes of clarity). For
    the German text see "Was ist Metaphysik?" in Heidegger, *Wegmarken*
    (Frankfurt-Main: Klostermann, 1967), pp. 1–19.

24 "What is Metaphysics?", p. 251.

25 "What is Metaphysics?", p. 256.

26 "What is Metaphysics?", p. 251. Regarding this correlation, Heidegger both
    follows and corrects Hegelian metaphysics. Referring to Hegel's statement
    that pure being and nothingness are "one and the same," he observes
    (p. 255) that this proposition "is correct. Being and nothingness hang
    together, but *not* because the two – from the vantage of Hegel's concept
    of thought – are one in their indefiniteness and immediacy, but because
    being itself is finite in essence and is only revealed in the transcendence of
    Dasein as projected into nothingness."

27 Heidegger, *Beiträge zur Philosophie (Vom Ereignis)*, ed. F.-W. von Hermann
    (*Gesamtausgabe*, vol. 65; Frankfurt-Main; Klostermann, 1989), pp. 67–8,
    75, 101, 266.

28 *Beiträge*, p. 79.
29 Heidegger, "Die Sprache" and "Das Wesen der Sprache" in *Unterwegs zur Sprache* (Pfullingen: Neske, 1959), pp. 19, 30–31, 200. For an English version see "Language" in *Poetry, Language, Thought*, tr. Albert Hofstadter (New York: Harper & Row, 1971), pp. 196–7, 207–8; "The Nature of Language" in *On the Way to Language*, tr. Peter D. Hertz (New York: Harper & Row, 1971), p. 72. Similar insights could also be derived from the later Wittgenstein. As Drucilla Cornell has pointed out: "The boundaries of our form of life ebb and flow like the sea; it is a sea upon which we are adrift. As Wittgenstein reminds us, when we appeal to communitarian standards in order to make sense, we cannot also delimit the entire repertoire of community standards . . . The constraints that enable meaning cannot be made determinate, foreclosing the reactivation of definition." See Cornell, " 'Convention' and Critique", *Cardozo Law Review*, vol. 7 (1986), pp. 682, 684.
30 Max Horkheimer, "Traditional and Critical Theory" and "Postscript", in *Critical Theory: Selected Essays*, tr. Matthew J. O'Connell et al. (New York: Herder & Herder, 1972), pp. 203, 244–5. For the German version see Horkheimer, *Kritische Theorie: Eine Dokumentation*, ed. Alfred Schmidt, vol. 2 (Frankfurt-Main: Fischer, 1968), pp. 152, 192–3.
31 *Critical Theory*, pp. 207–8, 244–5.
32 *Critical Theory*, p. 242. As he added: "In a historical period like the present, genuine theory is less affirmative than critical, just as appropriate social praxis cannot be 'productive'."
33 Max Horkheimer and Theodor W. Adorno, *Dialectic of Enlightenment*, tr. John Cumming (New York: Seabury Press, 1972), p. xiii (in the above and subsequent citations the translation has been slightly altered for purposes of clarity). The German original appeared first in 1947 in Amsterdam and was reissued as *Dialektik der Aufklärung: Philosophische Fragmente* (Frankfurt-Main: Fischer, 1969).
34 *Dialectic of Enlightenment*, p. xiv.
35 *Dialectic of Enlightenment*, pp. 9, 14.
36 *Dialectic of Enlightenment*, pp. 26, 36, 39–40, 42. The phrase regarding reason's "spials and intelligencers" is borrowed from Francis Bacon, "In Praise of Human Knowledge", in *The Works of Francis Bacon*, ed. Basil Montagu (London: Pickering, 1825), vol. 1, p. 254. As one may notice, the term "nature" is used in the study at least in a twofold sense: namely, in the sense of objective reality (as target of natural science), and in the sense of a non-epistemic field preceding the subject–object division (and thus as a synonym for "world" and "being").
37 Theodor W. Adorno, *Negative Dialectics*, tr. E. B. Ashton (New York: Seabury Press, 1973), pp. xx, 176–7, 179. 186 (in the above and subsequent citations I have slightly altered the translation for purposes of clarity). In transcending its "traditional self-understanding," Adorno elaborates (p. 186), enlightenment is "demythologization – no longer merely as a

reductio ad hominem, but conversely as a *reductio hominis*, as insight into the delusion of subjectivity styling itself as the absolute."

38 *Negative Dialectics*, pp. 6, 12, 27–8, 191, 277–8.

2

Adorno and Heidegger

Conversation and communication are among the guiding mottos of contemporary thought; but the meaning of these mottos is largely opaque. Can diverse voices or idioms readily be integrated into a common conversational framework – in a manner yielding transparent understanding of all points of view? Or, conversely, are idioms and perspectives necessarily divided by an unbridgeable gulf, by the "incommensurability" (as the saying goes) of linguistic and epistemic rules? Nowhere are the dilemmas of communication and non-communication more glaringly apparent than in the context of recent German thought – particularly in the conflictual relations between Frankfurt and Freiburg or between the "critical" paradigm initiated by Horkheimer and Adorno and the ontological concerns of Heidegger (and his followers). To a large extent, contacts between the two "schools" of thought have been marked either by neglect or indifference or else by polemical hostility and an insistence on incommensurability, often coupled with hegemonial claims. Thus, in the writings of Habermas, Heidegger's opus appears predominantly as a flawed or faulty type of argument, as a series of intellectual errors or mistakes – which can be remedied only through recourse to the critical paradigm and specifically to the model of communicative reason. Approached in this manner, to be sure, philosophical exchange has the character of moral indictment and error correction rather than of a mutual learning process.[1]

This, however, is not the end of the story. As it happens, relations between Frankfurt and Freiburg exhibit moments or episodes of rapprochement and latent affinity – no matter how repressed such moments may be by surface polemics. The foremost example of a subterranean linkage is the work of Adorno – a fact which has often been noted (and deplored) by other champions of the critical paradigm.[2] To be sure, rapprochement in this case was not the result of deliberate fraternization or of any overt sympathy for Heideggerian thought; nor was it the outcome of philosophical dialogue or communication – far from it. Throughout his life, Adorno maintained a relentless opposition to Heidegger's work and lavished on it an unending stream of polemical venom, a practice aggravated by personal distance. After a furtive meeting in 1929 (which failed to generate discussion), no personal contacts occurred between the two thinkers and neither side seemed interested in, or made overtures to initiate, dialogue. Although not responding polemically in kind, Heidegger in turn remained aloof from the Frankfurt School and at one point confessed complete ignorance of Adorno's writings. Clearly, aloofness and personal animosity augur ill for rapprochement and for the claimed intellectual affinity; they seem to militate frontally against communicative interaction. Yet overt behavior in this case – as in human affairs generally – cannot have the last word. Underneath open denials or rejections (in fact, through the medium of such denials) common concerns and shared agonies can readily be sensed or detected – concerns which even can be viewed as incipient modes of dialogue. This, in any event, is the thesis I want to explore here, a thesis which by now has more than idiosyncratic status. In 1981, the German philosopher Hermann Mörchen published a weighty tome entitled *Adorno and Heidegger* which was devoted precisely to their covert liaison – and which shall serve as guide in my own reflections. Subtitled "Examination of a Refused Philosophical Communication" the volume did not stop at the overt evidence of refusal but sought to unearth the lines of an almost involuntary complicity.[3]

While not entirely unique or isolated, Mörchen's volume strikes me as an exemplary study. As a former student of Heidegger who happened to live for many decades in Frankfurt, Mörchen was pre-eminently qualified to probe the complex misunderstandings and strategies of avoidance operative between the two schools as well as their underlying motives. The intent of his book was not to dissolve prevailing disputes or differences into cognitive transparency or consensual harmony. As attempted in *Adorno and Heidegger*, dialogue is not simply a "discursive" or epistemic venture, but rather a process of mutual engagement, predicated on a willingness to "suffer" one another – and to learn from suffering. As Mörchen writes in the conclusion of his study, efforts of mediation necessarily "fall short" of their aim if they fail to satisfy the first precondition of understanding: solidarity with the "agony" of the contestants.[4] In this respect his approach is entirely congenial to me. For some time, I have tried to correlate Heidegger and Adorno, not on the level of cognitive propositions or formulas, but on that of their guiding questions or worries, steadily attempting to read one opus through or in light of the other. As it seems to me, the two thinkers start from similar predicaments, but proceed to set diverse accents – accents which must be respected in their difference. Broadly put, Adorno is absorbed by the ills or wounds of our age, while Heidegger is more drawn toward wholeness and healing. But the contrast is not absolute: in the absence of attentiveness to wounds, healing becomes an abstractly speculative or esoteric pursuit, while total preoccupation with illness encourages cynicism and despair. In the following I shall explore the liaison cautiously in three steps. A first section shall deal with the main similarities and convergences linking Heidegger and Adorno on both an overt and covert level. A second section focuses on the chief differences between their perspectives and on the primary reasons of the "refused communication." By way of conclusion I shall probe the significance of their agonal relationship for philosophical reflection in general and for contemporary political thought in particular.

I

In *Adorno and Heidegger* Mörchen first discusses the conflicts and antagonisms between the two thinkers before turning to their latent affinities. I shall reverse this sequence here, for the reason that divergences only matter (and are sources of conflict) against the backdrop of some shared concerns – which does not imply a uniformity of beliefs. Mörchen is justifiably cautious at this point, sensing the danger of shallow homogenization or of a manipulative streamlining of views. Exploration of affinities, he affirms, cannot proceed in the manner that divergent perspectives are rashly subsumed under general categories or a higher denominator. In this he echoes his chosen authors. As Heidegger himself has observed, the shared ground of thinkers becomes visible only from a vantage which "does not superficially proclaim everything as identical but rather discovers commonality in concretely prevailing differences." This comment, in turn, is not far removed from Adorno's insistence on respect for non-identity – thus bringing into view a first element of rapprochement. In his presentation, Mörchen (correctly, I believe) locates possible convergences not on the plane of answers or doctrines but on that of problems or queries – which, he surmises, derive from a set of shared experiences. The notion of commonality, he writes, should not be misconstrued in terms of a "unity of results." Instead, the seriousness of the respective arguments is evident in "the passion of individually and even epochally divergent answers"; honoring this seriousness "we have to search for affinities less in similar results or opinions than in underlying or motivating *experiences*."[5]

In terms of experiential background, both thinkers took their point of departure from the dilemmas of late modernity, that is, from the predicaments engendered by the sway of modern science and technology. For Heidegger, this sway of science was an outgrowth of Cartesian and Newtonian metaphysics and much of his opus was devoted to the "overvoming" (*Verwindung*), though not elimination, of this metaphysical heritage. Viewed under ontological auspices, modern technology appeared to him not so much as a human instrument but rather as a comprehensive paradigm "enframing" and instrumentalizing human existence (*Gestell*). For Adorno, on the other hand, modern science was part and parcel of the "dialectic of enlightenment," a development in which human mastery of nature steadily rebounded on human life by subjecting modern society increasingly to technical-managerial controls. Taking aim at this development, Adorno severely castigated modern totalitarian trends, particularly the advent of the "totally administered society" with its corollary of "damaged human life" (*beschädigtes Leben*). In pondering the dilemmas of modernity, both thinkers took their bearings from the pre-eminent philosopher of modernity, Hegel – though appropriating his teachings differently. While critiquing or obviating a "dialectic" anchored in subject–relations, Heidegger found sustenance in Hegel's relentless inquiry into being and its "thoughtful experience" (*denkende Erfahrung*); in the movement from "natural" to "absolute" consciousness (developed in Hegel's *Phenomenology*) he perceived glimpses of the ontic–ontological difference. By contrast, Adorno embraced more readily dialectical thought seen as subject–object correlation – with the proviso that dialectic could not lead to absolute knowledge, that is, to the final synthesis or identity of knowing and being. Among Hegel's heirs, Adorno maintained at least some sympathy for Marx – while shifting the accent from economic production to culture and reinterpreting "materialism" as an emblem of bodily suffering. Construing production as instrumental fabrication, Heidegger's stance was more reserved; yet he appreciated Marx's historical acumen as well as his accent on the "wordly" context of human life (as an antidote to the traditional philosophical neglect of "worldhood").[6]

In Mörchen's view, one of the deepest and most pervasive affinities between Heidegger and Adorno resides in their departure (or turning away) from metaphysical foundationalism, particularly from modern metaphysics rooted in the category of subjectivity. For both thinkers, the central task of thought and experience was to venture beyond givenness or beyond the range of the familiar and safely appropriated into an uncharted terrain which Heidegger thematized in terms of "openness" and Adorno under the rubrics of "otherness" and non-identity. Ever since *Being and Time* Heidegger conceived human existence literally as ek-sistence or as standing out or ekstasis – namely, a standing out into the domain of "being" where every form of self-possession or appropriation simultaneously implies an expropriation (*Enteignung*). Similarly Adorno castigated as ideological the modern infatuation with selfhood and self-possession, and particularly the presumed centrality of "self-preservation" – applauding instead the readiness for dispossession or the willingness to "lose oneself" in the experience of strangeness (*schöne Fremde*). For both thinkers, the critique of egocentrism (and anthropocentrism) implied a distancing from modern "individualism" – to the extent that the latter amounts to a compact, ideological doctrine; in Mörchen's words: "both concur tacitly or implicitly in refusing to acknowledge the *primacy* of the individual and treating it instead as a 'historical category'." Closely linked with the decentering of subjectivity was the attack on modern "value" theory, that is, the reduction of all phenomena to targets of subjective valuation and appraisal. In Heidegger's work, such valuation appeared as outgrowth of the modern "oblivion of being" (*Seinsvergessenheit*); as he stated at one point, "being has turned into value" – a transformation he strongly deplored. Basically, value thinking for Heidegger was the source of modern nihilism, that is, of the epochal "devaluation" of Western culture; in this context, the treatment of God as supreme value was only a synonym for the Nietzschean phrase that "God is dead." Adorno proceeded from more social and economic concerns. Building on Lukács, he saw value theory as by-product of the "commodification" of social life under capitalist auspices – a process which denuded (and secularized) the world into calculable objects or commodities. "The element of calculation in value theory," Mörchen comments, "has for both Heidegger and Adorno a near-sacrilegious quality; this is evident even when – without theological overtones – the accent is placed on valuation in the market economy."[7]

Centered in subjectivity, value theory is only the other side of reification or the objectivism sponsored by modern, "value-free" science. Heidegger and Adorno were united in their opposition to "scientism" (seen as ideological world view), particularly in its positivist garb. From Heidegger's vantage, scientism was basically another evidence of the oblivion of being, of the levelling of the ontic–ontological difference into the one-dimensional mold of empirical givenness. In Adorno's view, scientism was vitiated by its political neutrality, its bent toward conformism and its complicity with social domination. As he wrote in his contribution to the *Positivismusstreit* (*The Positivist Dispute*), the scientistic "measure of all things" is the empirical fact seen as "the solid, irreducible bedrock which the inquiring subject must not question." For both thinkers, positivism or scientism had to be distinguished from science (as a delimited enterprise), and the latter in turn from philosophical reflection on the possibility and presuppositions of inquiry as such. The second distinction was highlighted in epigrammatic statements, such as Heidegger's phrase "science does not think" or Adorno's comment that "thinking is unscientific" – which should not simply be read as anti-scientific verdicts. Following in Husserl's footsteps, Heidegger deplored in modern science the progressive atrophy of philosophical reflection, an atrophy stifling the freedom of Socratic inquiry. For Adorno, the same decay was linked with the tightening of social and political constraints; as he wrote in his "metacritique" of science: "While initially promoting philosophy's emancipation from theology, the routinized ideal of science has in the meantime turned into a fetter prohibiting reflective thought." Both thinkers were adamant in refusing to equate philosophical reflection with a finite set of propositions or a closed "system" of ideas. Adorno presented his *Negative Dialectics* provocatively as an "anti-system," that is, as a series of reflections giving room to new experiences – in contrast to the bent to (intellectual and political) mastery implicit in system-building. While not shunning systematic coherence, Heidegger in turn traced system-building to Cartesian foundationalism and the search for absolute certainty – a search which was breached for the first time in Schelling's "system of freedom." Stylistically, Adorno preferred the essay genre to formal treatises, while Heidegger presented many of his inquiries as ambivalent-exploratory *Holzwege* or *chemins qui ne mènent nulle part.*[8]

Opposition to scientism was (directly or indirectly) linked with aversion to "representation" or "representational" thought according to which the world is nothing but a construct or conception of mind or else an external imprint on sense organs. In Heidegger's work, critique of representation (*Vorstellung*) was a corollary of his attack on modern metaphysics and its tendency to reduce phenomena to empirically given data or "beings-at-hand" (*Vorhandenes*). As he wrote in "The Epoch of the World Picture" ("Die Zeit des Weltbildes"), it was only in modernity that being has been identified with the "representedness of beings" and that the world as a whole is conceived as a mental "picture"; the source of this outlook lies in modern subjectivity, in the centerstaging of human mind before which "beings constantly have to present themselves and thus turn into pictures." Still more resolutely, Adorno castigated passive cognition or mirroring receptivity in favor of critical inquiry or the critical scrutiny of experience. In formulations echoing Heidegger's arguments, his "metacritique" denounced the "picture-character" of cognition, advocating instead the "idea of a pictureless (or imageless) truth." In overtly theological fashion, the latter point was connected by Adorno with the biblical "prohibition of images," that is, the prohibition against "representing"

God or the messianic kingdom. As Mörchen notes, the shared aversion
to representation was complicated, but not cancelled, by a certain divergence of accents, a divergence deriving mainly from Heidegger's continuing attachment to phenomenological method and particularly to the
phenomenological "intuition" of being. However, intuition (*Anschauung*)
in this case did not equal subjective fancy but rather a radical openness
to appearances and their modalities. In large measure, Heidegger accepted
Kant's notion of intuitive imagination as the common source of sensibility and reason and thus of the "inner kinship" of thought and experience.
While appreciating this same kinship, Adorno found the term "intuition" unacceptable owing to its "archaic traits"; therefore (Mörchen says)
he had to pursue the dialectical, socially critical path in order to "make
room for non-identiy."[9]
    In the case of both thinkers, anti-scientism and anti-objectivism were
related to their "linguistic turn" or their intensive concern with language –
a concern which was not merely marginal or episodic (as Habermas claims)
but an integral feature pervading their entire work. For both Heidegger
and Adorno, language was not simply a means or instrument of communication; on the contrary, both saw as one of the major dilemmas of our
time the progressive instrumentalization and corruption of language.
Countering this trend, Heidegger insisted that, prior to serving as a communicative means, language is a site of ontological disclosure, in the
sense that it "brings beings qua beings first of all into openness." Relying
on this ontological premise, Heidegger defended the linguistic character
of all thinking and reflection – in contrast to the reliance of modern metaphysics on a "pure" (or non-linguistic) consciousness. Moreover, language
for him was not simply a capacity of speakers or agents of speech acts;
rather, speech was overarched by the "primacy" of language itself or its
primary appeal – a circumstance which made speaking not so much a
spontaneous initiative as rather a mode of reply or responsiveness. As
Heidegger stated, language is always "ahead of us" and we only "repeat
after it": in speaking we "submit ourselves to the appeal [*Anspruch*] of
language." On all these points Adorno's position was not far apart. Together with Heidegger, he endorsed the basic "linguisticality" of thought
and also the primacy of language over speech – although dialectics (and
the refusal of ontology) entailed again divergences of accent. Thus he
shared Heidegger's endeavor to escape the alternatives of linguistic
"realism" and an arbitrary nominalism, but his fears about "fetishizing"
or hypostatizing language often drove him back to nominalist premises.
More specifically, the primacy of language – also termed the "language
of things" (*Sprache der Dinge*) – was sometimes treated as an objective,
sociological category dialectically juxtaposed to subjective speech, a

treatment distending the intimate correlation of appeal and response. In Mörchen's words, Adorno wanted to have "no truck with current ontological theories" elevating language to the "voice of being"; yet, at the same time, he clung resolutely to the "objectivity of language," the notion that through its signifying potency language is "more than a sign."[10]

For both Heidegger and Adorno, turning to language meant injecting a temporal or historical quality into reflective thought. In fact, the focus on time and temporality was perhaps the deepest, but also the most hidden (and overtly controverted) liaison between the two thinkers. From Heidegger's vantage, the temporal character of being (first adumbrated in *Being and Time*) constituted the decisive break with traditional metaphysics and its bifurcation of passing appearances and timeless essences. In his work, being does not hover beyond time or in a timeless present, but rather participates in the interplay of past, present and future and their reciprocal incursions. Moreover, for Heidegger, the future was in a sense privileged over the present owing to its "impending" character – its ability to lay claim to us in a manner eluding subjective appropriation. From the perspective of *Dasein*, this privilege was evident in the aspect of mortality and the "anticipation of death" as an event which cannot be managed or appropriated. Here again, resonances with Adorno's views are striking, despite the latter's overt reservations or apprehensions. Throughout his life, Adorno insisted on the temporality and finitude of human experience – in defiance of metaphysical claims of timeless truths. Repeatedly he spoke of the "temporal core" (*Zeitkern*) of truth, a core vitiated by the myth of atemporal or transtemporal permanence. Far from being simply a defect, finitude (*Vergängnis*) for Adorno lent sobriety and "dignity" to human life; it also demarcated the central point where nature and history "converge" or at least become "commensurable." With Heidegger, he saw death and its anticipation as an emblem of decentering and expropriation – although he never regarded death simply as an end, but always as a gateway and as token of a hidden (messianic) hope. Under the impact of Auschwitz and the holocaust, Adorno emphatically rejected any glorification or positive metaphysics of death, insisting on the sharp distinction between ordinary mortality and violent extermination. In the latter form, death was simply an instrument of the "totally administered society," terminating a totally damaged life. As he wrote, once human existence becomes "radically substitutable," death turns into a *"quantité négligeable."*[11]

As before, affinities in this case were again closely paired with contrasts of emphasis. The main contrast had to do with the issue of ontology, specifically with the alleged "ontologization" of time and history inaugurated in *Being and Time*. According to Adorno, Heidegger's ontological approach resulted in the clandestine revival, via "temporal metaphors," of basically atemporal and ahistorical essences. As a counterpoint to Heidegger's linkage of being and time, Adorno advanced the notion of a "natural history" where nature and history ultimately coalesce on the level of finitude – and where the two terms are obviously stand-ins for the traditional subject–object bifurcation and its dialectical mediation. Noting the metaphysical overtones of this bifurcation, Mörchen comments: "Only because, no matter how correlated, the two domains (nature and history) are presupposed as Platonically *separated* must the resulting 'division' of the world again be dialectically transcended [*aufgehoben*]." Heidegger's ontological treatment of time was prompted precisely by the aim to elude this metaphysical legacy, a goal accomplished through the temporalization of being itself. What barred Adorno from pursuing a similar course was his persistent, almost visceral dismissal of being and ontological inquiry. Being, for Adorno, was an empty concept, or else a foundational myth, a mystical quality or a theological subterfuge. In his successive writings he castigated being variously as a synonym for "unconditional solidity," for an atemporal "transcendence," for an "archaic" foundation, and for an empty vacuity – portrayals which augured ill for a calm exploration of relevant philosophical issues. To qoute Mörchen again: "Contrary to his own lived experience [*Seinserfahrung*] one can show how Adorno obviated the *question* of being – and thereby doubts directed at the traditional concept of being and its possible revision." By imposing his own metaphysical view of being on his counterpart or opponent, it was Adorno and not Heidegger who "carried the project of a renewed 'ontology' ultimately *ad absurdum*."[12]

II

The preceding comments arleady lead deeply into the terrain of contestation, a terrain marked by combative élan on the part of at least one of the contestants. Before taking up substantive disputes, Mörchen's *Adorno and Heidegger* explores sources or motives of the prevailing antagonism or "refused communication." One such motive, though probably not a central one, was the sense of competition or competitiveness between diverse orientations – a motive acknowledged by Adorno in his complaint that philosophical schools at all times have talked past each other and tried "to devour each other." During Adorno's own life-time, the two most prominent schools of Continental thought were positivism and what he called "existential ontology," the former led by Karl Popper and the second by Heidegger. Both schools were targets of his critical attacks. However, while the conflict with positivism was conducted in a relatively calm and even-handed spirit, the case of Heidegger was different. As Mörchen notes, "Heidegger was the enemy" and the language reserved for him far more bitter, occasionally vitriolic, than that applied to positivists. In some instances, irony tended to moderate the harshness of the opposition; but this did not always happen. More often than not, blunt polemical assaults undermined the possibility of reciprocal dialogue – to whose need they nevertheless testified: "Unrestrained invectives were expression of a bitterness which, heaped on the adversary, acknowledged *contre coeur* the inescapability of a communicative confrontation [*Auseinandersetzung*]."[13]

Another, perhaps more important motive was the desire for intellectual differentiation and a clear-cut profile – a desire particularly pronounced among positions marked by similarity or close proximity. Such differentiation was recognized by both thinkers as an urgent need. Thus, one of Adorno's postwar writings stated expressly that "the decisive differences between philosophers are concealed in nuances" and that conflict is most implacable between positions "resembling each other but nourished by different sources." Still more forcefully, the same view was expressed in a later study on Hegel: "Philosophical thought is never more allergical than against its closest ally which compromises it by concealing the difference in principle (or regarding the whole) in an inobtrusive nuance." Needless to say, Adorno considered his relation to Heidegger as a difference in principle (*Differenz ums Ganze*); by and large, he was content to stress the aspect of implacable conflict and allergical sensitivity – without reflecting on submerged affinities. In this relationship, Heidegger did not reciprocate in kind, although he was deeply aware of the nexus of difference and proximity (but in a manner unwilling to sacrifice the latter). A case in point was Heidegger's exchange with Ernst Cassirer in 1929. As Heidegger noted at that time, "communicative reflection" (*gesellige Besinnung*) accentuates neither "conflicting opinions" nor a pliantly "submissive consensus"; rather, it bows to the issue at stake (*Sache*). In such interaction, he added, it was important not to get bogged down in different positions or vantage points but to see "how precisely the differentiation of positions is the root of (common) philosophical labor." Later efforts of differentiation were directed at Cartesianism and more generally at modern metaphysics – but never for the sake of a simple exclusion of critiqued perspectives but for that of their agonal "overcoming" (*Verwindung*) which respects persistent continuities. Basically, a similar kind of agonal liaison was detected by Heidegger in the relation between philosophy and theology and, above all, in the connection between philosophy and poetry – two enterprises located "proximately on high mountain tops separated by an abyss." In Mörchen's words: "Compared with Adorno's outlook, the uniqueness of Heidegger's 'differentiations' resides not in a reduced sharpness of contours or an objectification of views, but in the linkage of delimitation *and* solidarity."[14]

Closely associated with these hidden or recessed motives were quasi-existential and social-political issues – a domain rapidly shading over into substantive disputes. One aspect – frequently noted – is the difference in life-style and habitat, with Adorno presumably favoring urban-industrial places and Heidegger more rural or small-town settings. Varying this theme, the difference is sometimes expressed as the contrast between cosmopolitanism and provincialism, between mobility and earth-bound "autochthony," or between modernity and tradition. Adorno himself was not averse to making such comparisons – as when he equated Heidegger's "being" at one point with "agricultural" or "agrarian" predilections. While recognizing evident divergences of life-patterns (epitomized in Adorno's emigré experience), Mörchen cautions against overestimating the theme or indulging in stark bifurcations. Even at the time of his political engagement (or debacle), Heidegger was no friend of the "blood and soil" ideology; more importantly, the claim of earth-bound autochthony militates against a central feature of his view of "being": namely, its "openness" toward otherness or unfamiliar horizons. On the other hand, Adorno was not so unambiguously a defender of modernization and enlightenment to warrant his clear-cut assignment to the camp of industrial modernity. One corollary of the claimed autochthony – easily the most notorious and widely discussed corollary – is the issue of racial biases, particularly of a possible anti-Semitism on Heidegger's part. According to Mörchen, racial disdain was not only absent in, but incompatible with Heidegger's teachings – a point supported by many indictments of "racial biologism" in his writings. At the same time, indications or recorded instances of anti-Semitic *behavior* are sparse and thoroughly controverted. "Adorno's opposition to Heidegger, in any event, does not seem to have been grounded (primarily) on this issue – given that many of his criticisms were formulated prior to Heidegger's overt political involvement.[15]

Needless to say, Adorno's antagonism was greatly deepened and intensified by Heidegger's pro-Nazi affiliation; there can also be no doubt that the episode (understandably) overshadowed all subsequent relations and that Adorno at least partially blamed Heidegger for the disasters occasioned by the regime. Mörchen makes no excuses for Heidegger's political blunder nor does he defend him against relevant attacks – although he does point to Heidegger's progressive distancing from this blunder (in his writings) and also to the aspect of "errancy" (*Irrgang*) which Heidegger always associated with philosophical radicalism or open-ended inquiry. These comments or passages clearly need to be supplemented by important recent studies on the details of Heidegger's political affiliation – whose contributions to the Adorno–Heidegger theme, however, are elusive. Regarding this theme, Mörchen astutely notes a point often overlooked in polemical literature: the fact that antagonism derived not only from Heidegger's overt politics but also from his "apolitics" or his aloofness from concrete political affairs. Together with Marcuse, Adorno repeatedly denounced the abstract quality of Heideggerian "historicity" and the lack of concreteness – or "pseudo-concreteness" – of his notion of "being-in-the-world." The same lack was also at least in part responsible for Heidegger's distance from Marx (*Marx-Ferne*), especially from issues of exploitation and class struggle. While sympathetic to some of Marx's early writings, Heidegger tended to identify Marxist materialism with instrumental productivity – shortchanging the dimension of social emancipation. Mörchen's comments in this area are judiciously weighed. While appreciating Heidegger's "mountain-top" perspective (in Todtnauberg) as an antidote to vulgar conformism, he also questions its strict congruence with the lessons of *Being and Time*. Once "submergence in temporality" is seen as consonant with the meaning of *Dasein*, he queries, does dedication to "the limited goals and varied struggles of mundane life not acquire a new kind of seriousness?" Can theoretical aloofness from praxis "still enjoy the privilege granted to it by the ontological tradition?" These questions are not raised to vindicate the thriumph of praxis. Moreover, one should note that – curiously – Adorno in his later years was himself charged with "theoreticism" or a lack of practical concreteness.[16]

Turning to substantive *philosophical* objections, Mörchen right away takes up an issue which was clearly crucial in obstructing debate: the issue of ontology. What chiefly aroused Adorno's antagonism in this respect was the ontic–ontological correlation, more specifically Heidegger's claim that *Dasein* is the kind of being which cares about "being" or whose "ontic characteristic" resides in its being "ontological." For Adorno, this claim was either a tautology or else a sleight of hand whereby mundane phenomena were magically "ontologized," that is, endowed with permanent essence or meaning. By means of this sleight of hand, Heidegger's thought was presumed to relapse into a traditional (Platonic) metaphysics and ultimately into a speculative type of foundationalism or essentialism. Moreover, from Adorno's vantage, "being" was simply a higher-level object to be grasped through cognitive or conceptual means – a grasp which was predicated on a constitutive subjectivity or an underlying subjectivism. As he wrote, Heidegger's ontology adumbrated an "object-realm of a quasi-higher order"; yet, as in the case of positivism or Husserl's eidetic inquiry, "rigid objectivism" was only a camouflage or the reverse side of a "hidden subjectivism." Commenting on these charges, Mörchen shows (convincingly, I believe) their largely misguided or untenable character. What is entirely missed or bypassed in Adorno's critique is Heidegger's radical revision of traditional metaphysics, his attempt to extricate being and ontology from objectivism and customary "two-world" theories. More importantly, being for Heidegger was never a doctrine or positive proposition but rather a question or problem – a question which had widely been forgotten in modern philosophy and which his work (at least in its early phase) sought to revive. According to Mörchen, Adorno's charge of "ontologization" involved at least three misconstruals: a misreading of the ontic–ontological difference; imputation of an atemporal meaning of being; and subsumption of ontic beings under atemporal essences. It is "difficult to imagine," he adds, that these misconstruals "resulted from a simple misunderstanding; for they conflict too obviously with Heidegger's texts."[17]

Fleshing out different dimensions of the topic, the study elaborates first on presumed motives of ontologization. In Adorno's view, a chief motive was the desire for fixity and "security" – a desire which Heidegger allegedly shared with "bourgeois" philosophy and its perennial striving for stability, secure property, and individual self-preservation. As Mörchen indicates, this claim is far from the mark – given that Heidegger's thought was basically averse to self-enclosure or egocentrism; security in his opinion meant basically "non-caring" (sine cura) or an unwillingness to care, in violation of Dasein's central existential characteristic. Desire for security was closely linked for Adorno with the strategy of "hypostasis" or hypostatization, that is, the elevation of passing or ephemeral phenomena into invariant structures and fateful constraints. One of the most objectionable features of traditional philosophy, in his portrayal, was its preoccupation with "permanent, unchanging" essences and, accordingly, its bent to hypostatize historical experiences into timeless truths; Heidegger's ontology was part and parcel of this attempt to "expel historical change from thought." In making these claims, Mörchen retorts, Adorno erases the distinctions between being and invariance and between invariance and lasting meaning; more importantly, he neglects Heidegger's resolute departure from metaphysics and his reformulation of "Wesen" (essence) as a transitive verb. In Heidegger's treatment, Wesen means "to permeate" or "to be steadily present with" (Anwesen); from a historical vantage, it means "past being" or what is present as past (Gewesen). Given these repeated statements, it is "hard to see" how the charge of hypostasis could be raised. The same holds true of the accusation of "pseudo-concreteness" (previously mentioned). For Adorno, the illusion of concreteness arose from the conflation of abstract conceptual categories (like being) and ontic-empirical phenomena, a process whereby Heideggerian thought acquired surreptitiously an aura of non-abstraction or concrete relevance. The issue could be clarified, Mörchen comments, if the presumed pseudo-concreteness were judged in light of Hegel's notion of concreteness – which presupposes that "being" not be seen as an empty concept or immediate intuition but rather as a "gathering" relating everything that is.[18]

A further defect of Heidegger's ontology – one particularly important to Adorno – was its presumed attempt to encompass all phenomena and thus to integrate reality into a uniform holistic structure. Approaching the term cognitively, he saw "being" as a "totalizing" concept destined to ride roughshod over concrete phenomenal differences or the realm of "non-identity." In Adorno's own view, wholeness or totality was basically a characteristic of modern social life or of the "totally administered society" – but as such it was precisely an emblem of domination and oppression from which critical thought was meant to seek an exit. As he stated in one of his more notorious passages: "the whole is the untrue" – an indictment which, in application to Heidegger, signified the untruth of an ontology camouflaging oppression and asserting the wholeness (or wholesomeness) of existing affairs. What this criticism neglects, Mörchen reminds us, is again the ontic–ontological difference – a distinction not unfamiliar to Adorno. While sharply castigating "totalitarian" oppression, his writings obstinately clung to holistic aspirations – provided they were given a critical or "negative" cast and limited to "gleaning holistic insight preferably from fragments." Yet for Heidegger too, wholeness was basically fragile or porous and by no means synonymous with positively given structures. As he affirmed in one of his early writings, "human existence is nothing whole" – to which he later added the rejection of a metaphysics pretending to render "the whole range of beings in its totality" accessible to finite *Dasein*. Basically, being in his treatment was a question through which human *Dasein* and cognition are themselves called into question – making completely illusory a conceptual grasp of the whole. Here is the "decisive point," Mörchen notes: "The 'whole' is no longer the *object* of our cognition but rather the context of our intensive questioning. If *we* try to encompass it, we miss that which encompasses *us* – more unambiguously: what *dawns* upon us."[19]

Adorno's conceptualism was the source of another charge, often repeated in his work: that of the supposed "immediacy" of ontological cognition, a directness violating the "dialectical" insight into the subjective mediation of all knowledge. By turning to the category of being, the charge holds, Heidegger "naively restored" the specter of immediacy in our complicated world, thus endowing ordinary human beliefs with the "dignity" of an immediate grasp (of essences). What his ontology bypassed of ignored was "dialectics," in its Hegelian or post-Hegelian mold: the realization "that no being can be thought without (human) being, nor the latter without mediation." In terms of Hegelian dialectics, being as such or in its immediacy was the most general and most empty notion – which, in order to gain concreteness as a concept, had to be mediated through subjectivity or "individual human consciousness." While modifying or revising Hegelian teachings (chiefly by truncating synthesis), Adorno clung to the dialectical subject–object correlation as a necessary philosophical schema. As Mörchen points out in his rejoinder, Heidegger was far from relinquishing the human element in cognition, as is evident in his treatment of "understanding" as a basic existential category. More importantly, Heidegger questioned Hegelian metaphysics and its subject-centered view of (conceptual) being – arguing that, far from being a constitutive source, subjectivity is primordially "mediated" by and through being. In this manner, Hegel's movement from unmediated abstractness to concreteness became a guidepost for ontological inquiry – but *beyond* Hegel's formulations. In Heidegger's own words: treated as "indefinite immediacy" grounded in a constitutive subject, being cannot be "released" from its relation to subjectivity, but only be viewed "in abstraction" form the latter. As a corollary, the relation of being and nothingness involved for him not a dialectic of thesis and antithesis or negation, but rather an ontological implication – predicated on the finitude of being and the exposure of *Dasein* to nihilation. Concealment and unconcealment, likewise, were not dialectical opposites but rather emblems of a primary "agon" (*Urstreit*) where being itself is at stake or contested as the "open middle." Seen against this background, Adorno's objection goes astray – although it remains potent (Mörchen says) against those misconstruing being in terms of Hegelian immediacy.[20]

In more polemical garb, the claimed immediacy of being was denounced by Adorno variously as a "cult of origins," as speculative "mysticism" or else as a general manifestation of "irrationalism." Since these labels are largely interchangeable and in many ways dependent on the issue of dialectics, their discussion here can be brief. By treating being as primordial givenness, Heidegger is said to have precipitated himself into the "abyss of archaism"; in fact, the "fallacy of origins" or primordiality is the aspect of his philosophy which "first and foremost requires critique." For Adorno, the project of a "fundamental ontology" (announced in *Being and Time*) involved a revival of *prima philosophia* with its concomitant claims of supremacy – claims which socially and politically were not innocent. For to reinstitute being as "highest catchword" means to sanction the pre-eminence of those able to determine the meaning of being; in this sense, return to origins or *"archai"* signifies submission to external authority – for *archē* means domination. Guided by critical-emancipatory aims, Adorno sought to break the "spell" of foundationalism, that is, to expose "the mighty claims of *prima philosophia* as empty." As Mörchen is able to show, this endavor was largely shared by Heidegger – though with less polemical élan (and with a bracketing of political connotations). Fundamental ontology in his treatment was not an exercise in foundationalism, but rather a preparatory step toward the "question of being" – which as question could not provide a solid ground. Likewise, *Dasein* for him was not an Archimedean point but the site of radical exposure and "dissemination" (*Streuung*). In addition, the term "origin" (*Ursprung*) has two possible meanings which Adorno fails to distinguish: namely, origin as the place from which thought proceeds and as a possibility to which it is underway (as a calling). Only the first meaning has the character of solid fixity while the second involves a journey into uncharted terrain. In Heidegger's words, ontological inquiry into origins or beginnings is a "foward or forward-directed" inquiry, not one looking "backwards." Still more clearly this view is expressed in *Der Satz vom Grund* where thinking is called "commemorative anticipatory thinking" (*andenkendes Vordenken*).[21]

Less attention need probably be paid to the charges of "mysticism" or a "mythology of being" – given the admittedly vague character of these labels and their widespread use in our century (for example, as a staple in the positivist arsenal). In turning to archaic origins, Adorno asserts, Heidegger took flight from history, entering instead into "complicity with myth" – where myth or "the mythical" means that which "has always been," which "as predestined or pregiven being determines historical life." Although suspicious of complete "demythologization," Adorno's own work aimed to undercut or dispel this mythical determinism, thereby dissolving the "nexus of blind fate" (*Verblendungszusammenhang*). In these polemical forays, ontology was again an ill-chosen target. While acknowledging the complex relationship of *mythos* and *logos*, Heidegger saw philosophizing as wedded to the "thinking of being" and not as a product of myth or mythology. Similarly with regard to mysticism, he insisted that philosophy "never arises" from the former – although mystical insight may well be a preamble or genuine partner of philosophy. In many respects, mysticism was a synonym for irrationalism – a label which again enjoys broad currency (and which, curiously, has been applied by positivist both to Heidegger and Adorno). In Adorno's usage, the label aimed basically at the opacity of being and a certain "contempt" for science allegedly present in "some of Heidegger's formulations." The charge, Mörchen retorts, is too vague to carry much weight – and can readily be refuted from Heidegger's texts which denounce the substitution of irrationalism for rationality as well as a sentimental anti-intellectualism or "slave rebellion" against reason. Actually, both thinkers acknowledged the correlation and mutual dependence of irrationalism and rationalism, especially where the latter stands as synonym for an instrumental or calculating rationality. Both thinkers likewise sought to find a path leading beyond this paired opposition – Heidegger by turning to "commemorative thinking" and Adorno to the "non-rational" rationality of mimetic art.[22]

Returning to social and political considerations, Mörchen finds conflict in this domain much more substantive and decisive – and accordingly offers detailed discussion of its various dimensions. The chief questions or issues examined at this point are: to what extent Heidegger's opus may be viewed as "proto-fascist"; more specifically, to what degree his thought was "affirmative" by urging conformity with the "powers that be"; whether, in line with some modern trends, he basically promoted "inwardness" (*Innerlichkeit*) and whether his notion of *Dasein* implied individual isolation, to the exclusion of social-political concerns. Contrary to many critics, Adorno did not accuse Heidegger of overt fascism or of directly endorsing the tenets of National Socialist ideology (some of which were implausible enough). Instead, he focused on latent, almost subliminal modes of complicity and affinity, modes deriving from his ontological, quasi-mythological bent and which lent to his thought at least a "proto-fascist" quality or potential. Foremost among these covert linkages was Heidegger's submission to being, that is, his acceptance of ontological "destiny" which translates politically into endorsement of dominant powers. According to Adorno, Heidegger's ontology was merely a doubling of existing reality, coupled with its uncritical "affirmation"; in this sense, his work stood in "objective accord with a society heading into the darkness of stark domination," thus providing an "apology of power from a supposedly higher vantage." In contrast to such complicity, Adorno's own work was wedded entirely to the task of critical negation; together with Horkheimer and Marcuse, he aimed to debunk the "affirmative character of culture," rejecting any positive depiction of truth or the "absolute" (as a kind of idolatry). In proceeding in this manner, Mörchen notes, Adorno occasionally ignored or at least slighted an important dialectical insight: the need for "determinate negation" – which cannot involve a total rejection of reality. In the case of total negation, does critique not leave room as an antidote only for a fancied "irreality," shading over into nothingness? Against this background, is there not a legitimate place for ontological reflection – on a plane preceding both affirmation and critical negation?[23]

Acceptance or affirmation of reality was only the reverse side of the charge of inwardness or an "inward turn" (*Verinnerlichung*) which Heidegger presumably shared with a long-standing tendency in German thought. Inwardness for Adorno meant basically a retreat into "a private sphere exempt from the power of reification" – but a retreat which precisely sanctioned or reinforced external constraints. While serving a progressive function in earlier times, this "inward turn" was nowadays "ideologically misused," by lending tacit consent to oppression. Heidegger's *Being and Time* was said to provide evidence of this turn, mainly in its focus on *Dasein*, its "mood" or existential tuning, and its precarious "authenticity" (divorced from "the They"); at least in its "basic approach" fundamental ontology was claimed to pay tribute to the "cult of inwardness" while relegating "world" or worldliness to a marginal position. Relying on numerous Heideggerian passages, Mörchen is able to counter this charge or at least to correct its pathos. Thus, Heidegger repeatedly portrayed existence as an "ekstatic standing out" – in opposition to a "subjective inner sphere" – while mood (*Stimmung*) in *Being and Time* signified a mode of being-in-the-world, one "arising neither from 'without' nor from 'within'" and thus at odds with the inner–outer bifurcation. Authenticity, on the other hand, meant a concerned or careful type of "in-being" which did not cancel but rather heightened relationships in the world (without leveling *Dasein* into social conformism). Similar passages could be cited with regard to individualism or individuation – terms which Adorno himself used gingerly and not without ambivalence. For Heidegger, individuation was a basic aspect of the "facticity" of *Dasein*, highlighted particularly in "being-toward-death" – but an aspect not simply antithetical to *Dasein*'s relational worldliness. As he stated in *Being and Time*, although *Dasein* involves the "possibility and necessity of radical individuation," this feature remains "equally primordial" with co-being or being-with-others (*Mitsein*) – because of joint participation in world and temporality. For Heidegger, the antidote to individual isolation was not social collectivity (seen as a subject-writ-large) but rather shared "in-being" – a view which needs to be compared with (and differentiated from) Adorno's postulated "dialectic" of individual and society.[24]

III

The preceding discussion has yielded a host of issues, a complex welter of antagonisms, misunderstandings, and possible convergences. In sifting through this welter, Mörchen displays a solid familiarity with texts as well as an impeccable fair-mindedness or equanimity – a rare quality among writers in this field. In terms of scholarship, his study is a rich storehouse of literary information, sometimes to the point that lines of argument are nearly overwhelmed by relevant citations and references. In carefully weighing charges and likely rejoinders, *Adorno and Heidegger* seeks to initiate or lay the groundwork for a "posthumous dialogue" between the two thinkers and the respective schools of thought, a dialogue which in actuality has never come to pass. Prospects for real-life dialogical exchanges are slim in our own time, owing to a deterioration of the intellectual climate.[25] As previously indicated, recent writings by Frankfurt theorists tend to be strongly polemical or vituperative in character, a trend fueled by intensified debates surrounding Heidegger's political past. Mörchen's choice of Adorno is felicitous and promising against this background: although an accomplished polemicist in his own right, his work was animated (at least in part) by rudiments of shared assumptions or concerns. Initiation of dialogue in this case is not only opportune, however, but also fruitful and important. More sharply than recent post-structuralist ventures, I believe, Adorno's agonal approach to Heidegger brings into focus an array of philosophical questions or problems, questions which are crucial to followers of both thinkers and more generally to students of contemporary Continental thought.

While fruitful and desirable, communicative exchange is complicated in numerous respects – which Mörchen does not ignore. One major obstacle is the notion of "communication" itself which both Adorno and Heidegger treated with considerable suspicion. Some of the former's pronouncements on the topic were stark and uncompromising. "Everything that today is called communication," his *Negative Dialectics* stated, "is without exception only the noise which drowns out the silence of the exiled." Faithful to his non-conformist stance, he lashed out against the "general euphoria of communication" promoted by modern mass media; his own thinking, in any case, sought to escape the "net of socialization and communication," to give expression to "what does not yet carry the imprint of universal communication." On this level, parallels can readily be detected with Heidegger's discussion of "the They" (*das Man*) as well as of everyday "chatter" or random talk (*Gerede*). In the case of both thinkers, to be sure, suspicion of communication was not equivalent to a rejection of dialogue or communicative interaction – provided room was made for otherness or the uniqueness of idioms and also for the "unsaid" (and perhaps unsayable). Adorno's aesthetics granted to art a special role here, namely, to communicate "through non-communication"; following the example of art, philosophical language likewise had to "cancel communication" where this was necessary to escape routinized conformism. For his part, Heidegger juxtaposed to chatter a more thoughtful, poetic mode of dialogue (*Gespräch*), a mode animated not so much by subjective speech acts as rather by attentiveness to the cues of language. In view of these reservations and provisos, attempts at conversation – even if posthumously and imaginatively staged – have to be wary of facile harmonization or consensualism. "There is no *total* communication," Mörchen admits; but there is a "limited" one which always presupposes exclusion of some other kinds of communication. To this extent, deficits of communication are "unavoidable."[26]

Limitations of this kind are aggravated by overt political contrasts, particularly by the different placement of the two thinkers on the prevailing political spectrum. Needless to say, Adorno and the Frankfurt School are solidly located on the "Left" – which seems to leave for Heidegger only a position on the "Right" (unless he is relegated to the vacuum of political irrelevance). This distinction is underscored by Adorno's long-standing Marxist sympathies, in comparison with Heidegger's more distant and often critical stance. In large measure, these political and ideological divisions are so entrenched today that the chances of loosening their hold are small. Yet, as Mörchen rightly insists, exploration of the Adorno–Heidegger liaison cannot fruitfully proceed unless some effort is made to erode the grip of traditional ideologies and nomenclature. Heidegger, he notes, cannot as readily or thoughtlessly be assigned to a Rightist position as is often done – particularly as long as the latter is identified with a backward-looking conservatism. On the other hand, Leftism is today undergoing an internal soul-searching and reassessment, a process placing in jeopardy its customary moorings in a Left-Hegelian (or humanist Marxist) type of "praxis" philosophy. More generally, the entire theory-praxis issue or conundrum is experiencing a thoroughgoing scrutiny and re-evaluation – whose effects were already clearly discernible in Adorno's case. These developments dictate at least caution with regard to political labels. In Mörchen words: "Whether the superficially useful Right–Left model still suffices in order to locate the partners of the dialogue (once it gets started), remains doubtful. Perhaps the political options inaugurated under Heideggerian auspices are *different* – and should at least initially be *kept open*."[27]

These comments cannot and are not meant to provide a political alibi.

While eluding customary labels, Heidegger was probably too reticent (outside his overt political blunder) to ponder the social and political implications of his thought – a fact which even his supporters must find disturbing. In the conclusion of his study, Mörchen explores the possible "limits" or blind spots of Heidegger's work and the extent to which they were correctly pinpointed by Adorno. He finds some merit in the charge of "pseudo-concreteness" and of certain "counter-enlightenment" tendencies. However, the main limit or deficiency resides for him in the "bracketing of the social field of conflict" or of concrete social-political struggles. In fact, this bracketing constitutes for him the central target of Adorno's critical objection, and he complains himself of Heidegger's "embarrassing insensitivity for problems of social and international oppression, of unjust privileges and modes of domination." This complaint does not by itself vindicate Adorno's position – whose reverse blind spot was the neglect of ontology – but it carries an element of ferment into Heidegger's perspective and his (loosely defined) school of thought. Strictly speaking, such ferment is not so much "carried into" his perspective (from outside), but is rather endemic or intrinsic to his focus on temporality and worldliness; given his departure from traditional metaphysics, mundane social life cannot possibly be excluded from ontological inquiry. As Mörchen observes, the "weakest" point in Heidegger's work – in light of his own "understanding of being" – is the fact that his neglect of the "concrete tasks" of social and political life, his "untimely" attitude à la Nietzsche, *may* be construed as an "escape from a concrete immersion into temporality." While opening up an "unusual breadth of horizons," his mountain-top perspective in this respect carried a price: namely, that of loosening the nexus of being and time. This loosening was either not seen or not acknowledged by Heidegger as a philosophical problem. In any event, he seemed to have "difficulty" in admitting the relevance of mundane social affairs for his question of the temporality of being. Although perceiving everywhere the symptoms of ontological oblivion and technological enframing (*Gestell*), he did not integrate their effects so thoroughly into his thought as to erase "a remnant of unconquered metaphysics, namely, distance from time."[28]

As Mörchen recognizes, however, time for Heidegger did not simply mean clock-time – an aspect which injects some ambivalence into his presumed "distance from time." At another point, his study speaks of social distance or "distance from society" (*Gesellschaftsferne*), a term borrowed from Adorno – but with an open admission of the double-edged or ambivalent character of this distance. Following Adorno, Mörchen deplores his teacher's aloofness from concrete social-political dilemmas. "Overly preoccupied by his central experience of the oblivion of being," he writes, Heidegger seems to have no more room left "for the (seemingly) different question regarding the inveterate, anti-human power of societal constraints – and regarding the connection, perhaps the identity of the two questions." As a result, Heidegger does not give us concrete guidance in political contexts, in situations "where we need to ponder the dangers likely to result from mutually conflicting political tendencies which solicit our support." Yet the verdict is not entirely clear cut or free from doubt. While shielding him from ongoing political debates, social distance or distance from existing society also had a liberating effect for Heidegger – by bringing into view social possibilities or vistas which would have remained hidden from a more thoroughly integrated or socially embedded vantage. The ambivalent relation of nearness and distance, of the proper and alien is a persistent theme in his opus. Thus, *Being and Time* describes being as both closest to and farthest removed from *Dasein*; while concretely inserted into the world, the latter is also termed a "creature of distance" shot through with otherness. As Mörchen concedes, philosophical distance from reality is "not to be condemned if it helps us to become the 'creature of distance' which we are" – an admission complicating his (and Adorno's) central objection. Perhaps, he adds, the presumed limits or deficits of Heidegger's thought are conditioned also by "our prejudices and fixed categories": while, more open to the "things themselves," he "experienced more strangely and expressed more originally" what we deem to be excluded.[29]

Ambivalence of this kind, one should add, was not entirely foreign to Adorno. Closeness to society in his case was never a synonym for pliant adaptation or for a "realism" shunning distant possibilities or utopian hopes. From this perspective, the relation between the two thinkers involved not so much a "total" difference (or *Differenz ums Ganze*) as a difference of accent – but one which remained crucial and reverberated through all facets of the respective works. Basically, Adorno preferred always to stay close to the agonies of his time and to the dilemmas and conflicts of present-day industrial society: although straining beyond present ills (toward "reconciliation"), he forbade himself any cognitive-philosophical conception of the "good life" or of a reconciled condition. It was the focus on suffering and real-life oppression – and not any kind of doctrinaire materialism – which attracted him to Marxist thought seen as a program of ideological critique. It was the same emphasis which prompted him to embrace features of traditional "dialectics" viewed as tensional subject–object relation – because most people in present-day society find themselves mired in subject–object splits and resulting modes of alienation. Even when – as in his aesthetic theory – he allowed himself to insert glimpses of a reconciled or "undamaged" life, these glimpses were fragile, fragmentary and elusive. Adorno's fixation on present-day ills has earned him the reputation of melancholy or pessimism – not entirely without justification. As he stated in *Minima Moralia*, "there is no right or good life in the midst of the wrong life" (of our time) – implying that present-day society is completely and irremediably wrong or corrupted. Rebelling against the eternal "truths" of traditional metaphysics, he calimed at another point that what is invariant or unchanging is not truth or happiness but only human suffering and misery. Undoubtedly, one of the strongest motivations of this outlook was the experience of Auschwitz and the holocaust. In the face of this experience, he argued, relentless opposition to and "hatred" of evil, not sympathy, was the only viable response: "It is one of the grimmest features of our age that nearly all those gestures through which goodness is directly proclaimed – such as love of neighbor – turn imperceptibly and willy-nilly into evil, while those persisting in relentless defiance acquire the reputation of inhumanity, misanthropy, skepsis and destructiveness."[30]

What emerges in such statements is a negative ontology or rather antiontology potentially jeopardizing being as such. In some of his writings, Adorno castigated the traditional notion of "essential being" (*Wesen*) as a synonym for corruption and deformity (*Unwesen*), a deformity to be combatted and abolished rather than being accepted as invariant. His *Negative Dialectics* talked about the present world as "wrong or rotten to its core" (*bis ins Innerste falsche Welt*), while portraying its own approach (of critical dialectics minus synthesis) as an "ontology of the wrong or corrupt reality." By contrast, Heidegger's thought was accused of offering a "positive" or uncritical ontology, one presenting existing reality basically as already redeemed or reconciled.[31] While provocative and evidently the outgrowth of deep agony, these formulations are hazardous and fraught with profound philosophical quandaries. Clearly, if existing reality is wrong or evil in its essential being (*Wesen*) or its core, then goodness becomes entirely un-real or chimerical – while change for the better can be expected only from a radical apocalypse. What lurks behind these views is an incipient Manicheism, a concept of two opposed principles, with this-worldly reality entirely in the grip of corruption – until it is destroyed by other-worldly intervention. If Manicheism is to be avoided, then ontology cannot be restricted to wrong or deformed reality (*Unwesen*); accordingly, thought of being cannot exclusively be negative or critical in character but must include thought of "undamaged" or reconciled being – yielding an ontology of the intertwining of wholeness and deformity, or of the interplay of presence and absence, being and nothingness. In theological terms, the issue harkens back to disputes surrounding the effects of the "fall": disputes highlighted by the opposing labels of "*corruptio naturae*" and "*vulnera naturae*," where the notion of a wounded nature intimates a damaged but not irremediably corrupt this-worldly reality.

These comments obviously do not vindicate a "positive" or entirely uncritical ontology, one bypassing the widespread experience of corruption and oppression. One of Adorno's most relentless objections – which supporters of Heidegger should carefully heed – is the charge of an "affirmative" stance blindly endorsing existing conditions or the "powers that be." Perhaps, in cultivating his social distance, Heidegger did not always sufficiently guard against the peril or lure of this stance – despite his general indictment of technological domination (*Gestell*). Yet, ontologically, the situation is more complex. As Mörchen reminds us (correctly, I believe), some sort of "primary confidence" or pre-cognitive acceptance is necessary for human living and thinking to proceed – in line with what Merleau-Ponty called "perceptual faith." In Heidegger's own formulation: "every negation is only the affirmation of the Not," that is, the acceptance of "not-being" in being – which does not detract in any way from the reality of not-being and from the deformation and oblivion of being. At least occasionally, Adorno himself spoke of the dialectic of affirmation and negation, and of the need to recognize and affirm, no matter how intermittently, the redeemed quality or potential of being – or, in Benjamin's phrase, the "chips of messianic time." Perhaps, as Mörchen notes again, buried deeply underneath philosophical disputes there hovers another theological difference: namely, the demarcation between Jewish and Christian Messianism, the latter characterized by affirmation of divine redemption and incarnation, the former by indefinite postponement of the messianic event. If this assumption is correct – and there is evidence in the writings of both thinkers – then there is a need to recognize and accept the demarcation, while simultaneously making room for a possible reconciliation. Insistence on postponement shields against complacency and against complicity in prevailing modes of injustice; at the same time, however, absolute or infinite postponement acts as a barrier to the hoped for event. Conversely, shunning false euphoria and mundane complicity, Christian belief must cultivate sober expectancy or a sense of lying in wait – without relinquishing trust in incarnation and in a temporal existence transfigured, every so often, by chips of messianic time.[32]

NOTES

1 Compare especially the discussion of Heidegger's work in Jürgen Habermas, *The Philosophical Discourse of Modernity: Twelve Lectures*, tr. Frederick Lawrence (Cambridge, MA: MIT Press, 1987), pp. 131–60. See also Habermas's Preface in Victor Farias, *Heidegger und der Nationalsozialismus*, tr. Klaus Laerman (Frankfurt-Main: Fischer, 1989), pp. 11–37.

2 As Habermas observes at one point, Adorno's aesthetics comes "shockingly close" to Heideggerian ontology; see Habermas, *The Theory of Communicative Action*, vol. 1: *Reason and the Rationalization of Society*, tr. Thomas McCarthy (Boston: Beacon Press, 1984), p. 385.

3 Hermann Mörchen, *Adorno und Heidegger: Untersuchung einer philosophischen Kommunikationsverweigerung* (Stuttgart: Klett-Cotta, 1981). The meeting occurred in January of 1929 in Frankfurt after a lecture presented by Heidegger; the confession of ignorance was made to Richard Wisser in 1969. See *Adorno und Heidegger*, pp. 13, 17, note 11; also Günther Neske, ed., *Erinnerung an Martin Heidegger* (Pfullingen: Neske, 1977), p. 283.

4 Mörchen, *Adorno und Heidegger*, p. 659.

5 *Adorno und Heidegger*, pp. 484–7. The citation is taken from Heidegger's (so far unpublished) lectures of 1926–7 on the history of philosophy from Thomas Aquinas to Kant.

6 *Adorno und Heidegger*, pp. 489, 492. As Mörchen adds, both Heidegger and Adorno were much less sanguine than Marx about the possibility of a theory–praxis coincidence or the sublation of theory into praxis. Regarding Heidegger's stance compare Chapter 6 below ("Heidegger and Marxism").

7 Mörchen, *Adorno und Heidegger*, pp. 490, 493, 504–6. Emphasizing the theological component in Heidegger's case he observes (p. 505): "Here is the *decisive* motivation of Heidegger's critique of valuation: it is directed against such 'slighting or downgrading of God' and against 'the greatest blasphemy which can be committed against being'." The Heidegger citation is taken from *Holzwege* (Frankfurt-Main: Klostermann, 1950), pp. 238–9.

8 Mörchen, *Adorno und Heidegger*, pp. 506–12, 515–23, 528–30. Compare Adorno et al., *The Positivist Dispute in German Sociology*, tr. Glyn Adey and David Frisby (New York: Harper & Row, 1976), pp. 30–31; Adorno, *Minima Moralia: Reflexionen aus dem beschädigten Leben* (Frankfurt-Main: Suhrkamp, 1951), p. 161; *Zur Metakritik der Erkenntnistheorie* (Frankfurt-Main: Suhrkamp, 1971), p. 49; *Negative Dialectics*, tr. E.B. Ashton (New York: Seabury Press, 1973), p. xx; Heidegger, *Vorträge und Aufsätze* (Pfullingen: Neske, 1967), Pt. 2, p. 7; *Schellings Abhandlung Über das Wesen der menschlichen Freiheit* (1809) (Tübingen: Niemeyer, 1971), p. 58.

9 Mörchen, *Adorno und Heidegger*, pp. 543–8, 554–7. Compare Heidegger,

Holzwege, pp. 69, 82–4; Adorno, *Zur Metakritik der Erkenntnistheorie*, pp. 141, 148.

10 Mörchen, *Adorno und Heidegger*, pp. 562–4, 566–75. Compare Heidegger, *On the Way to Language*, tr. Peter D. Hertz (New York: Harper & Row, 1971), pp. 75, 111–12; *Holzwege*, p. 60; Adorno, *Negative Dialectics*, pp. 85–6, 111. For both thinkers, the primacy of language involved not only overt sayings, but also the dimension of the unsaid or unsayable – a corollary (at least in Heidegger's case) of the interplay of unconcealment and concealment. On Adorno's conception of language (and its relation to Walter Benjamin) see also Martin Jay, "Habermas and Modernism", in Richard J. Bernstein, ed., *Habermas and Modernity* (Cambridge, MA: MIT Press, 1985), pp. 128–36.

11 Mörchen, *Adorno und Heidegger*, pp. 588–94, 598, 602–8. Compare Adorno, *Negative Dialectics*, pp. 350, 371; *Minima Moralia*, p. 312; *Prismen: Kulturkritik und Gesellschaft* (Frankfurt-Main: Suhrkamp, 1969), p. 147.

12 Mörchen, *Adorno und Heidegger*, pp. 613–16, 625–8. Compare Adorno, *Negative Dialectics*, pp. 107, 110, 117–18, 129, 396; *Minima Moralia*, p. 202; *Zur Metakritik der Erkenntnistheorie*, pp. 29, 137; *Noten zur Literatur*, vol. 3 (Frankfurt-Main: Suhrkamp, 1965), p. 171.

13 Mörchen, *Adorno und Heidegger*, pp. 209–11. Compare Adorno, *Negative Dialectics*, p. 32.

14 Mörchen, *Adorno und Heidegger*, pp. 212–14, 220–30. Compare Adorno, *Prismen*, p. 286: *Drei Studien zu Hegel* (Frankfurt-Main: Suhrkamp, 1963), p. 86; Heidegger, *Kant und das Problem der Metaphysik* (1929; 4th edn, Frankfurt-Main: Klostermann, 1973), pp. 259, 268; *Aus der Erfahrung des Denkens* (Pfullingen: Neske, 1954), p. 11: *Wegmarken* (Frankfurt-Main: Klostermann, 1967), p. 107. The only exception to Heidegger's blending of delimitation and solidarity can be found in some of his writings on Nietzsche (which accentuate antagonism).

15 Mörchen, *Adorno und Heidegger*, pp. 245–9, 251–2, 254 (note 128). Compare Adorno, *Philosophische Terminologie*, vol. 1 (Frankfurt-Main: Suhrkamp, 1973), p. 163. The charge of "provincialism" was raised, among others, by Habermas in his *laudatio* for Hans-Georg Gadamer; see Habermas, "Urbanisierung der Heideggerschen Provinz", in Gadamer and Habermas, *Das Erbe Hegels* (Frankfurt-Main: Suhrkamp, 1979), pp. 9–31.

16 Mörchen, *Adorno und Heidegger*, pp. 255–71. The simple triumph of praxis was rejected by Adorno repeatedly, as in this statement: "*Humanitas* awakens with the separation of theory and praxis; it is alien to that non-differentiation which in reality bows to the primacy of praxis." See *Stichworte: Kritische Modelle 2* (Frankfurt-Main: Suhrkamp, 1969), p. 178. For recent studies on Heidegger's politics compare Victor Farias, *Heidegger und der Nationalsozialismus*, and Hugo Ott, *Martin Heidegger: Unterwegs zu seiner Biographie* (Frankfurt-Main: Campus, 1988); for an English version

of the former study see *Heidegger and Nazism*, ed. Joseph Margolis and Tom Rockmore, tr. Paul Burell and Gabriel R. Ricci (Philadelphia: Temple University Press, 1989).

17 Mörchen, *Adorno und Heidegger*, pp. 291–6, 302 (note 44). Compare Adorno, *Negative Dialectics*, pp. 76, 109–10, 115–16; *Zur Metakritik der Erkenntnistheorie*, pp. 82, 192; Heidegger, *An Introduction to Metaphysics*, tr. Ralph Manheim (Garden City, NY: Anchor Books, 1961), pp. 32–3. For critical discussions of Adorno's conception of ontology see also my "Phenomenology and Critique: Adorno", in Dallmayr, *Critical Encounters* (Notre Dame: University of Notre Dame Press, 1987), pp. 39–72.

18 Mörchen, *Adorno und Heidegger*, pp. 297–302, 306–13, 315–18. Compare Adorno, *Negative Dialectics*, pp. 52, 93, 103–4; *Philosophische Terminologie*, vol. 2 (Frankfurt-Main: Suhrkamp, 1974), p. 233; Heidegger, *Holzwege*, pp. 80, 275; *Wegmarken*, pp. 96, 225; *Zur Sache des Denkens* (Tübingen: Niemeyer, 1969), p. 12.

19 Mörchen, *Adorno und Heidegger*, pp. 324–34. Compare Adorno, *Minima Moralia*, p. 57; *Negative Dialectics*, p. 369; *Noten zur Literatur*, vol. 4 (Frankfurt-Main: Suhrkamp, 1974), p. 45; Heidegger, "Anmerkungen zu Karl Jaspers' *Psychologie der Weltanschauungen*," in Hans Saner, ed., *Karl Jaspers in der Diskussion* (Munich: Fink, 1973), p. 86; *Wegmarken*, p. 7. In *Being and Time*, Heidegger termed "equally primordial" the statements that "*Dasein* is in the truth" and that "*Dasein* is in the untruth"; see *Sein und Zeit* (11th edn; Tübingen: Niemeyer, 1967), par. 26, p. 122.

20 Mörchen, *Adorno und Heidegger*, pp. 336–42, 346–50, 363. Compare Adorno, *Negative Dialectics*, pp. 71, 106–8, 115–16, 124; Heidegger, *Wegmarken*, pp. 263, 269; *Holzwege*, p. 43.

21 Mörchen, *Adorno und Heidegger*, pp. 365–73, 388–9. Compare Adorno, *Negative Dialectics*, pp. 80–81, 118–19, 278; *Zur Metakritik der Erkenntnistheorie*, pp. 42, 46; *Philosophische Frühschriften* (Frankfurt-Main: Suhrkamp, 1973), p. 339; *Prismen*, p. 288; Heidegger, *Der Satz vom Grund* (Pfullingen: Neske, 1957), p. 159; *Heraklit* (*Gesamtausgabe*, vol. 55; Frankfurt-Main: Klostermann, 1979), p. 108; *Metaphysische Anfangsgründe der Logik im Ausgang von Leibniz* (*Gesamtausgabe*, vol. 26; Frankfurt-Main: Klostermann, 1978), p. 173.

22 Mörchen, *Adorno und Heidegger*, pp. 392–8, 412–21, 425–30. Compare Adorno, *Philosophische Frühschriften*, pp. 346, 368; *Noten zur Literatur*, vol. 3, p. 173; *Eingriffe: Neun Kritische Modelle* (Frankfurt-Main: Suhrkamp, 1972), pp. 51, 278; *Philosophische Terminologie*, vol. 1, p. 89; *Negative Dialectics*, p. 84; *Aesthetic Theory*, tr. Christian Lenhardt (London: Routledge & Kegan Paul, 1984), pp. 79–80, 440; Heidegger, *Holzwege*, p. 325; *Wegmarken*, p. 177; *Metaphysische Anfangsgründe der Logik*, p. 5. Mörchen (p. 423) also discusses critically the charge of an irrational "decisionism" leveled at Heidegger's early work.

23 Mörchen, *Adorno und Heidegger*, pp. 431–44. Compare Adorno, *Zur Metakritik der Erkenntnistheorie*, p. 40; *Negative Dialectics*, p. 307; *Ohne*

Leitbild (Frankfurt-Main: Suhrkamp, 1967), p. 188; *The Jargon of Authenticity*, tr. Knut Tarnowski and Frederic Will (Evanston: Northwestern University Press, 1973), pp. xxi, 4–5; *Noten zur Literatur*, vol. 1 (Frankfurt-Main: Suhrkamp, 1963), p. 26.

24 Mörchen, *Adorno und Heidegger*, pp. 453–68. Compare Adorno, *Kierkegaard: Konstruktion des Ästhetischen* (3rd edn; Frankfurt-Main: Suhrkamp, 1966), pp. 87, 277; *Stichworte*, p. 42; *The Jargon of Authenticity*, pp. 73–6, 138; *Negative Dialectics*, p. 305; Heidegger, *Sein und Zeit*, pp. 38, 114, 125, 329; *Holzwege*, pp. 81, 85; *Wegmarken*, p. 203; *Grundprobleme der Phänomenologie* (*Gesamtausgabe*, vol. 24; Frankfurt-Main: Klostermann, 1975), par. 15, p. 241, tr. by Albert Hofstadter as *The Basic Problems of Phenomenology* (Bloomington: Indiana University Press, 1982), pp. 169–70.

25 There are some hopeful studies, however, pointing broadly in the direction charted by Mörchen; see, e.g., the contributions by Adolf Polti, Josef Früchtl, and Hauke Brunkhorst in Forum für Philosophie/Bad Homburg, ed., *Martin Heidegger: Innen- und Aussenansichten* (Frankfurt-Main: Suhrkamp, 1989), pp. 273–338.

26 Mörchen, *Adorno und Heidegger*, pp. 230–4, 242–4, 659. Compare Adorno, *Negative Dialectics*, p. 348; *The Positivist Dispute*, p. 35; *Impromptus* (Frankfurt-Main: Suhrkamp, 1968), p. 119; *Noten zur Literatur*, vol. 2 (Frankfurt-Main: Suhrkamp, 1961), p. 114; *Aesthetic Theory*, p. 7; Heidegger, *On the Way to Language*, pp. 30–1.

27 Mörchen, *Adorno und Heidegger*, pp. 647–52.

28 Mörchen, *Adorno und Heidegger*, pp. 481–2, 639–42, 651.

29 Mörchen, *Adorno und Heidegger*, pp. 469–74, 478–80, 654. Compare Adorno, *The Jargon of Authenticity*, pp. 111–12; Heidegger, *Sein und Zeit*, par. 5, p. 15; *Wegmarken*, p. 71.

30 Adorno, *Minima Moralia*, p. 42; *Negative Dialectics*, p. 352–3; *Philosophische Terminologie*, vol. 1, p. 201. Compare Gillian Rose, *The Melancholy Science: An Introduction to the Thought of Theodor W. Adorno* (New York: Columbia University Press, 1978).

31 Adorno, *The Jargon of Authenticity*, pp. 102, 129–30; *Negative Dialectics*, pp. 10, 30, 176–7.

32 Mörchen, *Adorno und Heidegger*, pp. 441–7, 559. Compare Heidegger, *Wegmarken*, p. 189; Adorno, *Aesthetic Theory*, pp. 2, 123, 196, 358; Maurice Merleau-Ponty, *The Visible and the Invisible*, ed. Claude Lefort, tr. Alphonso Lingis (Evanston: Northwestern University Press, 1968), pp. 3–4, 28, 50.

3

Critical Theory and Reconciliation

Turris fortissima nomen . . .

Proverbs

As I understand it, the term "practical theology" signals a complex interlacing of theology or thought of the divine and human praxis or practical engagement. Bypassing segregation and coincidence, such interlacing means that theology is not divorced from the world of practical and political concerns, just as human praxis does not shun or cancel its linkage with the divine (or the transcendent). Taken in this sense, the term itself points already to the theme of this chapter: the theme of reconciliation, and more particularly of the relation between critical theory and reconciliation. The motivation undergirding my choice of the theme is its broad significance. On the one hand, reconciliation plays a crucial and even central role in Christian theology – and perhaps in all religious thought tracing its roots to the Scriptures. On the other hand, reconciliation is a prominent topic in some forms of Western philosophy and social-political thought. Not being a theologian, I shall limit myself to allusions in that field. In the New Testament, reconciliation has chiefly two meanings – which, however, are closely connected: reconciliation between a human being and God (initiated through a divine act of redemption) and reconciliation between human beings (on the basis of the same redemptive act). In both cases the assumption is that of an initial breach or enmity which then requires a process of healing or mediation leading to restored friendship. As Paul writes in 2 Corinthians (5:19) regarding people's relationship to God: "In Christ God was recon-

This essay was first presented at a conference on practical theology or "theology of the public realm" held at the University of Chicago Divinity School in October 1988.

ciling the world to himself, not counting their trespasses against them, and entrusting to us the message of reconciliation." Divine redemption at the same time furnishes the ground for a new fellowship among people formerly divided by enmity. Thus, Paul says in Ephesians (2:11–14): "Remember that at one time you Gentiles in the flesh were separated from Christ, alienated from the commonwealth of Israel . . . But now you who once were far off have been brought near in the blood of Christ; for he is our peace, who has made us both one and has broken down the dividing wall of hostility."[1]

In Western philosophy, reconciliation is not an uncommon theme – even outside the range of medieval philosophical theology; traces of it can be found in Plato's notion of *eros*, in Aristotle's ontological conception of *dynamis*, and in socialist utopias from Thomas More to Marx. In the modern context, however, the foremost philosophical spokesman of the theme is Hegel with his focus on dialectical "mediations" and their consummation in the "absolute spirit." In an eloquent and captivating passage, Gadamer once portrayed Hegel as the philosopher of reconciliation *par excellence* – a description which meshes not accidentally with his status a "Christian" thinker. According to Gadamer, the basic experience triggering the entire labor of Hegel's system was the experience of division or enmity (*Entzweiung*). "As the starting point of Hegel's thought," he writes, "division [*Entzweiung*] entails as its corollary the reconciliation of division or, in his own terms, the 'reconciliation of corruption.' Thus, the task which Hegel pursues as a thinker is the reconciliation of all forms of divisiveness, accomplished in the medium of philosophical reflection." Gadamer illustrates his comments primarily by reference to the "phenomenology" of everyday experience – to the twists and turns of interpersonal relationships – reaching the conclusion that reconciliation is "the secret of Hegelian dialectics." Yet he also recognizes that this dialectics is predicated on the premise of divine intervention or the redemptive power of the absolute. To this extent, he notes, Hegel's philosophy also seeks to embrace the "truth of Christianity" and thus to achieve a reconciliation of faith and reason. The latter point has been corroborated by another leading Hegel scholar of our time, Michael Theunissen, particularly in his study entitled *Hegel's Doctrine of the Absolute Spirit as Theological-Political Treatise*. According to Theunissen, "mediation" is a vernacular term for reconciliation just as "absolute spirit" is a translation of the divine redemptive spirit made manifest in Christ's ministry. As he states: "God's concrete incarnation reveals the truth of the spirit, especially by highlighting the incommensurability of divine glory and human servitude." Operating in the same medium of the spirit, the goal of philosophy (for Hegel) was hence to represent conceptually "nothing else but the actual reconciliation effected by Christ in objective reality."[2]

My own focus here is not directly or centrally on Hegel's philosophy; but his impulses are bound to reverberate in the following presentation. As is well known, Hegel's system has cast a long shadow (or rather a long light) on subsequent developments – an influence which is by no means exhausted. Immediately after his death, Hegel's legacy was appropriated by Left and Right Hegelian factions, and through the former it was bequeathed to Marx and his heirs. In this somewhat circuitous way, the legacy finally left its imprint on the Frankfurt School, and particularly on its founders, Horkheimer and Adorno. To be sure, in the course of its travels or peregrinations, Hegel's opus was liable to undergo changes or shifts of accent; foremost among these modifications was the eclipse of the notion of a final synthesis accomplished on the level of absolute spirit – an eclipse inaugurated by the Left Hegelians and later seconded and intensified by most existentialist and neo-Marxist writers. Notwithstanding this change, however, the Hegelian notion of reconciliation continued to play a powerful role in the work of the early Frankfurt School; only more recently has the notion come to share the apocryphal status of the absolute spirit. I shall proceed in three steps. First of all, I want to show the centrality of reconciliation in "early" critical theory, by concentrating on selected writings of Horkheimer and Adorno (from *Eclipse of Reason* to *Negative Dialectics*). Next I want to turn to Habermas's reformulation of critical theory and to his progressively sharpened critique of his predecessors, a critique which in large part centers on their notion of reconciliation. Finally, I shall try to assess the successive phases of critical theorizing and conclude by vindicating an unorthodox (linguistically transformed) Hegelian conception of absoluteness and redemptive reconciliation.

I

As a distinctive outlook or perspective, critical theory was first developed by Frankfurt theorists after the demise of the Weimar Republic during the initial years of their exile. As formulated by the school's founders, the perspective was designed as an antidote to the dominant bourgeois mentality or social-theoretical paradigm of the time which they designated as "traditional theory" – which basically was a synonym for positivism or positivist empiricism. From the vantage of positivism, reality (including nature and society) was perceived as an array of neutral facts or external data amenable to "objective" analysis by the scientist or human observer. Given the underlying subject–object dichotomy, reality could be transformed – and in fact was progressively transformed in modernity – into a target of technical control serving the supposed survival needs of subjects or the human species. Paralleling this transformation, reason as reflective insight was increasingly streamlined into a calculating or instrumental capacity geared toward enhanced mastery or power over nature. Anticipated in Bacon's equation of knowledge and power, the project of technical control reached its culmination in twentieth-century positivism and scientism – and finally revealed its dark or sinister side in fascism. Opposing the instrumentalism of positivist science, critical theory narrowed the subject–object gulf by marshalling some of the resources of dialectics – a dialectics construed largely along Left-Hegelian lines with the accent on emancipatory social praxis.[3] Yet, almost from its inception, critical theorizing found itself challenged or contested by a steadily darkening global horizon. The outbreak of World War II and the intensification of technological imperatives cast doubt on the prospect of even modest dialectical mediations – without succeeding, to be sure, in cancelling the founders' critical-oppositional stance. Both the gloom of the war years and the founders' desperately maintained hope found eloquent expression in a study written by Horkheimer in 1944 and subsequently published under the title *Eclipse of Reason*.

In line with early impulses of critical theory, Horkheimer's study focused again on the rise of modern scientism, and particularly on the triumphant sway of positivism or logical empiricism with its celebration of a purely abstract-formal type of rationality (in contrast to substantive reasoning). This scientific ascendancy, in his view, was paralleled in the social domain by the structure of capitalist or market economy as a network of causal, quasi-objective relationships juxtaposed to the individual producer and consumer. On both levels, the consequence of modern developments was the radical split or division between subject and object, inside and outside, man and nature.

> As the end result of the process, we have on the one hand the Self, the abstract ego emptied of all substance except its attempt to transform everything in heaven and on earth into means for its preservation, and on the other hand an empty nature degraded to mere material, mere stuff to be dominated, without any other purpose than that of this very domination.[4]

Under the impact of these developments, reason itself was increasingly both formalized and instrumentalized – formalized through the expulsion of all substantive ends, and instrumentalized through the equation of purpose with mastery and control. Although seemingly holding the promise of greater latitude and emancipation, these changes actually were the harbingers of a new closure – by stunting the human capacity to appreciate the dimension of the non-instrumental (or non-purposive). As Horkheimer added:

The story of the boy who looked up at the sky and asked, "Daddy, what is the moon supposed to advertise?" is an allegory of what has happened to the relation between man and nature in the era of formalized reason. On the one hand, nature has been stripped of all intrinsic value or meaning. On the other, man has been stripped of all aims except self-preservation; he tries to transform everything within reach into a means to that end.[5]

According to the study, modern (instrumental) rationality unleashed not so much a benign as rather a destructive dialectic – in the sense that domination of nature rebounded or boomeranged on the human subject or agent of control. "In the process of emancipation," we read, "the human being shares the fate of the rest of his world: domination of nature involves domination of man. Each subject not only has to take part in the subjugation of external nature (human and nonhuman), but in order to do so must subjugate nature in himself: thus domination becomes 'internalized' for domination's sake." Internalization of control is closely tied to the ascendancy of the abstract-rational ego or *cogito* with its tendency to repress internal instincts and the imaginative potential of the unconscious. Following the dictates of survival or self-preservation, the ego serves simultaneously the function of inner-psychic self-management and that of effective adaptation to external constraints in an increasingly rationalized and instrumentalized world. Apart from the effects of internal repression, ego-centered instrumentalism further rebounds on interhuman or social relations by forcing the latter into a rigid structure of super- and subordination. In Horkheimer's words: "The history of man's efforts to subjugate nature is also the history of man's subjugation by man. The development of the concept of the ego reflects this twofold history." In its endeavor to triumph over external nature, over internal impulses and over fellow beings in society, the ego is generally perceived to embody the functions of "domination, command, and organization"; its characteristic gesture is the "out-stretched arm of the ruler, directing his men to march or dooming the culprit to execution." Social domination, in turn, is frequently camouflaged through internalization or sublimation – and sometimes through a combination of mastery and the (partial) release of instinctual frustrations (as in fascism).[6]

Regarding the prospect of healing or mediating modern divisions, *Eclipse of Reason* was circumspect and subdued. As Horkheimer insisted, subject–object or man–nature splits could by no means be overcome by collapsing the tension into one of the constitutive poles. "The later development of rationalism and of subjective idealism," he noted, "tended

increasingly to mediate the dualism by attempting to dissolve the concept
of nature – and ultimately all the content of experience – into the ego,
conceived as transcendental" – which was a solution by fiat rather than
reflection. Under liberal-pragmatic auspices, the ego's role was expanded
into a collective or anthropocentric enterprise geared toward the "ideas
of progress, success or happiness" – without greatly improving matters.
The reverse strategy consists in the suppression of reason in favor of a
simplistic "return to nature" or else the revival of "old doctrines" and the
creation of "new myths" – which is a recipe for primitivism if not barbarism.[7] Just as modern dilemmas could not be cured through one-
sided contractions, the remedy could not be found in unitary visions or
instant types of synthesis bypassing the labor of mediation:

> The dualism of nature and spirit can no more be denied in favor of their
> alleged original unity than the real historical trends reflected in this
> dualism can be reversed. To assert the unity of nature and spirit is to
> attempt to break out of the present situation by an impotent *coup de
> force*, instead of transcending it intellectually in conformity with the
> potentialities and tendencies inherent in it.[8]

In Horkheimer's view, the dilemmas brought about by modernity could
not simply be undone, set aside, or magically wished away – because (as
he said) "we are, for better or worse, the heirs of the Enlightenment and
technological progress." To ignore the latter or to cancel them through
recourse to crude formulas or regrees to more primitive stages was bound
to aggravate rather than alleviate the "permanent crisis" of our age.
Instead, without truncating one side or "committing the fallacy of equating nature and reason," mankind was challenged "to reconcile the
two" – which can only happen through radical reflection attentive to
nature as its "seeming opposite."[9]
    Reconciliation through genuine mediation thus was the proper remedy
of modern divisions. According to the study, subject–object or man–
nature rifts had as a corollary the conflict between "subjective" and
"objective" modes of rationality – with the one tending to spontaneity
and romanticism and the other to alienation and reification. "The task
of philosophy," we read, "is not to play the one stubbornly against
the other, but to foster a mutual critique and thus, if possible, to pre-
pare in the intellectual realm the reconciliation of the two in reality."
Hegel's philosophical system owed its "incomparable force" to his critical
awareness of the pitfalls of one-sided perspectives. In Horkheimer's
presentation, the rifts between subject and object, spirit and nature were
both a "mere" appearance and a "necessary" appearance created by a

dialectical momentum. To move beyond the level of appearances it was imperative to grasp both the "separateness" and the "interrelatedness" of the polar opposites, that is, to penetrate to their tensional correlation. Subjugation of nature, he stated, was bound to imply human subjugation and vice versa "so long as man does not understand his own reason and the basic process by which he has created and is maintaining the antagonism that is about to destroy him." Reason or spirit could be "more than nature" only by concretely realizing "its own 'naturalness'," that is, its own "trend to domination, the same trend that paradoxically alienates it from nature." In this manner, reason could become "an instrument of reconciliation," and indeed "more than an instrument." The latter prospect was advanced if, instead of exerting control, reason allowed nature to mirror itself peacefully in reflective thought and language – differently phrased: if it recaptured some of the playful-mimetic (that is, non-purposive or non-instrumental) impulses of childhood and pre-cognitive existence. If, through reflective and linguistic sublimation, Horkheimer wrote, nature becomes able to "mirror itself in the realm of spirit," it thereby gains "a certain tranquillity by contemplating its own image" – a process which is "at the heart of all culture." In sum, channeling mimetic impulses into the "general medium of language" rather than regressive behavior means "that potentially destructive energies work for reconciliation."[10]

A similar perspective, sketched in even bolder, more dramatic strokes, emerges in a book composed roughly at the same time: Horkheimer's and Adorno's *Dialectic of Enlightenment*. Like Horkheimer's study, *Dialectic of Enlightenment* concentrates on modern conflicts and divisions, particularly on the growing gulf between subject and object, man and nature. Again, the rift is ascribed to an inner momentum of reason which cannot simply be reversed or cancelled but which urgently demands mediation and reorientation. According to the authors, the advancement of knowledge and social progress inevitably involve a retreat or exodus from unreflective naturalism, that is, from primitive-natural forces and mythical constraints; however, precisely by exiting from and superimposing itself on nature, reason becomes an instrument of domination – thus entangling itself in reification and turning into a "second nature." Basically, the program of rational enlightenment, they write, was always "the disenchantment of the world, the dissolution of myths, and the substitution of knowledge for fancy." Yet, by equating itself with power and with the sway of causal-natural laws (fixed by science), reason was in a sense remythologized and redogmatized. Thus, enlightenment revealed its own darkness or dark underside, and progress its nexus with regress. In the authors' words: "We are wholly convinced – and therein lies our *petitio principii* – that social freedom is inseparable from enlightened thought. Nevertheless, we believe just as clearly to have recognized that this very way of thinking – no less than the actual historical forms (the social institutions) with which it is interwoven – already contains the seed of the reversal universally apparent today. If enlightenment does not accommodate reflection on this regressive element, it seals its own fate."[11]

In terms of the study, the regressive counterpoint of enlightenment – its dialectical underside – results from the equation of knowledge and power, an equation which in turn reflects the growing division between human beings and nature. Ever since the time of Bacon, Horkheimer and Adorno note, the linkage of reason and science has shown a "patriarchal" face: by conquering superstition, mind or reason is meant to "hold sway over a disenchanted nature." In the course of modernity or modernization, this patriarchal legacy has led to a progressive widening of the Cartesian rift between *res cogitans* and *res extensa* – which coincides with the gulf between inside and outside, between logical form and substantive content. Increasingly, they write, "being divides into the *logos* (which with the advance of philosophy contracts to the monad, to an abstract point of reference), and into the mass of all things and creatures without. This single distinction between inner existence and external reality engulfs all others." On the subjective side, the *cogito* in modernity is steadily stylized into a sovereign selfhood, a self-contained identity which ejects from itself all forms of otherness as modes of reification; in large measure, modern emancipation has this connotation of self-recovery or self-possession. It is only through retreat into inwardness, we read, that man obtains "self-identity," a selfhood that cannot be "dissipated through identification with others" but "takes possession of itself once and for all as an impenetrable mask." Under the impact of this self-enclosure, disenchanted or disqualified nature turns into the "chaotic matter of abstract classification," while the sovereign self becomes addicted to "mere having or possession, to abstract identity." The upshot of this bifurcation is the radical subordination of matter to mind, that is, the domination of rationally emancipated humankind over nature. "Systematizing spirit or reason and the creator-God resemble each other as rulers of nature," the study observes. "Man's likeness to God consists in the sovereignty over the world, in the countenance of mastery, and in the ability to command." Modern science in particular considers objects only to the extent that they are "makeable," producible and controllable: "In this metamorphosis the nature of things reveals itself as always the same: as target of domination."[12]

Reason or rationality in modernity shares the fate of the *cogito*: by being truncated into a self-contained logical formula through which means–ends relations can be deductively or inductively pinpointed. This tendency was first evident in the sequence of modern philosophical "systems"; later it became virulent in functional-sociological models seeking to grasp the totality of social life. In the authors' words: "From the start, enlightenment recognizes as being and occurrence only what can be apprehended in unity; its ideal is the system from which all and everything follows." The primary means for accomplishing unification – a means extolled especially by positivism and the "unified science" movement – is number, that is, the reduction of all qualitative differences to quantitative measurement. "Number," the study notes, "became the canon of enlightenment: the same equations govern bourgeois justice and commodity exchange." In excising qualitative differences, formal–quantitative reasoning also prepared the ground for the streamlining and homogenization of social life and thus for the establishment of various social controls and disciplines. While being wedded to universal categories, formal rationality also promoted a distinctive hierarchy, by defining "truth" as the rule of (universal) form over (particular) content, of rational knowledge over non-rational experience – a schema which exacted a price: namely, the alienation of reason from the goal of genuine cognition. In exorcizing "mimetic magic," we read, the rational ego also "tabooed the kind of knowledge which really reaches its object; its hatred extended to the image of the vanquished pre-history and its imaginay bliss." This tabooing (of the non-rational) was intensified in the same measure as the ego was progressively internalized and transcendentalized: sensuality was exiled from the reign of reason. According to the judgment of enlightenment (as well as Protestantism), regress into "prehistory" is the lot of anyone abandoning himself to life "without rational reference to self-preservation." From the vantage of reason, instinct is "as mythical as superstition," serving a God not postulated by the self "as irrational as drunkenness." For both prayer and submergence in naturalness, progress has prepared the same fate: "by anathematizing the self-oblivion of reason as well as that of pleasure."[13]

As in Horkheimer's work, exposing the "dialectic of enlightenment" is not meant as a plea for primitivism. Some help in avoiding the twin pitfalls of regression and rational triumphalism can be found in Hegelian dialectics, and particularly in his notion of "determinate negation." With that notion, Horkheimer and Adorno assert, Hegel "revealed an element that separates the Enlightenment from the positivist decay with which he lumps it together." Yet, this endorsement is qualified: by ultimately "absolutizing" the outcome of negation, namely his system and historical totality (they say) Hegel himself "contravened the prohibition (of images) and lapsed into mythology." As a result, the authors recommend a more subdued, post-Hegelian dialectics – but one clearly geared toward the healing of modern divisions. Again, hope cannot and must not be pinned on instant solutions or magical reunions of opposites. "All mystical unification," the authors state, "is deception, the impotent-inward trace of a missed radical renewal." Only through relentless reflection – one mindful of its complicity with power – can thought break the spell of reification. Precisely by forestalling any "hypostatization of utopia" and by unfailingly exposing domination as division, the rupture between subject and object – which thought does not allow to be obscured – becomes simultaneously "the index of its own untruth and of the truth." At this point, enlightenment is more than enlightenment: namely, "nature which becomes perceptible in its alienation" (or otherness). In the self-cognition of reason as predicated on division, nature begins to be reconciled with spirit and with itself. By curtailing itself and acknowledging its natural premises, reason "abandons the claim to dominion which precisely subjects it to nature." Thus, healing of divisions is at least initiated (if not completed) through radical "self-reflection of thought" pushing beyond instrumentalism, differently phrased: through a "recollection of nature in the rational subject" – a remembrance which holds the hidden key to the "truth of all culture." As the authors conclude, enlightenment fulfills and "sublates" itself when the means–ends nexus is suspended – at the point where the "nearest practical ends" reveal themselves as the "most distant goal" and where repressed nature is remembered as the "land of origin" as well as the portent of hope.[14]

Qualified endorsement of Hegelian dialectics is the hallmark also of Adorno's later writings, particularly his postwar essays on Hegel and his *Negative Dialectics*. "Qualified" here means acceptance of healing mediations *minus* resort to the "absolute" or to any kind of comprehensive synthesis (especially a synthesis presumed to be operative in reality). This ambivalence is clearly evident in the essay on Hegel's notion of "experience" or "experiential content" (of 1958). As Adorno observes there: "Hegel's thought – more than that of any previous philosopher – suffered from the alienation between subject and object, between consciousness and reality." Yet, instead of regressing backward or retreating into some kind of immediacy, Hegel trusted in the healing power of mediations: in the ability of rationality to reflect upon itself and to discover the "wounds of unreason" in its own dominion. The chief means of mediation – the inner "nerve of the dialectic" – is again located in "determinate negation," in the sustained engagement and labor of thought with concrete conditions. However, while applauding these and related aspects of Hegelian dialectics, Adorno in the end distances

himself from its "idealism": its tendency to soar into a realm of absoluteness where real conflicts or divisions are already synthesized or reconciled
(though only in thought). Opposing this escapist tendency, Adorno's
essay underscores the conflictual, torn, and fragmented character of real-
life experience. "The history of this unreconciled age," he writes, "cannot
be one of harmonious development: the latter is only the figment of an
ideology which ignores historical antagonisms. Conflicts and contradictions – its only true ontology – are the governing law of history which
only proceeds antagonistically and through untold suffering" – as Hegel
himself recognized when he called history a "slaughter bench." Once this
grim reality is bypassed, idealism turns into an ideological legitimation
of prevailing conditions; even determinate negation at this point is
placed into "the service of an apologetic function, the justification of
existing reality."[15]

Adorno's chief reservation in the essay has to do with the presumed
"rationality of the real" (as asserted in the Preface to Hegel's *Phenomenology*). "Such a philosophy," he complains, "marches with the stronger bat-
talions," treading under its heels alternative possibilities and utopian
hopes. At this point the truth of Hegelian dialectics turns into its
"untruth" – an untruth rightly denounced by Left-Hegelian critics. By
postulating a merely abstract-theoretical reconciliation, Hegel is said to
have shortchanged real-life opportunities and political tasks. A philosophy, we read, which dissolves everything "into spirit" and celebrates
"the identity of subject and object on a grand scale," is bound to become
quietistic and to serve as alibi for prevalent modes of domination. Particularly in the higher reaches of Hegel's system, the difference between
"contingency and absoluteness" is cancelled (through subsumption of the
former under the latter) – in a manner violating real-life experience. In
all these respects, Adorno's essay provides a strict counterpoint. Reality,
he affirms, is definitely "not rationality or the rational" but its reverse.
Above all, the "division between subject and object" cannot be overcome
through mere theory – as long as the conflict persists in concrete reality.
In effect, he claims, the grand synthesis envisaged by Hegel is nothing
but a replica of the existing social totality with its built in domination
and coerced conformism: "The subject–object identity to which his
philosophy ascends is not a system of reconciled absolute spirit but a
synonym for the real world experienced as system. Absolute spirit is the
name for the relentless unification of all parts and particular moments
of bourgeois society into a totality under the auspices of the exchange
principle." Countering Hegel's conception of absolute truth, Adorno's
essay culminates in the thesis that "totality or the whole is untruth" –
while Hegel's conception merely absolutizes domination. Only with a view

toward the future can the truth of the whole be recovered – but as redemptive task: "The ray of light revealing the whole in all its parts as untrue is none other than the ray of utopia–the utopia of a whole truth still to be accomplished."[16]

On a broader scale and with more subtlety, a similar perspective is outlined in the *magnum opus* of Adorno's later life: his *Negative Dialectics* (of 1966). Its "negative" character here means that dialectics confines itself to the (determinate) negation of existing ills and divisions while foregoing the imagination and portrayal of a completely reconciled condition. As before, the thrust of this outlook – while accepting the task of mediation – is directed against Hegel's "absolutism," against his presumed identification of subject and object on an abstract-speculative level. Although recognizing non-conceptual otherness, Adorno observes, Hegel's system "pre-thinks" or conceptually prearranges every concrete particularity; thus, objects and phenomena are streamlined and integrated into a grand synthesis or harmonious order – which is the order of pure thought. Despite protestations to the contrary, phenomena ultimately congeal into "exemplars of concepts"; notwithstanding the proclaimed need of objectification, thought remains contained in its own domain, endlessly rehearsing its own categories. In Adorno's view, the only way to rupture this self-enclosure is through thought's attentiveness to non-thought or reason's turn toward the "non-identical" – which precludes a premature synthesis. In his words: "If thought really yielded to its object, if it focused on the thing rather than its categories, then things themselves would turn articulate under its lingering glance." In this manner, thinking would regain (in Hegel's own terms) its "freedom to the object" – a freedom lost under the spell of the subject's "meaning-giving autonomy." Basically, philosophy's genuine concern in our time, he adds, is with those matters in which Hegel, at one with the tradition, expressed his disinterest: namely, "nonconceptuality, singularity and particularity" – things which ever since Plato have been dismissed as "transitory and insignificant." Philosophy's theme thus consists of "those qualities it downgrades as contingent, as a *qualité négligeable*."[17]

According to Adorno, the corrective to Hegel's speculation is the rigorous and persistent reliance on the notion of (determinate) negation. Only negation is able to break through the enclosure of thought and the reification of objects. This fact lends pre-eminence to "negative" dialectics over its idealistic variant. "To change the direction of conceptuality, to turn it toward non-identity," we read, "is the hinge of negative dialectics. Insight into the constitutive character of the nonconceptual in the concept would end the compulsive identification which the concept entails unless halted by such reflection." Confined within the domain of thought, traditional idealism offered a truncated dialectics ultimately unable to overcome modern divisions. In its idealist version, dialectics was tied to the "sovereign subject" as source of conceptualizations. However, this primacy of the subject is now "historically obsolete," even in its Hegelian guise; none of the reconciliations proffered by absolute idealism were "tenable" or stood the test of time. Only a negative dialectics holds out promise under present circumstances; by being attentive to the otherness (or other side) of thought it undermines ingrained divisions – without granting access to instant conceptual synthesis. In Adorno's words: Being mindful of the "breach between subject and object" and its traces or furrows in all experience, such dialectics "in the end turns its face toward reconciliation – one which would release the non-identical, ridding it even of mental coercion, and thus would open the road to the multiplicity of differences." In this sense, reconciliation would be "recollection of the manifold seen as no longer hostile – something which is anathema to subjective reason." Dialectics, properly understood, is "in the service of such reconciliation."[18]

In ridding itself of its idealist legacy, dialectics also extricates itself more thoroughly from the nexus of domination, in regard to both nature and society. In terms of the study, idealism by privileging subjectivity merely "spiritualized" the Darwinian struggle for survival, thus reinstating a repressive naturalism. By proclaiming itself the Baconian master and even idealist creator of all things, the epistemological-metaphysical subject participates and entangles itself in this nexus: "In exerting mastery it becomes part of what it believes to master, succumbing like the lord" (in Hegel's master–slave relationship). In relinquishing subjectivity and identifying rationality negative dialectics softens and heals the enmity between thought and reality, humans and nature. Dialectical thinking, Adorno writes, "respects that which is to be thought – the object or subject matter – even where the latter does not heed the rules of logic." Instead of being narrowly confined by its own rules, thinking is able "to think against itself without self-cancellation. If dialectics allowed definition, this would be one worth suggesting." Thus, in making reality its target, thinking does not solely obey a modified Darwinism; although doing violence to things through its synthetic constructs, reason also is able to "heed a potential slumbering in things," thereby "making amends" to them for its own acts. Differently phrased: "irreconcilable reasoning is matched by the hope for reconciliation" – a hope predicated on the fact that the resistance of thought to mere thingness intends in objects even that which eludes reification. This elusive element is the domain of otherness or difference – a domain captured in Eichendorff's phrase of "beautiful strangeness" (*schöne Fremde*). As Adorno states:

"The reconciled condition would not annex the alien through an act of philosophical imperialism; instead, its happiness would consist in allowing it to remain distant and different even in proximate surroundings, beyond the pale of heterogeneity and sameness."[19]

II

The preceding discussion, I believe, revealed new and captivating vistas – but probably also some dilemmas besetting "early" critical theory. While correcting speculative hyperbole, the turn to negation undoubtedly exacted a price. For, if the "whole" is entirely untrue and beyond the pale of redemption, how can even parts be reconciled or redeemed – without resort to a *creatio ex nihilo* (which further aggravates instrumentalism or the plight of willful fabrication)? How, in other words, can thought recover the potential slumbering in nature if the latter is hopelessly corrupt? Moreover, who could serve as agent of transformative healing – given the general nexus of perversion? These and other aporias – to which I shall return later – do not detract, in my view, from the authors' basic élan: their undaunted plea for an emphatic type of reconciliation, construed in unorthodox Hegelian terms. By comparison, Habermas's work has always been more circumspect and subdued, more intent on mapping out knowable terrain than on exploring *terra incognita*. Regarding Hegel's legacy, Habermas shares with Horkheimer and Adorno – and with Left Hegelians in general – the aversion to absolutes (especially the "absolute spirit") and the pervasive shift from speculation to human praxis or pragmatics. Going beyond his predecessors, however, he also casts doubt on the prospect of comprehensive "reconciliation" (in Hegel's sense) – preferring to reduce it to more limited or manageable proportions, chiefly under the heading of intersubjective "communication." The latter change is accompanied by a dramatic upgrading of the function of reason or rationality, that is, by a de-emphasis of the "*dialectic* of enlightenment" in favor of a restored (though linguistically reformulated) Enlightenment rationalism. Habermas's opus as a whole can be seen as a precarious blend of praxis-orientation and quasi-Kantian rationalism – with the latter ingredient tending to ascend and prevail over the former (without cancelling a broadly pragmatic framework). A few examples must suffice to illustrate this point.

One of Habermas's earliest writings which attracted wide attention was a critique of Marxist "philosophy," that is, of dialectical theorizing, from the vantage of a Left-Hegelian praxis focus. Remnants of this outlook were still present – though mixed with rationalist features – in his first major work, published shortly before Adorno's death: *Knowledge and Human Interests* (1968). While the linkage of knowledge and interests postulated in this work was an attack on postivist and other modes of detached theorizing, the concern with epistemology or knowledge theory concurred uneasily (if at all) with Left-Hegelian or pragmatic premises. In fact, Kant was singled out in the study as the last great practitioner of modern epistemology – a form of cognitive reflection which fell on bad days already with Hegel's turn to the absolute and subsequently with Marx's privileging of labor (until it finally dissolved under the weight of positivism). In a loose variation on Kant's three Critiques, *Knowledge and Human Interests* differentiated between three basic types of knowledge or cognitive inquiry – science, hermeneutics, and reflective critique – which in turn were correlated with the interests in technical control, in practical understanding, and emancipation. Soon after publication of this study, the ascendancy of rationalism began. In several "postscripts" or epilogues to his earlier writings, Habermas introduced an emphatic distinction or dichotomy: namely, the distinction between rigorous knowledge and pragmatic interests, or between the ordinary life-world and the domain of "discourses" wedded to rational validity claims. A similar bifurcation occurred in the field of emancipatory critique, where "rational reconstruction" (a theoretical enterprise) was contrasted with therapeutic experience. The primary focus of Habermas's subsequent work has been on discourses – which are rationally disciplined forms of communication – and on the rational reconstruction of various types of "competences" (cognitive, moral, communicative). Discourse analysis has led to the formulation of a discursive theory of knowledge as well as a "discourse ethics," tied respectively to the standards of "truth" and "rightness." Apart from probing cognitive and moral development, reconstructive inquiry has yielded a theory of "universal pragmatics" and a framework of "communicative action" and rationality (to mention only the most prominent titles of recent investigations).[20]

It is precisely in the fields of universal pragmatics and communicative interaction that the redemptive quality of contemporary critical theory is said emerge. Basically, universal pragmatics seeks to pinpoint the general preconditions or required "capabilities" undergirding rational communication or discourse as such. In Habermas's presentation, rational communication implies or is premised on four general validity claims: the claims to truth, rightness, truthfulness, and comprehensibility. While truth claims govern the denotative or referential aspects of speech, that is, statements referring to "external nature" (or the external world), rightness claims apply to intersubjective relations, that is, to the normatively regulated domain of "society" (or the social world). Claims to truthfulness – not discursively redeemable – point to the speaker's "internal nature" (or inner world), while comprehensibility involves the transparency of the chosen medium of communication. Thus, universal pragmatics shows human speech as furnishing a network of relationships: to outer and inner nature, to society, and to language itself. In Habermas's words, the model is that of "a communication in which grammatical sentences are embedded, by way of universal validity claims, in three relations to reality, thereby assuming the corresponding pragmatic functions of representing facts, establishing legitimate interpersonal relations, and expressing one's own subjectivity." Language itself in the model is conceived as "the medium of interrelating three worlds."[21] The model was fleshed out in *The Theory of Communicative Action* into a general philosophical and sociological framework. In terms of that study, communicative action is differentiated from a variety of more subject-centered and purposive activities, including "teleological" and "dramaturgical" actions. Communicative rationality in turn is rigorously demarcated from the sphere of "cognitive-instrumental rationality," that is, a calculative reasoning dedicated to the expansion of technical control. If at all, antidotes to divisiveness can only be found in the communicative domain:

> This concept of communicative rationality carries with it connotations based ultimately on the central experience of the unconstrained, unifying, consensus-producing force of argumentative speech – a speech in which different participants overcome their merely subjective views and, owing to the mutuality of rationally motivated convictions, assure themselves of both the unity of the objective world and the intersubjectivity of their life-context.[22]

The theory of communicative rationality also serves as launching pad for an attack – carried out with growing intensity – on the older Frankfurt School and its notion of reconciliation. According to Habermas, traditional philosophy – including "early" critical theory – was basically a monological enterprise, that is, one rooted in the category of "subjectivity" or subjective "consciousness"; drawing on Wittgenstein and other analytical thinkers, his own perspective promises a "paradigm shift" from consciousness to language and thereby a settlement of previously unresolved (and irresoluble) dilemmas. *The Theory of Communicative Action* initially sketches the background and motivations of the older Frankfurt School, before proceeding to a critical assessment. In Habermas's presentation, the concept of "instrumental reason" – the school's central focus – involved in essence a radicalization of Lukács' notion of "reification," a radicalization which expanded the latter notion from the domain of commodity exchanges to the broad range of cognitive rationality and progressive historical rationalization. From the perspective of Horkheimer and Adorno, all conceptual reasoning – including idealist dialectics – is bent on identification and the truncation of otherness, thereby betraying "the utopian goal of cognition." Rationalization accordingly appears as an encompassing process – leading to the thesis of the "untruth" of the whole. The pacemaker of this total streamlining of the world is the cognitive ego or subject, a subject wedded entirely to the principle of self-preservation and using this principle as a warrant for unlimited domination – whose effects, however, prove to be self-destructive. In Habermas's words: "Horkheimer and Adorno understand 'control of nature' not merely as a metaphor; the label of 'mastery' or 'domination' serves as the common denominator for the control of external nature, the command over human beings, and the repression of one's own internal nature." In this manner, construed as conceptual-identifying thought, the concept of instrumental reason is meant to disclose the mechanism or "logic" governing the mastery of nature and human beings alike. According to the immanent dialectic of this logic, "victories over outer nature are paid for with defeats of inner nature," as well as defeats of (less rational) social groups. The dialectic of enlightenment and rationalization ultimately derives from "the structure of a reason that is instrumentalized for the sake of self-preservation" – an instrumentalization which marks every progress or advance simultaneously as a regress.[23]

As Habermas notes, this somber scenario is not without a ray of hope – a ray cast basically by the notion of reconciliation. Referring specifically to the "dialectic of enlightenment," he writes:

> This philosophy of history yields a catastrophic view of the relation between spirit and nature, a relation distorted beyond recognition. Yet we can speak of distortion only insofar as the original relation of spirit and nature is secretly conceived in such a way that the idea of truth is linked with that of a universal reconciliation – where reconciliation includes the interaction of humans with nature, with animals, plants, and minerals.[24]

In this notion of reconciliation, Habermas discovers first of all a tension with the Hegelian legacy; for Horkheimer and Adorno clearly distance their view from a grand conceptual or metaphysical synthesis (achieved on the level of objective or absolute spirit). As he states: "The dialectical reconciliation of the universal and the particular remains, in Hegel's own terms, metaphysical because it does not give its due to the 'non-identical' dimension in the particular." In clinging to the notion of reconciliation, Horkheimer and Adorno thus both embrace and simultaneously bracket the idealist legacy of philosophy: the latter by rejecting synthesizing world-views and the former by keeping alive the prospect of a philosophical overcoming of divisions in a new guise. Their work, we read, was paradox-ically motivated by a dual conviction: on the one hand, the conviction "that 'great' philosophy (culminating and terminating in Hegel) could no longer of itself develop and systematically ground the idea of reason, the idea of a universal reconciliation of spirit and nature – because this idea had perished with metaphysical-religious worldviews"; on the other hand, the belief that philosophy – whose moment of realization (in Marx's sense) had passed – "nevertheless constitutes the only available memorial to the promise of a humane social life," that under its ruins (so to speak) lay buried "the truth from which thought could draw its negating, counter-reifying power." Given these two convictions or assump-tions, the problem was how to correlate or harmonize their evident con-flict or contradiction – a task Horkheimer and Adorno failed to solve, and inevitably so owing to their underlying premises. For, Habermas asks, "how can the idea of reconciliation, in whose light alone Adorno is able to expose the shortcomings of idealist dialectics, still be explicated – if negative dialectics offers itself as the only (but discursively inaccessible) path of retrieval?"[25]

According to Habermas, the only hint or clue provided by Horkheimer and Adorno regarding the character of non-instrumental thought is the notion of *"mimesis"*; yet, under the spell of traditional philosophy with its implicit conceptualism, the notion cannot be coherently stated or developed – but only opaquely be invoked like a quasi-natural (and non-rational) power. "As place holder for that primordial reason (which later was diverted from truth)," we read, "Horkheimer and Adorno specify a capacity, *mimesis* – about which they can speak only as they would about a piece of unintelligible nature: they characterize the mimetic capacity, in which instrumentalized nature remonstrates silently against its plight, as an 'impulse'." At this point, the dilemma of early critical theory comes starkly into view: the divisions produced by thought or reason are to be healed by something beyond the range of thought. In terms of that perspective itself, domination is to be recognized as "unreconciled nature even within thought." However, Habermas asks, even if thought were capable of such an idea of reconciliation, "how could it transform mimetic impulses into insights, discursively in its own element and not merely intuitively in speechless 'recollection' " – given that "thought is always identifying thought, tied to operations devoid of specifiable meaning outside the bounds of instrumental reason?" The paradox of early critical theory consequently rests in its non-theorizable claim: in the fact that Horkheimer and Adorno "would have to put forward a *theory* of mimesis, which in their own terms is impossible." This impasse was not and could not be overcome in their work. Thus, instead of explicating "universal reconciliation" – as Hegel had done – as the "unity of identity and non-identity of spirit and nature," they are content to let the notion stand "as a cipher, almost in the manner of *Lebensphilosophie*." This aspect is particularly evident in Adorno's writings. More consistently still than Horkheimer, Adorno in the end no longer "wanted to show a way out of this aporia." His *Negative Dialectics* was both an "attempt to circumscribe what cannot be said discursively" and a "warning against seeking refuge in Hegel at this point." Basically, the book was a mental "exercise": by reflecting once more on dialectics, it demonstrates what otherwise remains clouded, namely, "the aporetic status of the concept of non-identity." In this manner, Adorno cancelled every "theoretical claim."[26]

Moving beyond the critique of his predecessors, Habermas in his study proceeds to delineate his alternative solution – an alternative designed to rescue critical theory from its self-abandonment as "theory." In pondering the paradoxes and aporias of the older Frankfurt School, he says, we come to appreciate the reasons and need for a "paradigm shift" in contemporary social theorizing. Ultimately, the aporias of the older generation are attributed to its failure to perform this shift and thus to gain access to new resources. "I want to maintain," Habermas writes, "that the program of early critical theory foundered not on this or that contingent circumstance, but from the exhaustion of the paradigm of the philosophy of consciousness. I shall argue that a change of paradigm to communication theory makes possible the return to the enterprise that was *disrupted* by the critique of instrumental reason, thus allowing the recovery of the *since-neglected* tasks of critical social theory." In terms of the study, the paradigm change actually occurs on two levels: that of concrete action theory – where it involves a shift from purposive or "goal-directed" to "communicative" action – and that of cognitive thought or rationality; given the context of modern rationalization, the accent falls squarely on the latter. "What needs to be explicated today," we read, "is no longer cognition and the *mastery* of objectified nature as such but rather the intersubjectivity of possible consensual *agreement* [*Verständigung*] – at both the interpersonal and intrapsychic levels"; the focus of investigation thereby shifts "from cognitive-instrumental to *communicative rationality*." In Habermas's view, the shift was vaguely intimated in the notion of *mimesis* – but foiled due to its intrinsic aporias. The "rational core" of the notion, he insists, can be recovered only once we abandon the paradigm of the "philosophy of consciousness" – based on subjects representing and producing objects – in favor of the paradigm of "language philosophy" centered on intersubjective understanding and communication, thereby "subordinating the instrumental-rational aspect to a more comprehensive *communicative rationality*." This change also permits a rational grasp of the issue of reconciliation. In some (isolated) passages, Adorno actually linked the issue with that of an "undamaged intersubjectivity"; but the latter can only be established and maintained "through the reciprocity of consensual *agreement* based on free mutual recognition."[27]

III

As it seems to me, the dispute among spokesmen of critical theory is not of minor or marginal import, but touches at the heart of the school's enterprise. If the somber scenario sketched by Horkheimer and Adorno is correct, then critical theory is involved or enmeshed in a "crisis" of culture, indeed in a crisis operative in reality itself whose resolution can only dimly be gleaned and only partially be advanced through purposive human means. On the other hand, if Habermas's version is accepted, then critical theory is part of the ongoing critical self-correction of rational inquiry and culture – a self-correction routinely performed by scientific communities wedded to the principle of fallibilism and evidently required for cognitive and societal progress. The question remaining in that case is only what (if any) relation this principle of fallibilism has to the issue of reconciliation as formulated by Hegel and later by the early Frankfurt School. In my view, a major strength and attraction of that first generation resided in its resolute attachment to this issue, notwithstanding the difficulties of its articulation. As previously indicated, this articulation can be questioned and faulted in many ways – a point I want to take up now. The central problem, as I see it, consists in the totalization of the "nexus of corruption," a feature which is closely linked with, and actually a corollary of, the expulsion of absolutes (chiefly Hegel's absolute spirit). On this score, the older Frankfurt School is actually more consistent than Habermas who, while sharing the expulsion of absolutes, still maintains the possibility of harmonious development and social progress. Perhaps a brief glance back at Hegel may be helpful at this juncture.

In Hegel's system, the absolute spirit designates that point where all human strivings, all forms of willfulness and subjective intentionality come to rest; after having undergone multiple kinds of alienation, having struggled along the "highway of despair" and suffered the "reversal of consciousness," human spirit in the end comes to blend with the absolute spirit – which Theunissen quite correctly treats as a synonym for God (specifically the God of Christianity). It is this absolute alone – which as the end is simultaneously a perpetual beginning – which for Hegel heals and overcomes divisions and furnishes a warrant for reconciliation. Once this warrant is cancelled or removed, the world necessarily sinks into divisiveness and darkness, into a totalized "nexus of corruption" where aggression and willful caprice relentlessly perpetuate themselves in a web of domination. This, in large part, is indeed Horkheimer's and Adorno's scenario – at least on its most manifest, rhetorical level. Hence the dilemmas and aporias noted by Habermas and many other readers – and which can easily be sharpened under the rubric of instrumental reason. If the world is totally corrupt and perverse, then this world must be destroyed and replaced by a completely new one through some kind of *creatio ex nihilo*; moreover, given the removal of absolutes, such creation can only be the work of human agents or producers. In this manner, reconciliation and redemption become the target of goal-directed activity, that is, of purposive fabrication, thereby blending imperceptibly into what William Connolly has called the "civilization of productivity." At the same time, being themselves part of the corrupt world, human agents can only perpetuate or re-create the state of corruption; thus, instrumentalism becomes inescapable and self-destructive.[28]

As it happens, Horkheimer's and Adorno's scenario is not one-dimensional in this sense, but contains another, more recessed level – precisely the level on which reconciliation becomes pertinent. As Habermas correctly observes, their work at this point secretly pays tribute to Hegel's legacy – although they do so in a new guise and a radically revised vocabulary. This change is itself subtle and multi-dimensional. In my view, the departure from Hegel is not solely due to Left-Hegelian influences, that is, to the postulated move from theory to praxis (which remains entirely external to Hegel's notion of spirit). Although this may be part of the story,[29] there is also, I believe, a deeper and more cogent motivation: namely, the realization that the absolute in our time can no longer be couched in terms of a self-transparent "subjectivity" or a univocal "reason" or *Vernunft*. Horkheimer's and (especially) Adorno's writings give evidence of ceaseless experimentation, of persistent efforts to recapture or reformulate the defunct and yet not completely exhausted or disposable legacy. Some of the terms used in this search are "*mimesis*," "remembrance of nature in the subject," and "thought thinking beyond itself." No doubt some of these terms are enigmatic – given the stark background of instrumentalism and the subject–object bifurcation. However, I do not agree with Habermas's charge of inarticulateness; while providing less than a clear road map (a strange demand in this case), eatly critical theory surely did more than simply letting these terms "stand like a cipher." *Mimesis* is a case in point. In none of the reviewed writings is the term a synonym for a regressive naturalism or a lapse into natural impulses; instead, it denotes a reflective sublimation or "sublation" of nature in thought. As we read in *Negative Dialectics*: "To represent the cause of what it repressed – that of mimesis – conceptuality has no other way than to adopt something mimetic in its conduct, *without* abandoning itself." In this adoption or receptivity, philosophical thought is akin to aesthetics or the "aesthetic moment." Yet, Adorno adds, the affinity of philosophy and art does not simply support their confusion. The task of philosophy is rather "to sublate the aesthetic into real thought or thought of the real; the latter and play are its two poles."[30]

The last phrase prompts a few additional comments on *mimesis*. In Horkheimer's and Adorno's usage, the term designates initially a child-like playfulness and delight in imitation – before conduct is disciplined by the rigors of adulthood and rational thought. In this sense, *mimesis* cannot permanently be maintained without regression. However, in the view of early critical theory, adulthood and reason cannot simply cancel or eliminate playfulness – without becoming instruments of repression and domination (of inner and outer nature). This seems to me persuasive and entirely compatible with reflective insight. The stark antipode of instrumentalism (or instrumental reason) is a conduct and mode of thought which is non-purposive, non-goal-directed, not purposely intentional – which is precisely the domain of play or playfulness. With this notion of play, Horkheimer and Adorno recover a good deal of the spirit (if not the letter) of Hegel's legacy; while expelling the absolute on the level of "idea," they recover it on a different, quasi-sensual or quasi-material level – and quite necessarily so. One might say (and I would in fact claim) that instrumentalism can only be overcome by some such move; differently put: that without "absoluteness" in some guise instrumentalism is inescapable. To be sure, "absolute" at this point does not mean being removed or aloof, but rather being entangled in and permeating everything (which does not equal immanentism).[31] This entanglement, moreover, has a temporal dimension, by linking past and future, beginning and end. This is the good sense of the notion of a recollection or "remembrance of nature in the subject." For without remembrance of this sort, reconciliation or redemption readily slide into the mold of purposive fabrication. In some fashion, reconciliation must already have happened and be happening continuously so as to elude the culture of productivity. In this case, however, we (human agents) are at best partners in and not producers of reconciliation.

The point can serve as transition to Habermas's perspective. As indicated, communicative action and rationality are offered as remedy or solution for the problem of divisiveness. However, there are ample reasons for doubting the viability of this remedy. In fact, it might be said that the "solution" is only successful by dissolving the issue of reconciliation or by putting it out of reach. This aspect can be elucidated in several ways. First of all, it is clear that communication is restricted to the intersubjective domain (the so-called "social world") and not meant to extend to the domain of nature. Ever since *Knowledge and Human Interests*, Habermas has stipulated a sharp distinction between understanding and empirical science, consistently maintaining (against Marcuse and others) that the only cognitively "promising" way of dealing with external nature is that of technology or technical control. This acceptance of control, however, cannot readily be confined or isolated from other domains; it certainly is not as such mitigated by communicative rationality. It is not only conceivable but current practice that human society collectively (at least in its large majority) concurs consensually that exploitation of nature is in the common interest and required for further progress; even restrictions of control are advocated basically for the sake of long-range survival needs. This communicatively established or sanctioned control, however, reverberates beyond its initial target – first of all into the sphere of inner or "internal nature"; for, as we know at least since Freud, societal progress and rationalization are inevitably purchased at the price of instinctual repression. From there – and this was one of the main insights of the older Frankfurt School – the road is not far to social and political domination. For advances in rationalization and modernity necessarily produce a division between more rational and less rational groups, between the more modernized and "developed" and the less modernized or "underdeveloped." As Connolly observes soberly: "Modernity does not appear, in either its capitalist or its socialist form, to be a universalizable form of life. These civilizations of productivity depend upon the continued existence of areas with 'undeveloped' economies and ecologies." Thus, Hegel's judgment of the Greek world is repeated on a new plane: "It 'creates for itself in what it suppresses and which is at the same time essential to it, an internal enemy' – a third world."[32]

In large measure, the contagion of control can be traced to the dubious character of the proclaimed "paradigm shift": the shift from consciousness or subjectivity to language. Although reiterated emphatically, the change is actually disavowed at crucial junctures of Habermas's argument. Thus, the difference between "communicative" and "teleological" action is basically a difference of performative attitude or goal orientation, with action being directed in one case to efficiency of control and in the other toward understanding. As Habermas admits, every action is at its core teleological, that is, governed by purposive intentionality and goal-direction.[33] The same can be said about the distinction between "instrumental-cognitive" and "communicative" rationality. However, intentionality and goal-directedness can only be the attributes of agents or subjects – which shows the continued role of subject-philosophy (or the paradigm of consciousness). The same paradigmatic continuity is also evident in the theory of universal pragmatics. The four dimensions (of validity) listed above are clearly centered or positioned around the subject construed as speaker or performer of speech acts. As Habermas himself writes, universal pragmatics involves a series of "fundamental demarcations." According to this scheme, "the subject demarcates himself (1) from an environment that he objectifies in the third-person attitude of an observer; (2) from an environment that he conforms to or deviates from in the ego-alter attitude of a participant; (3) from his own (inner) subjectivity that he expresses or conceals in a first-person attitude; and finally (4) from the medium of language itself." The labels chosen to designate these four dimensions are "external nature, society, internal nature, and language." Not surprisingly, the continued invocation of subject-philosophy gives rise to various splits or divisions (other terms for "demarcations") – between humans and nature, ego and alter, ego and id – which in turn promote various modes of mastery and control. Again, Habermas himself serves as witness to this fact. "A general theory of speech acts," he states, "would thus describe exactly that fundamental system of rules that adult subjects have to master so as to fulfill the conditions for the successful employment of sentences in utterances."[34]

Paradigmatic continuity is particularly evident in the field of language itself, seen as a "medium" of communication. Treated as a system of rules mastered by speakers or speaking agents, language appears as a pliant tool readily amenable to cognitive theorizing and propositional (or quasi-propositional) statements. In contrast with willful designs, communicative action and rationality are said to yield a transparent consensus couched in univocal terms or identical meanings – a notion presupposing a streamlined language stripped of intrinsic ambiguity. Thus, to the extent that there is a "linguistic turn," it is at best a partial or half-hearted shift: one accentuating communication while bypassing the inner complexity of the field – what Hamann and others have called the "abyss" of language. In this respect, the older Frankfurt School has actually made a more resolute move toward language, and away from traditional subject-philosophy. As Horkheimer observed already in *Eclipse of Reason*: "Philosophy must become more sensitive to the silent testimonies of language and plumb the layers of experience preserved in it." In this endeavor, philosophy could not simply trust streamlined concepts tailored to the principles of identity; neither philosophy nor language, he said, can be reduced to a "formula." Instead, without shunning concepts, thinking has to recover and sublate in language the traces and marks of experience: "Philosophy is at one with art in reflecting suffering through language and thus transferring it to the sphere of experience and memory." In his *Negative Dialectics*, Adorno links this memory of suffering with the dimension of "naming" or "names," that is, with the metaphorical and rhetorical character of (ordinary) language through which it inheres in the concrete world. "What remains to be thought instead," he writes, turning against traditional epistemology, "has linguistically its distant and vague archetype in the names which do not preempt their target through categories." Language, he continues, is not simply a sign system designed to serve "epistemic functions"; going beyond abstract categorial definitions it rather seeks to release or rescue "non-identity" from the "spell of its exile." For this end, philosophy enlists the resources of rhetoric (without collapsing into the latter). In his words: "Rhetoric represents within philosophy that which cannot be thought except in language. It asserts itself in the imperatives of concrete presentation through which philosophy transcends the communication of already known and fixed contents."[35]

In my own view, contemporary thought is indeed marked by a paradigm shift engendering a host of new philosophical problems; but it can be such a shift only as move to language in the strong and comprehensive sense. While not excluding them from view, the shift cannot be contained within the bounds of communication and speech-act theory. First of all, as an intentional performance, speech-acting does not make sufficient room for listening. In his stress on performative "competence," Habermas consistently privileges speaking over hearing or listening – basically suspecting the latter as a carrier of heteronomy (or a danger to autonomous reason). However, apart from being required for ordinary dialogue, listening or receptive sensitivity is implied in language on numerous levels. Every word spoken or written down evokes or carries in its wake a whole host of other words and phrases, that is, a whole range of synonyms, antonyms, and close and distant allusions. Thus, every speech act or communication resonates with the whole dense web of ordinary language – which accounts for the difficulties of interpretation. Moreover, every spoken or written word conjures up the unspoken and unwritten – what might have been and what has not been (perhaps never can be) spoken or written; thus, language or speech reverberates with its own silence, with what Horkheimer called the "silent testimonies of language" – to which he exhorted philosophy to become attentive. In large measure, this complexity of language is sedimented in metaphor, in the poetic-rhetorical and idiomatic texture of speech; attentiveness to this fabric means basically a "remembrance of nature" (language's nature) in thought – which does not equal a simple fusion of reason and literature.[36] It is only through such remembrance and in terms of such language-thought that reconciliation can be sensibly articulated (if it can be articulated at all). Along the same lines, language alone today can claim absoluteness or assume the role of Hegel's absolute spirit – with the proviso again that absoluteness does not mean separation (nor reducibility to a conceptual formula).[37]

Such a view of language in its emphatic and unrestricted (or un-pruned) sense – and replete with Hegelian resonances – has been articulated by Gadamer in the final part of his *Truth and Method*, devoted to the portrayal of an ontological, language-based hermeneutics. Like Adorno, Gadamer links language with "naming" and the rendition of concrete experience. As he writes: "The word is not merely a sign; in a sense that is hard to grasp it is also something almost like an image" or name manifesting experiential content. The latter is not initially "wordless" and then (so to speak) subsumed under a term or concept; rather, it is part of experience itself "that it seeks and finds words which disclose it." Together with Adorno, Gadamer also vindicates concrete-idiomatic language against its reduction to abstract categories and conceptual schemes; like the former, he perceives this reduction as an exercise of mastery or control (of logic over content). "The logical ideal of the systematic order of concepts," we read, "triumphs progressively over the living metaphoric texture of language on which all ordinary concept-formation depends. For only a grammar governed by logic will want to distinguish between the 'real' and the 'metaphorical' meaning of words."[38] In his portrayal of ordinary language, Gadamer eloquently invokes Hegel's legacy of "speculative" thought – although the latter, in his view, remained himself confined within the field of propositional statements without reaching the domain of linguistic experience as such. In a sense akin to Hegel's but on a new level, Gadamer observes, "language itself has something speculative about it" – namely, as the enactment of meaning or the happening of speech. Speculative is such a process, he adds, "in that the finite possibilities of a word are linked with the intended sense in a direction toward the infinite." For to speak or to say something means "to correlate what is said with an infinity of the unsaid in a comprehensive synthesis of meaning which alone grants understanding.[39]

Against this background, the issue of reconciliation comes again into view – both in its philosophical and its religious or theological sense. For if language involves not only speaking but also listening to (others and) its speculative complexity, then thought can also recuperate the notion of a primordial naming or calling – which is not a fixed point but a perpetual beginning: namely, the word(s) through which things and creatures were called into being. From this event or in pursuance of it, the same calling reverberates through history, as a call to all humans to reconciliation and atonement – a call addressed to them "by their name." For Christians, this summoning reaches its fulfillment in Christ – who is nothing but the embodiment of this word or call and who through his effective reconciliation holds out the same promise to all believers and to humankind at large. In Gadamer's words, language is operative first of all in creation seen as "the word of God." Most importantly, however, the actual redemptive or reconciling deed – "the sending of the Son, the mystery of incarnation" – is itself "presented in St John's prologue in terms of the word." As elaborated by medieval and later theology, Christ as Son is also the midpoint or "center of language," a notion in which "the mediation of the incarnation event achieves alone its full truth."[40] Yet Christ's redemptive act was performed not for his own sake but for the sake of the world – upon which he calls not from the platform of a doctrine or abstract principle, but in his capacity as the exemplary "name," the name of names, in whom the concrete suffering of existence is manifestly inscribed. Both his own suffering and that of the world, in turn, are not ends in themselves, but urgent pleas for transformative mediation, for the healing of brokenness and divisiveness. Until his return, this plea has to be the heart of all human speech and action – which, however, cannot proceed without the grant of absoluteness and absolution. As Paul wrote to the Colossians (1:19–20): "For in him all the fullness of God was pleased to dwell, and through him to reconcile to himself all things, whether on earth or in heaven, making peace by the blood of his cross."

NOTES

1   The passage continues by saying (2:16) that Christ's redemptive act was meant to "reconcile us both to God in one body through the cross, thereby bringing the hostility to an end." As used in these passages, reconciliation seems to be akin to "atonement" in the Old Testament (e.g., Leviticus 16:20; Ezekiel 45:17–20; Daniel 9:24).

2   See Hans-Georg Gadamer, *Reason in the Age of Science*, tr. Frederick G. Lawrence (Cambridge, MA: MIT Press, 1981), pp. 27–9, 34–5 (translation slightly altered); Michael Theunissen, *Hegels Lehre vom absoluten Geist als theologisch-politischer Traktat* (Berlin: de Gruyter, 1970), p. 100. Among

many other passages Theunissen cites Hegel's statement: "It is the general interest of philosophy to reproduce in thought the same reconciliation which we accept in faith." He also points to a (limited) Hegel revival in the confines of Christian theology: e.g., Hans Küng, *Menschwerdung Gottes* (1970), tr. by J. R. Stephenson as *The Incarnation of God: An Introduction to Hegel's Theological Thought as Prolegomena to a Future Christology* (New York: Crossroad, 1987). On Theunissen see my "Dialogue and Otherness" in Dallmayr, *Critical Encounters* (Notre Dame: University of Notre Dame Press, 1987), pp. 209–23, also my introduction to his *The Other*, tr. Christopher Macann (Cambridge, MA: MIT Press, 1984).

3 See especially Max Horkheimer, "Traditional and Critical Theory" (1937), in *Critical Theory: Selected Essays*, tr. Matthew J. O'Connell et al. (New York: Herder & Herder, 1972), pp. 188–243. Although adopting the notion of dialectics largely from Lukács, Horkheimer even then expressed doubt in the existence of a privileged emancipatory subject or class (i.e., the proletariat).

4 Horkheimer, *Eclipse of Reason* (1947; New York: Seabury Press, 1974), p. 97. The study was translated into German by Alfred Schmidt and published together with later essays under the title *Zur Kritik der instrumentellen Vernunft* (Frankfurt-Main: Fischer, 1967).

5 *Eclipse of Reason*, p. 101.

6 *Eclipse of Reason*, pp. 93–4, 105. Regarding the last point Horkheimer added (p. 121): "In modern fascism, rationality has reached a point at which it is no longer satisfied with simply repressing nature; rationality now exploits nature by incorporating into its own system the rebellious potentialities of nature. The Nazis manipulated the suppressed desires of the German people."

7 *Eclipse of Reason*, pp. 107–9.

8 *Eclipse of Reason*, p. 169.

9 *Eclipse of Reason*, pp. 126–7. According to Horkheimer, neither monism nor dualism offer a satisfactory philosophical solution (p. 171): "The real difficulty in the problem of the relation between spirit and nature is that hypostatizing the polarity of these two entities is as impermissible as reducing one of them to the other . . . The assumption of an ultimate duality is inadmissible – not only because the traditional and highly questionable requirement of an ultimate principle is logically incompatible with a dualistic construction, but because of the content of the concepts in question. The two poles cannot be reduced to a monistic principle, yet their duality too must be largely understood as a product."

10 *Eclipse of Reason*, pp. 174–5, 177, 179. On *mimesis* and mimetic impulses see pp. 114–16, especially the comment (p. 115): "In the present crisis the problem of mimesis is particularly urgent. Civilization starts with, but must eventually transcend and transvaluate, man's mimetic impulses."

11 Max Horkheimer and Theodor W. Adorno, *Dialektik der Aufklärung* (first published 1947; Frankfurt–Main: Fischer, 1969), pp. 3, 9; tr. by John

Cumming under the title *Dialectic of Enlightenment* (New York: Seabury Press, 1972), pp. xiii, 3. (In the above and subsequent citations I have slightly altered the translation for purposes of clarity.)

12 *Dialectic of Enlightenment*, pp. 4, 8–10. As the authors add grimly (pp. 9, 32): "Enlightenment behaves toward things like a dictator toward men: He knows them insofar as he can manipulate them . . . The essence of enlightenment is the alternative whose ineradicability is that of domination. Men always had to choose between their subjection to nature or the subjection of nature to the self . . . Under the pressure of domination human labor has always led away from myth – into whose jurisdiction it has always relapsed under the spell of domination."

13 *Dialectic of Enlightenment*, pp. 7, 14, 29.

14 *Dialectic of Enlightenment*, pp. 24, 39–40, 42. Compare also their comment on the sense of remembrance (p. xv): "The issue is not the conservation of the past but the redemption of the hopes of the past."

15 Theodor W. Adorno, "Erfahrungsgehalt" in *Drei Studien zu Hegel* (Frankfurt-Main: Suhrkamp, 1963), pp. 90, 96–9.

16 *Drei Studien zu Hegel*, pp. 99, 102–4. A very different interpretation of the notion of the "rationality of the real," namely along theological (and Christological) lines, had been given earlier by Franz Rosenzweig in *Hegel und der Staat* (Munich and Berlin: Oldenbourg, 1920), vol. 2, p. 79.

17 Adorno, *Negative Dialektik* (Frankfurt-Main: Suhrkamp, 1966), pp. 17–18, 36; tr. by E. B. Ashton as *Negative Dialectics* (New York: Seabury Press, 1973), pp. 8, 27–8. (In the above and subsequent citations I have slightly altered the translation for purposes of clarity.)

18 *Negative Dialectics*, pp. 6–7, 12. The above does not simply mean a substitution of multiplicity for unity and of particularity for universality. As Adorno adds (p. 158): "Like Kant and the entire philosophical tradition including Plato, Hegel is a partisan of unity. Yet, an abstract denial of the latter would not befit thinking either. The illusion of grasping the manifold directly would mean mimetic regression and a lapse into myth, into the horror of diffuseness – just as unitary thinking, imitating blind nature through its repression, ends in mythical dominion at the opposite pole. Self-reflection of enlightenment is not its revocation."

19 *Negative Dialectics*, pp. 19, 141, 179–80, 191. In a later passage (p. 207), Adorno links negative dialectics with a (non-objectivistic) materialism, finding in negativity (and the prohibition of images) an affinity of the latter with theology: "At its most materialistic, materialism concurs with theology. Its central aspiration would be the resurrection of the flesh – a notion utterly foreign to idealism, the realm of the absolute spirit."

20 See Jürgen Habermas, "Zur philosophischen Diskussion um Marx und den Marxismus" (1957) in *Theorie und Praxis* (Neuwied: Luchterhand, 1963), pp. 261–335; *Knowledge and Human Interests*, tr. Jeremy J. Shapiro (Boston: Beacon Press, 1971); "Introduction" to *Theory and Practice*, tr. John Viertel (Boston: Beacon Press, 1973), pp. 1–40; "A Postscript to

Knowledge and Human Interests", in *Philosophy of the Social Sciences*, vol. 3 (1975), pp. 157–89; "Wahrheitstheorien," in Helmut Fahrenbach, ed., *Wirklichkeit und Reflexion* (Pfullingen: Neske, 1973), pp. 211–65; "What is Universal Pragmatics?" (1976) in *Communication and the Evolution of Society*, tr. Thomas McCarthy (Boston: Beacon Press, 1979), pp. 1–68; *Moral Consciousness and Communicative Action*, tr. Christian Lenhardt and Shierry Weber Nicholson (Cambridge, MA: MIT Press, 1990), pp. 43–115; *The Theory of Communicative Action*, 2 vols, tr. Thomas McCarthy (Boston: Beacon Press, 1984 and 1988).

21 "What is Universal Pragmatics?", p. 67.

22 *The Theory of Communicative Action*, vol. 1: *Reason and the Rationalization of Society*, p. 10. (In the above and subsequent citations I have slightly altered the translation for purposes of clarity.)

23 *The Theory of Communicative Action*, vol. 1, pp. 373, 378–80.

24 *The Theory of Communicative Action*, vol. 1, pp. 380–81.

25 *The Theory of Communicative Action*, vol. 1, pp. 373–4, 377. In another formulation of the conflicting assumptions the study states (p. 383): On the one hand, early critical theory "shares with the tradition of great philosophy (which, in however refracted a manner, it continues) certain essential features: the insistence on contemplation, on a theory divorced from practice; the direction toward the totality of nature and mankind . . . On the other hand, Horkheimer and Adorno regard the systems of objective spirit as ideologies; the latter succumb hopelessly to a critique which ceaselessly moves back and forth between subjective and objective reason."

26 *The Theory of Communicative Action*, vol. 1, pp. 382–5. Habermas in this context levels strong accusations against Adorno, chiefly the charges of approximating Heideggerian views and of betraying the motivations of the very beginning of the Frankfurt School (pp. 385–6): "As opposed as the intentions behind their respective philosophies of history are, the later Adorno and Heidegger resemble each other in their position on the theoretical claims of objectifying thought and of reflection: remembrance of nature comes shockingly close to the recollection [*Andenken*] of being . . . A philosophy that withdraws behind the lines of discursive thought to the 'remembrance of nature' pays for the evocative powers of its exercises by renouncing the goal of theoretical knowledge – and thus by abandoning that program of 'interdisciplinary materialism' in whose name critical social theory was first launched in the early thirties."

27 *The Theory of Communicative Action*, vol. 1, pp. 366, 386, 390, 392. The polemic against the older Frankfurt School is continued in Habermas's more recent *The Philosophical Discourse of Modernity: Twelve Lectures*, tr. Frederick Lawrence (Cambridge, MA: MIT Press, 1987), chapter 5. However, the presentation there does not yield much for present purposes – in part because nearly half of the chapter entitled "The Entwinement of Myth and Enlightenment" is devoted to a discussion of Nietzsche (whose "regressive-archaic" outlook is designed to cast a shadow on the older

Frankfurt School). According to the chapter, Horkheimer and Adorno radicalized modern enlightenment by unleashing a relentless "ideology critique" against enlightenment itself; thereby they became trapped in aporias, now called "performative contradictions" (p. 119): "The radicalization or totalization of enlightenment denounces the latter with its own tools. Adorno was quite aware of the performative contradiction inherent in totalized critique. His *Negative Dialectics* reads like a continuing explanation of why we must circle within this performative contradiction and indeed should remain there." Again, there is the accusation of the atrophy of "theory" (pp. 127–8): Horkheimer and Adorno choose the option of "stirring up, holding open, and no longer wanting to overcome theoretically the performative contradiction inherent in a totalized ideology critique. Since, on this level of reflection, any attempt to formulate a theory would slide into an abyss, they eschew theory and practice determinate negation on an *ad hoc* basis." In this manner they miss the alternative solution of communicative rationality (p. 129): Like historicism, Horkheimer and Adorno "surrendered themselves to an uninhibited skepticism regarding reason, instead of weighing the reasons casting doubt on this skepticism itself. In this way, perhaps, they might have laid the normative foundations of critical social theory so deep that they would remain untouched by any decomposition of bourgeois culture (like the one happening then in Germany for all to see)."

28   Regarding the "civilization of productivity" compare William Connolly, *The Politics of Ambiguity* (Madison: University of Wisconsin Press, 1987), pp. 76–86.

29   There is, I believe, an element of Left Hegelianism in the departure from Hegel (but only on one level). Suspicious of idealism and a mere reconciliation within the sphere of "mind," Horkheimer and Adorno shift the accent to non-mental "reality" and praxis. However, this is a misunderstanding of the notion of (absolute) "spirit" – which, for Hegel, designated the very core or essence of reality. Exiled from the absolute, external "reality" and human praxis are not only unreconciled but indeed irreconcilable and unredeemable. For a critique formulated along similar lines see Theunissen, *Hegels Lehre vom absoluten Geist*, pp. 24–36.

30   *Negative Dialectics*, pp. 14–15. Contrary to the above (and similar statements elsewhere), Habermas accuses Adorno of confusing reason and art, philosophy and aesthetics; see *The Theory of Communicative Action*, vol. 1, pp. 384–5. The notion of *mimesis*, to be sure, is further developed in Adorno's *Aesthetic Theory*, tr. Christian Lenhardt (London: Routledge and Kegan Paul, 1984), pp. 79–83, 166–71, 453–5; but even there "thinking" about art is not simply equated with art. The work clearly seeks to articulate a "theory," though not in Habermas's sense (who hardly has a monopoly on the term).

31   The "absolute" is indeed removed from willfulness and purposive intentionality; but precisely in this way is it able to participate in everything in

a non-domineering, sympathetic way.

32 William Connolly, *Political Theory and Modernity* (Oxford: Blackwell, 1988), p. 133. The polemic against Marcuse is developed in Habermas, "Technology and Science as 'Ideology'", in *Toward a Rational Society*, tr. Jeremy J. Shapiro (Boston: Beacon Press, 1970), pp. 81–122, and "Psychic Thermidor and the Rebirth of Rebellious Subjectivity", in Richard J. Bernstein, ed., *Habermas and Modernity* (Cambridge, MA: MIT Press, 1985), pp. 67–77.

33 Habermas, *The Theory of Communicative Action*, vol. 1, p. 101.

34 "What is Universal Pragmatics?", pp. 26, 66. The continuity of subject-philosophy in Habermas's theory – his tendency to replace "the subject" by a plurality of subjects – was noted by Theunissen early on; see his *Gesellschaft und Geschichte* (Berlin: de Gruyter, 1969). For a brief summary of the study's argument see my "Critical Epistemology Criticized", in *Beyond Dogma and Despair* (Notre Dame: University of Notre Dame Press, 1981), pp. 251–3.

35 Horkheimer, *Eclipse of Reason*, pp. 165–6, 179; Adorno, *Negative Dialectics*, pp. 52, 55, 162–3. In turning to rhetoric, Adorno does not propose its complete fusion with philosophy (p. 56): "Dialectics – literally: language as the organon of thought – means the attempt to rescue critically the rhetorical moment, that is, to approximate thing and expression mutually to the point of indistinction . . . In dialectics, contrary to popular opinion, the rhetorical element is on the side of content." In his emphasis on "naming" (and the mimetic element of language) Adorno shows his indebtedness to Walter Benjamin. On the latter's language theory, and Habermas's ambivalent relation to it, see Martin Jay, "Habermas and Modernism", in Bernstein, ed., *Habermas and Modernity*, pp. 125–39, esp. pp. 129–34. In my view, Habermas tends to confuse the mimetic and metaphorical element with expressiveness (of a speaker's inner life).

36 The charge of fusing philosophy and literature is leveled by Habermas chiefly against Jacques Derrida and his followers; see his *The Philosophical Discourse of Modernity*, chapter 7 with its excursus on the "Levelling of the Genre Distinction between Philosophy and Literature", pp. 161–210. Habermas concedes that ordinary language is "ineradicably rhetorical" and that the "illuminating power of metaphorical tropes" radiates into more "specialized languages"; but he insists (pp. 209–10) on the strict separation of metaphor from reason, of rhetoric from philosophy (or the subordination of the former to the latter): "Whoever transposes the radical critique of reason into the domain of rhetorics in order to blunt the paradox of self-referentiality, thereby dulls the sword of the critique of reason itself." But where, if not from ordinary language, does reason derive its vocabulary? Strict separation seems to be predicated on the assumption of a purely mental language (which is disavowed by the "linguistic turn").

37 As Adorno writes, with some exaggeration: "Hegelian dialectics was a dialectics without language – although dialectics in its most literal sense

postulates language; to this extent Hegel remained an adept of the prevalent mode of science. He did not need language in an emphatic sense since everything, including the speechless and opaque, was supposed to be spirit and spirit the comprehensive synthesis. This supposition cannot be salvaged." These lines should be read in conjunction with comments on the retrieval of (Hegelian) "infinity" and "speculation" on a new level: "An idea bequeathed to us by idealism – corrupted by it more than any other – needs to be rethought today: the idea of the infinite . . . Even after breaking with idealism, philosophy cannot do without speculation which was extolled by idealism and tabooed with it – though speculation needs to be taken in a sense broader than the overly positive Hegelian one." See *Negative Dialectics*, pp. 15–16, 163.

38   Gadamer, *Truth and Method*, 2nd rev. edn, tr. and rev. Joel Weinsheimer and Donald G. Marshall (New York: Crossroad, 1989), pp. 416–17, 432. The beginning of this logical ideal is traced to Aristotle. However, Gadamer also acknowledges another side in Aristotle – where language appears as a mid-point between "naturalness" and logical artifact (p. 431): "When Aristotle says of sounds or written signs that they 'signify' in becoming a 'symbolon', this means that they do not exist naturally but according to convention (*kata syntheken*). But this is by no means an instrumental sign theory. Rather, the convention according to which spoken sounds or written signs mean something is not an agreement on a means (or instrument) of communication – which would always already presuppose language – but it is the basic concord on which human community and its agreement on what is good and just are founded." In a telling footnote (p. 431, note 59) Gadamer adds that Aristotle's thoughts on language should be read "in the light of his *Politics*."

39   *Truth and Method*, p. 469. As Gadamer continues, this speculative quality is found "in an intensified way" in poetry or poetic language. Poetry is the most "absolute" or speculative form of language because it is least subject to control or least at our (instrumental) disposal. In all these respects Gadamer is very close to Heidegger's philosophy of language. On the latter compare Gerald Bruns, *Heidegger's Estrangements: Language, Truth and Poetry in the Later Writings* (New Haven: Yale University Press, 1989).

40   Gadamer, *Truth and Method*, pp. 419–20, 428–9. Regarding the speculative or absolute dimension of language, Gadamer's hermeneutics has also accorded a central place to the notion of "play" or (serious) playfulness; see esp. pp. 91–9. For a vindication of play in the sense of non-purposiveness or non-utility compare also Klaus-M. Kodalle, *Die Eroberung des Nutzlosen* (Paderborn: Schöningh, 1988).

4

Kant and Critical Theory

Kant's legacy still reverberates powerfully in contemporary thought. Basically, his "Copernican Revolution" signaled a shift of accent from a seemingly self-contained universe to the constitutive role of human faculties – a shift preceded, to be sure, by Descartes' resolute turn to the *cogito* (which in a sense inaugurated modern philosophy). Instead of relying on passive reception and contemplation, Kant's move underscored the function of *a priori* categories – implanted in mind or reason – as prerequisites of cognition and scientific analysis; instead of accepting traditional beliefs or shared customs, the same move foregrounded the potency of unsullied (or "noumenal") freedom as guidepost for moral conduct and social action. Seen from this vantage, Kant's opus stands virtually as a synonym for the Enlightenment project, that is, for the ambition to liberate mankind from external bonds, oppressive traditions, and generally from all modes of "self-induced immaturity."[1] Given this internal linkage, his work understandably came to exert a strong impact on subsequent progressive thought in the West – a trajectory stretching from Left Hegelianism over Marx to the contemporary Frankfurt School. The impact or affinity, one may note, is evident not only in the general intellectual orientation but also in the adopted vocabulary, particularly in the stress on "critique" – as can be seen in Bruno Bauer's "critical criticism," in Marx's "critique of political economy," and in the more recent program of "critical theory." This same stress, one should add, has also steadily emerged as a fulcrum of philosophical controversy or contestation. From a variety of angles – including phenomenology and ordinary language philosophy – questions have been raised regarding the primacy accorded to critique over receptive thought, to reason over the practices of a shared life-world.

The promise and predicaments of Kantian rationalism are nowhere as instructively displayed as in the context of the Frankfurt School. As originally formulated by Max Horkheimer, the program of "critical theory" relied on constructive human intervention and design in opposition to the passive replication of existing empirical reality. Construed in its traditional sense, he wrote in his programmatic essay of 1937, theory "organizes experience in the light of questions connected with the reproduction of life within the framework of existing society." By contrast, critical social theory focuses on "men as the producers of the totality of their historical life-forms." Prevailing social conditions, from this vantage, depend "not only on nature but also on the power humans exert over it"; consequently, "objects (of inquiry), modes of perception, questions asked, and the meaning of answers all bear witness to human activity and the degree of human control." Given this focus on constitutive human capacities, critical theory according to Horkheimer was a direct descendant of German idealim, and particularly of Kant's critical philosophy. In relating seemingly irreducible facts or data to "human production," we read, "critical social theory is in accord with German idealism; ever since Kant, the latter has marshalled this dynamic moment against the worship of facts and the attendant social conformism." The difference between idealism and critical theory, in Horkheimer's account, resided basically in the conception of human agency – with critical theory accentuating social labor and production in contradistinction from the idealist-Kantian stress on (subjective) consciousness. This difference, however, did not impair an underlying and persisting congruence: namely, the shared critical thrust of thought and the shared moral intent of a liberation from oppressive traditions. In Horkheimer's words, critical theory is "wholly distrustful of the rules of conduct which society as presently constituted provides its members." Under the auspices of capitalism, late industrial society is marked by the contrast between sporadic individual freedom and overall social determinism: "Critical thought has a view of man as self-divided until this opposition is removed," that is, until a condition is reached "where whatever humans will is also necessary and where objective necessity is the necessity of rationally mastered events."[2]

In the decades following Horkheimer's essay, critical theory underwent manifold changes and revisions – changes which modified or muffled but scarcely eliminated the Kantian legacy. In the context of the older Frankfurt School, a major development was Horkheimer's and Adorno's progressive disaffection with the project of human mastery and control, a project now traced to the ambitions of instrumental reason; as a corollary of this development, Adorno sought to counterbalance human construction with a renewed receptiveness – a move reflected in the stress placed on "otherness" or "non-identity" and on the artful "mimesis" of natural inclinations. For present purposes I shall not pursue Adorno's complex path from materialist production to negative dialectics – although I shall invoke some of his insights at a later point. Instead, my focus here shall be on Habermasian critical theory, particularly its moral or ethical dimension and its linkage with the Kantian heritage of critique. As one may note, Habermas – like Horkheimer in 1937–pays tribute to Kantian thought in all his writings while simultaneously trying to extricate himself from its idealist moorings; in lieu of Horkheimer's shift to social labor, Habermas turns from consciousness to communicative interaction, that is, to the constitutive role of intersubjective deliberation (while relegating labor to a monological-instrumental domain). Although at odds with Kantian idealism, communicative interaction is said to be pregnant with strict or context-free normative standards whose status is at least loosely akin to Kant's categorical imperative. My intent in the following is to explore the lingering Kantianism in communicative ethics. A first section shall examine Habermas's effort to vindicate his ethical program against other, more context-dependent perspectives, particularly the perspective of Hegelian *Sittlichkeit*. Next, I shall assess critically the strengths and shortcomings of this vindication as compared with Hegelian and post-Hegelian considerations. By way of conclusion, I shall return to Adorno and his critique of Kantian thought (as found in *Negative Dialectics*), in an effort to adumbrate possibilities of a post-metaphysical or negative-dialectical ethics.

I

Kantian resonances have permeated Habermas's opus from the beginning. His ground-breaking epistemological treatise, *Knowledge and Human Interests*, explicitly paid tribute to Kant as the last great practitioner of a critical theory of knowledge. The study's main thesis was in fact that, after Kant, cognitive or scientific inquiry was "no longer seriously comprehended" or reflected upon by philosophy; recent empiricism or positivism, in particular, had completely relinquished the epistemological task – "which is why it generally has regressed behind the level of reflection represented by Kantian thought." The model of cognition outlined in the study – the tripartition of interests and corresponding knowledge claims – was distantly patterned on Kant's threefold critical enterprise, although critique was now communicatively recast or reformulated (and although the *Critique of Judgment* was largely sidestepped or left unexplored). About a decade later, Kant's legacy surfaced again in Habermas's program of a "universal pragmatics," in the sense that linguistic interaction was said to be predicated on deep-seated or generative validity claims redeemable through communication. Abandonment of the concept of the "transcendental subject" in Kant's sense, Habermas noted at the time, "does not mean that we have to renounce universal-pragmatic analysis of the application of our concepts of objects of possible experience, that is, investigation of the constitution of experience." The difference from Kantian premises at this point was seen to reside chiefly in the fact that strict *a priori* demonstration is replaced by quasi-transcendental or formal-universal analysis of "the conditions required for argumentatively redeeming validity claims that are at least implicitly related to discursive vindication." Similar quasi-transcendental concerns animated formulations of cognitive and moral development published at the same time, where Habermas paid homage to Piaget's genetic structuralism, to Kohlberg's moral psychology, and to cognitive theories from Kant to Peirce.[3]

Subsequently, aspects of universal pragmatics and of the theory of moral development coalesced in Habermas's proposal of a "discursive" or "communicative ethics" – certainly one of the most innovative and ambitious contributions to ethical theorizing in our time. Reacting against a prevalent mood of moral skepticism or non-cognitivism, Habermas inserted his proposal squarely in the cognitivist tradition – a tradition which ultimately can be traced to Kantian initiatives. As Habermas observed in 1983: "*All* cognitivist theories of ethics draw on an intuition which Kant expressed in his categorical imperative." In line with this intuition, ethics on cognitivist premises is construed in such a manner as to endorse only norms which can muster "the qualified consent of all possible participants," that is, norms which "embody a *general will* or, in Kant's frequently repeated formula, can become 'general law'." While invoking Kant's moral intuition, Habermas's own proposal did not simply follow the strategy of transcendental deduction – a divergence due mainly to the "linguistic turn" in recent philosophy, that is, the turn from consciousness to language or communication. Given its intimate linkage with the overall design of Kant's system, he observed, Kant's conception of the categorical imperative can "no longer be readily defended under changed circumstances." Relying at least in part on insights culled from Apel's transcendental hermeneutics, Habermas at this point translated Kant's "general law" into a universal principle of communicative interaction, that is, a principle presupposed by and constitutive for argumentation which participants cannot refuse to accept without committing a "performative contradiction." Under normative auspices, this principle – by santioning free and equal participation – provides a kind of categorical standard or yardstick for the evaluation of actual communicative exchanges, namely, the yardstick of a "rationally motivated consensus" or of an "ideal" or "unlimited" speech community. Summarizing these and related points, Habermas in the end condensed the gist of discursive or communicative ethics into the "parsimonious" formula that "only such norms can claim validity which obtain (or might obtain) the consent of all those affected as participants in a practical discourse."[4]

Rounding out his presentation in 1983, Habermas also defended his proposal against alternative approaches, particularly against more contextualized theories of ethics including the Hegelian conception of *Sittlichkeit*. Basically, *Sittlichkeit* at this juncture was identified with the actual moral practices and beliefs of a concrete "life-world," while discursive ethics served the function of a quasi-transcendental validation of norms. A few years later, Habermas specifically addressed this issue or tensional relation in greater detail in an essay entitled "Morality and *Sittlichkeit* [Ethical Life]," subtitled "Does Hegel's Critique of Kant Also Apply to Discourse Ethics?" Better and more succinctly than other writings, this essay (in my view) sharpens and profiles the significance of Kant's legacy for contemporary critical theory. As Habermas states at the beginning of the essay: "In recent years Karl-Otto Apel and I have undertaken the attempt to reformulate Kant's moral theory by grounding moral norms in communication – a venture to which I refer as 'discourse ethics'." The paper is divided into two main parts or segments. The first part discusses the meaning of discourse ethics and the moral intuitions animating or guiding the discursive approach. The second part addresses the issue thematized in the essay's title by focusing on four main objections which Hegel raised against Kantian morality: namely, first, the objection to the "formalism" of Kant's ethics, that is, to the abstraction of the categorical imperative from the "concrete content of maxims and duties"; secondly, the critique of Kant's abstract "universalism," that is, the segregation of moral judgment from individual cases and the "particular problem context"; thirdly, the attack on the "impotence of the mere ought" (*Ohnmacht des blossen Sollens*), that is, its incapacity to deal with the "practical implementation" of moral insights; and lastly, Hegel's remonstration against the "terrorism of pure conviction" (*Terrorismus der reinen Gessinnung*), that is, the possible resort to violent or immoral strategies in order to impose pure moral postulates on a recalcitrant social and historical reality.[5]

Before elaborating on the distinctive meaning of discourse ethics, Habermas initially highlights the salient features of Kantian ethics and of all moral theories indebted to that legacy; briefly put, such theories are "deontological" (rather than ontological), "cognitivist" (rather than skeptical), "formal" (rather than material), and "universalist" (rather than particularist) in character. While classical, especially Aristotelian ethics had dealt with all questions of the "good life," Kant's approach was deliberately restricted to the problem of "right or just action"; instead of embracing all modes of human conduct, his attention was focused on the normative validity or "ought-status" (*Sollgeltung*) of norms (that is, on their deontological quality). For Kant, this ought-status was not merely a matter of intuition or arbitrary decision, but amenable to cognitive insight; although differentiating between theoretical and practical reason, he regarded normative validity as at least analogous to theoretical truth claims (and, like the latter, as cognitively justifiable). By treating moral norms as rules or principles distinct from actual conduct, Kantian ethics distinguished between form and content, between abstract principle and rule-application; by stressing free (or noumenal) will-formation, it provided a formal-procedural rather than substantive grounding of norms. Finally, Kantian ethics was universalist in scope and intent: namely, by virtue of its claim that, far from reflecting merely "the intuitions of a particular culture or epoch," the categorical imperative (or a similar moral principle) could function as "general law." As Habermas points out, discourse ethics shares these salient features of the Kantian approach – though modifying some of its accents. Basically, the modifications or innovations of discourse ethics have to do with the sense of formalism and universalism. In lieu of the transcendental deduction of the categorical imperative, discourse ethics introduces the notion of a communicative grounding of norms, that is, the procedure of moral argumentation. As mentioned before, this notion can be condensed into the formula that "only those norms may claim validity which could obtain the consent of all concerned, in their role as participants in a practical discourse." In accordance with this formula, discourses must be structured in such a way that all concerned can "participate freely and equally in a cooperative search for truth, a search bowing only to the force of the better argument." Rigorously applied, this formula ties in with the aspect of universalism – an aspect further buttressed by considerations of "performative contradiction," that is, the view that participants in discourses must implicitly (and even counterfactually) accept the normative premises of argumentation.[6]

Regarding the moral intuitions captured by discourse ethics, Habermas refers broadly to anthropological and sociological insights concerning the exposure and vulnerability of human beings under conditions of socialization or social coexistence. "Moral," he writes, "I call all such intuitions that teach us how best to conduct our lives so as to counteract the *extreme vulnerability* of human beings by means of thoughtfulness and considerateness. Anthropologically viewed, morality is a safety device compensating for human vulnerability built into socio-cultural life-forms." Human exposure or vulnerability derives from a process of identity-formation where humans are progressively individuated and particularized while simultaneously being related to or integrated in large social contexts. In Habermas's words: "Humans capable of speech and action are constituted as individuals by growing into an intersubjectively shared life-world and by becoming members of an existing language community." This process of growth or maturation, however, is not regularly smooth or unproblematic. Rather, with advancing stages of individuation, the individual subject becomes entangled in a "steadily more dense and more subtle fabric of reciprocal vulnerability and safety needs"; this fact accounts for the "quasi-constitutive insecurity and chronic fragility" of human identity under conditions of socialization. Discourse ethics (like other theories of a Kantian type) proceeds from these anthropological and sociological concerns. Being tailored to the needs of fragile and vulnerable creatures, ethical theory must be attentive simultaneously to individuation and socialization, that is, the protection of individual identity and the validation of intersubjectively binding norms. In Habermas's presentation, these two ethical tasks can be captured under the respective headings of "justice" and "solidarity" (or else of equal respect and benevolence). The distinctive contribution of discourse ethics is to show that both dimensions have "one and the same moral root: namely, the vulnerability and safety needs of creatures which are individuated through socialization." Basically, all moral theories revolve around these crucial concerns; in doing so, they tap insights deriving from expectations of symmetry and reciprocity governing communicative action.[7]

Turning to Hegel's critique of Kantian ethics, Habermas takes up first the issue of "formalism" or of the purely formal and ultimately vacuous character of Kant's imperative (and of ethical principles patterned on this precedent). In his treatise on *Natural Law*, Hegel had argued that Kant's imperative was purged of all substantive content and that, as a purely formal or "analytical" proposition, it lapsed into tautology. Habermas initially rejects this charge as untenable – although he qualifies this rejection subsequently in several ways. "Neither Kant nor discourse ethics," he writes, "lay themselves open to the charge that their formal or procedural definition of morality yields only tautological statements." The reason for this immunity lies in the fact that Kantian or quasi-Kantian moral principles demand not only logical and semantic consistency – "as Hegel wrongly contended" – but also the application of a "substantive moral perspective," or rather the application of principles to substantive moral issues; the latter issues, however, arise not from moral philosophy but from life experience. Practical conflicts which need to be morally assessed and consensually resolved, we read, "grow out of the communicative praxis of everyday life"; they are "found or encountered, but not generated" by ethical reason or the participants of moral discourse. Having thus blunted or seemingly obviated Hegel's objection, Habermas in a second move grants a certain validity to concerns about formalism. Every procedural or deontological ethics, he concedes, must separate "the structure from the content" of moral judgment. In line with this separation or abstraction, such an ethics distills or extracts from the vast range of practical issues those questions which are amenable to rational debate and hence to a process of rational validation. At this point, normative statements about presumably "just" or "right" actions and norms are segregated from evaluative notions or preferences regarding the "good life" in the context of a given cultural tradition. For Hegel, it was precisely this separation of rightness from the good life which was morally dubious and a source of the vacuity of Kantian ethics – a point, Habermas admits, which has not "satisfactorily been resolved" (although it might be through a purely negative formulation of moral rules).[8]

A similar two-step reply is given to Hegel's critique of abstract "universalism." In his *Phenomenology*, Hegel had argued that Kant's focus on absolute duty, encapsulated in the categorical imperative, entailed the neglect or devaluation of particular situations or concrete human virtues. "Neither Kant nor discourse ethics," Habermas asserts again firmly, "expose themselves to the charge that the stress on the generalizability of norms leads to neglect or even repression of the plurality of existing social conditions and concrete interests." Actually, modern society in Habermas's view is marked by a parallel development of growing proliferation or diversification and universalization: "The more particular interests and value preferences are differentiated in modern society, the more abstract and general are those morally justified norms which regulate the individual's scope of behavior in the common interest." To the extent that Hegel's charge is pertinent, he adds, it applies only to the "rigorism" of Kant's ethics with its abstraction from concrete consequences, and not to discourse ethics (which includes consequences in its argumentative procedure). On the other hand – and this is the second part of the reply – Hegel's objection is said to be also "correct" in another respect. As Habermas points out, moral theories of the Kantian or quasi-Kantian type are "specialized in questions of justification," while bracketing or leaving unanswered "questions of application." The problem here (as Hegel clearly perceived) is that no norm or rule contains within itself "the rules for its own application." As a result, moral arguments are of little avail unless the "decontextualization" effected for purposes of normative validation can be remedied again in concrete instances, that is, on the level of application. Like Kantian theory, Habermas admits, discourse ethics has to "face up to the difficult issue whether the application of rules in concrete cases does not require a type of *prudence* or reflective judgment" which remains tied to the context of parochial pre-understandings, thereby undercutting the "universalist claim of validating reason." Although acknowledging the plausibility of this train of thought, Habermas quickly distances himself from prudential judgment (mainly due to its neo-Aristotelian overtones). In contrast to such contextualism, we are told, "discourse ethics is emphatically opposed to any retreat behind the philosophical level achieved by Kant, namely, his differentiation or dissociation of normative validation from the application and implementation of moral insights."[9]

Closely associated with abstract universalism is the issue of normative "impotence" or of the inefficaciousness of categorical standards. Noting Kant's sharp separation of "ought" from "is," of moral duty from inclination and happiness, Hegel had accused "noumenal" morality as necessarily lacking impact in the concrete "phenomenal" world. In Habermas's presentation, this objection applies validly to Kant but not properly to discourse ethics. Given the division between duty and inclination, reason and sense experience, he notes, Kantian morality is vulnerable to the charge of practical inefficacy. The immunity of discourse ethics is ascribed to its attenuation (and even abandonment) of the noumenal-phenomenal division and to its reliance on broad-scale argumentation which includes discussion of interests and practical consequences. On the other hand – and here is another two-step movement – Hegel is said to be correct on a certain level even with reference to discourse ethics. Practical discourses too, Habermas concedes, "disengage problematic norms and actions from the substantive *Sittlichkeit* of their life-world contexts" in order to permit their testing or scrutiny "without regard to existing motives or institutional settings." This testing involves a process of decontextualization or "demundanization" (*Entweltlichung*) of norms which is unavoidable for purposes of normative validation; however, the question remains how this abstraction can be remedied or compensated for to facilitate practical implementation. Moral theories, Habermas adds, "must indeed remain practically ineffective unless they can rely on the supportive strength of motives and socially accepted institutions"; in Hegel's terms, they must be "translatable into the concrete obligations of everyday life." This then was Hegel's correct insight: every universalistic ethics depends upon "supportive life-forms" which sustain it a good stretch of the way. Luckily, in Habermas's view, modern Western society exhibits such supportive life-forms or life-contexts. In fact, moral universalism as inaugurated by Rousseau and Kant is itself "historically grown," namely, in the context of societies steadily fostering such supportive moral features.[10]

Hegel's final objection also had to do with the practical dilemmas or frustrations of a noumenal morality. Unless seen as a counsel of abstinence or passivity, he argued, such a morality was likely to induce its adherents to impose abstract principles on a recalcitrant world – if necessary by means of political terror (as exemplified by Jacobin policies in France). Habermas is firm in rejecting this charge both with reference to Kant and to discourse ethics – this time without a second-step qualification. Neither Kant nor discourse ethics, he insists, are open to the charge of justifying or even indirectly abetting repressive or "totalitarian" political strategies: precisely in regard to the political implementation of universalist legal or constitutional norms, "the maxim that the end justifies the means is incompatible with the letter and the spirit of moral universalism." The danger of repression or terrorism is attributed at this point not to Kantian or quasi-Kantian theories but rather to mistaken historical speculations postulating an inexorable "march of history" guided or accelerated by a social-political vanguard. The error of this view, we read, is to construe society as a "subject-writ-large" and then to identify "the morally accountable actions of the vanguard with the trans-moral praxis of this higher-level social subject." To be sure, rejection of historical speculations does not by itself resolve the dilemmas of moral praxis in real-life contexts. As Habermas acknowledges, the discursive validation of norms cannot simultaneously account for either the genesis or the implementation of such norms. "By themselves," he writes, "discourses cannot fulfill the conditions required for enabling all those concerned to participate regularly in practical discourse." In real-life situations, these conditions are frequently lacking – which leads to the question how innovative moral praxis bent on changing social conditions can itself be morally justified. As before, the development of moral life-forms in the West comes to the rescue at this juncture, by obviating the need for radical change. In our Western societies, we read, "questions of revolutionary ethics – never satisfactorily resolved even in Western Marxism – are happily not acute or pressing."[11]

By way of conclusion, Habermas reassesses the status of discourse ethics in light of Hegel's combined objections. In his view, these objections affect not so much Kantian or quasi-Kantian theories as such as rather a host of "corollary problems" associated with such theories. As he recognizes again, every ethics defining itself as at once deontological, cognitivist, formalist and universalist purchases its moral stringency with a number of abstractions. As a result, the question arises immediately whether issues of justice or rightness can at all be detached from concrete contexts of the good life. Even if this problem can be resolved – and Habermas believes that it can – the further problem emerges whether at least the application of valid norms in concrete cases does not require the replacement of universal reason by a "contextually nurtured prudential judgment." Assuming again a resolution of this problem – an assumption Habermas makes – discourse ethics still faces the dilemma whether the principles of a universalist ethics are at all amenable to implementation in real-life situations – given that such an ethics depends indeed on supporting or "accommodating" life-forms. These dilemmas are aggravated by additional predicaments not previously mentioned, having to do with the constitutive limitations of discursive argumentation. One such limitation concerns the exclusion of previous generations whose hopes for justice or rightness may have been dashed or brutally obstructed. In Habermas's words, discourse ethics is not equipped with a teleological assurance which would cancel the "irreversible sequence of historical events." But how can later generations, as potential beneficiaries of norms, expect the "posthumous assent of the slain and degraded victims" of past ages? Equally problematic is the exclusion of nature and nature's creatures or their reduction to targets of argumentation. "In the compassion with tortured animals, in the pain caused by destroyed biotopes," Habermas comments, "moral intuitions come to the fore which cannot seriously be satisfied by the collective narcissism of a lastly anthropocentric approach." The lesson he draws from these predicaments is the need for self-limitation or a subdued self-understanding of ethical theory. What such a theory can be expected to accomplish, he concludes, is "the clarification of the universal core of moral intuitions and thus the refutation of value skepticism." Beyond this, it must renounce the ambition to make substantive contributions.[12]

II

Habermas's vindication of discourse ethics – in the face of Hegelian and more broadly contextualist challenges – is no doubt impressive and in some respects engagingly appealing. I find particularly attractive some of the concluding comments, including the reference to the "collective narcissism" of contemporary anthropocentric thought (which also affects ethical theorizing). The statement about the "slain and degraded victims" of the past is a reminder which is bound to haunt all types of ethics and meta-ethics no matter how circumspectly contrued. Similarly jolting is the allusion to ecological problems, particularly the passage about tortured creatures, about destroyed biotopes, and more generally about the havoc wreaked by technological progress on the ecological fabric of the globe. Ethical theories in the future, I believe, will increasingly be measured by the degree to which they confront and address those issues. My appreciation or sympathy extends also to the discussion of the moral intuitions guiding discourse ethics, especially the stress placed on human vulnerability in the context of socialization and the resulting need for thoughtful considerateness. This vulnerability, I would add, is not so much relieved as rather intensified or abetted by the prevailing anthropocentrism of Western culture – which suggests to me a certain urgency of combatting manifestations of both individual and collective narcissism. Whether this urgency is congruent with ethical "self-limitation" in Habermas's sense is at least questionable. Although applauding intellectual modesty in all domains, I find dubious Habermas's concluding counsel – to the extent that it seems to excise substantive concerns from moral reflection. In restricting moral theory to a "universal core," this counsel appears to erect a gulf between theory and praxis, principles and life-world which is hard to sustain (and which conflicts with his own earlier insights). While it may be true that "philosophy cannot relieve anyone of practical responsibility," it seems to me equally correct to say that moral praxis cannot relieve anyone of a sensible, contextually nurtured reflectiveness. This reflectiveness, moreover, cannot be replaced by social science information, and even less by a "materialist theory of society" as a supplement to Kantian idealism.[13]

These considerations prompt a closer look at the premises and status of discourse ethics. As indicated, this ethics – despite some modifications – shares the salient features of Kantian morality, that is, its deontological, cognitivist, formalist and universalist character. A question which arises immediately at this point concerns the philosophical warrant or plausibility of these features or accents. Deontology separates duty from inclination, rightness from the good life, while cognitivism opts in favor of knowledge over sensibility, of rational transparency over ambivalence; likewise, formalism relies on the division between form and content just as universalism on that between rules and particular contexts. All these divisions, one may recall, are categorial distinctions endemic to the Western metaphysical tradition – a tradition which today is contested or under siege. In formulating a quasi-Kantian ethical theory, Habermas tacitly endorses the categorial divisions of metaphysics; moreover, he does so without providing a philosophical warrant for them – and even while claiming to offer a post-metaphysical or "non-metaphysical" account. In his own way (though with insufficient radicality) Hegel sought to overcome the bifurcations of traditional metaphysics – as

Habermas recognizes when he writes: "Theories of duty accentuate justice while theories of moral goodness stress common welfare. Hegel already recognized that the unity of ethical life is missed if the two aspects are isolated from each other and erected into opposing principles; his own concept of *Sittlichkeit* accordingly proceeds from a critique of the two respective types of one-sidedness." While applauding the broad intent of Hegel's initiative, Habermas retreats from its implications – namely, by reinstating the categorial accents of Kantian metaphysics. "Discourse ethics," he writes, "picks up the basic intent of Hegel's thought – in order to redeem it with Kantian means." This dual if not antinomial move, it seems to me, accounts in large measure for the strained and often puzzling character of Habermas's vindication – a strain approximating his argument sometimes to the sleight of hand ascribed by Hegel to the , "practical legislation of [Kantian] pure reason."[14]

The chief device designed to accomplish Hegelian intentions "with Kantian means" is the process of argumentation – whose mediating capacity, however, is doubtful. Emulating the objectives of Hegelian *Sittlichkeit*, discourse ethics is said to produce "substantive results through procedural methods" and even to capture the "inner linkage between justice and the good life." These objectives are claimed to be achieved through recourse to communicative interaction – which on closer inspection reveals distinctly Kantian traits. The strategy of discourse ethics to derive principles from argumentation, Habermas asserts, is "promising" because discourses represent a "more exacting mode of communication exceeding concrete life-forms – a mode in which the premises of consensual-communicative action are generalized and rendered abstract, namely, by being extended to an ideal communication community embracing all subjects capable of speech and action." The consensus expected in the latter context, he adds, "transcends the limits of any concrete-actual community." What surfaces here is a strong distinction between discourses and ordinary speech, between ideal and actual communication, in a manner replicating the Kantian form–content or "ought–is" division; in ethical terms, normative validity is assigned to ideal premises and procedures of discourse – while Hegelian *Sittlichkeit* is relegated to the domain of factual or "concrete life-forms." Somewhat later Habermas describes the pragmatic "universals" of speech as an "a priori structure" shared by participants – and thus not in turn as a result of speech or argumentation. In light of these considerations, I would question the claim that discourse ethics "abandons the doctrine of two realms," that is, the Kantian dichotomy between noumenal (or intelligible) and phenomenal domains – seeing that the dichotomy resurfaces in communication itself or (to use Habermas's words) "within everyday communicative praxis." This aspect, in my view, decisively shifts the balance from Hegel to Kant or away from the Hegelian mediation. Not surprisingly, Kantian or neo-Kantian philosophers have tended to accuse discourse ethics of redundancy (if not disingenuousness) – namely, of deriving its normative force entirely from Kantian (or noumenal) premises while disguising this fact behind linguistic practices.[15]

Irrespective of the latter charge, the uneven balance affects the cogency of Habermas's defense against Hegel; it also may account in part for the curious structure of the defense: the two-step movement of rejection and admission. This can be seen by a glance at Habermas's specific rejoinders. With regard to the "formalism" issue, I am not convinced that Hegel's concern about semantic tautology has really been put aside. As indicated, Habermas counters this concern by pointing to the application of a substantive perspective or rather the application of norms to substantive moral problems. However, the application of principles to concrete issues clearly does not render the former themselves substantive or non-formal. Nor is this situation changed by the fact that practical conflicts in need of resolution grow out of "everyday life" and thus are "encountered, but not generated" by ethical reason. As Habermas himself has repeatedly insisted (in a quasi-Kantian vein), issues of genesis and of validation must not be blended or contaminated – which leaves normative validity non-historical and hence again formal. In the second step of his rejoinder, Habermas expressly concedes the formal character of every procedural ethics, that is, its need or necessity to segregate structure or form from moral content. By virtue of this separation, he adds, such an ethics is able to extract reason from unreason, random or contingent practices from normatively justified practices. Given their non-substantive character or their separation from concrete content, normative principles inevitably seem to acquire a purely analytical status; ample philosophical arguments, however, are available to show the tautological bent of pure "analyticity" (quite apart from Quine's attack on the very distinction between analytical and synthetic statements). In trying to rescue his rejoinder to Hegel, Habermas in the end invokes the possibility of an indirect or negative but non-contextual definition of morality, namely, one focused on the overcoming of "damaged life." However, negation or opposition of this kind relies at least on an embryonic understanding of goodness or undamaged life – which corroborates Hegel's preoccupation with *Sittlichkeit*.[16]

The strength of Hegelian insights emerges also with regard to the issue of universalism. In his rejoinder, Habermas absolves discourse ethics from this objection by pointing to the steady proliferation of particularistic interests and life-forms accompanying the growing generalization of

norms in modern society. This argument, however, reinforces rather than
refutes Hegel's point. Precisely the generalization and growing abstractness of rules tends to expel or remove particularistic settings from the
frame of a more broadly shared *Sittlichkeit*; differently phrased: the more
abstractly universal rules are construed, the less particularly is accessible
to "mediation" in Hegel's sense. In a way, Habermas acknowledges this
fact when he writes that *"merely* particular interests" are amenable only
to the negotiation of interest-based compromises, a negotiation remaining outside of "discursively achieved consensus." The dilemma of abstract
universalism – or of the divorce of universal rules from particularity – is
aggravated in the field of "application" or the transfer of rules to concrete
situations. As Habermas recognizes in the second step of his rejoinder,
Kantian or quasi-Kantian theories bracket or bypass this field while focusing entirely on validation or justification; moreover, no rule – he admits –
carries with itself "the rules for its own application." This admission, I
believe, is grievous given the practical thrust of ethics (as distinct from
pure intellectualism) – more grievous than the rejoinder suggests. For,
in the absence of shared meanings guiding application, "decontextualized" rules retreat into the sphere of empty analyticity (unless they are
repressively imposed). Sensibly and quite cogently, Gadamer's *Truth and
Method* has portrayed application not as a mere accessory but as contitu-
tive part of the understanding of rules; by means of application (and only
through this process), he has insisted, general rules are reintegrated into
a shared fabric of *Sittlichkeit*. The same point has been made by philosophers more closely attuned to Habermas's opus. Thus, relying on Wittgensteinian insights, Herbert Schnädelbach has argued in favor of the
"inseparability" of rules and rule application and ultimately for the
replacement of pure reason by a "historical rationality" akin to Hegelian
mediation and prudential judgment. At the end of his rejoinder,
Habermas briefly ponders the role of prudence – only to dismiss it as a
regression behind Kantianism. General principles of reason, he says,
operate even in prudential judgments – neglecting the dependence of
principles on a context of shared understandings.[17]

    Neglect of this dependence also had motivated Hegel's charge of the
"impotence" of Kantian imperatives or of their inability to penetrate into
mundane-phenomenal reality. As mentioned before, Habermas's rejoinder exempts discourse ethics (though not Kantian morality) from this
charge by pointing to its abandonment of the noumenal–phenomenal
bifurcation and its recourse to broad-scale argumentation extending to
interests and practical consequences. As I have also indicated, however,
this rebuttal is weakened if not entirely undermined by the reinscription of Kantian divisions in argumentation itself, chiefly through the

distinction between actual and ideal (or counterfactual) modes of communicative interaction. Following his two-step procedure, Habermas's second step actually confirms this reinscription by speaking of the disengagement of norms from "the substantive *Sittlichkeit* of their life-world contexts" and of the need to validate the former by abstracting from "existing motives and institutional settings." Underscoring this need, the essay insists on the decontextualization and even "demundanization" (*Entweltlichung*) of norms for purposes of normative justification. To offset this abstraction from life-worlds, Habermas subsequently appeals to the "supportive strength of motives and socially accepted institutions" and to the correlation of moral principles with "supportive or accommodating life-forms" – such as can happily be found in modern Western societies. While concurring with the stress on supportive life-forms, I find Habermas's argument at this point inordinately benign and hardly congruent with the thrust of discursive generalization. Surely, this thrust – an outgrowth of Enlightenment rationalism – has tended not so much to strengthen as rather to weaken or erode supportive life-forms; to the extent that there are still enclaves of *Sittlichkeit*, they persist less because than in spite of decontextualized universalism. More importantly and disconcertingly, enclaves of moral life have increasingly been cognitively denuded or stripped of prudential-rational resources; Enlightenment principles at this point exact a price: the more reason is abstracted and universalized, the more concrete life-forms are reduced to fideist convictions.[18] Invoking the needed viability of moral life-contexts, in any event, means to endorse basic Hegelian premises – whose overall cogency is simultaneously denied.

Supporting life-forms and their continued viability also function prominently in the retort to Hegel's final concern: the danger of an oppressive (perhaps terroristic) moralism. I shall not pursue this issue further – except to point again to the strategy of redeeming Kantian intentions "with Hegelian means" (to reverse the earlier formula). Instead I want to draw attention to a prominent or guiding feature of Habermas's argument. All his successive rejoinders to Hegel rely crucially on the postulate of decontextualization: namely, the abstraction of rightness or justice from the good life, of normative validation from problems of application, and of universal principles from concrete life-forms. Decontextualization, however, inevitably also involves "delinguistification" (*Entsprachlichung*) in the sense of an abstraction from the fabric of ordinary language. This feature is curious in light of Habermas's strong emphasis on the "linguistic turn" and on the linkage of his approach with the "paradigm shift" from consciousness to language – a shift jeopardized by his universalist leanings. Awareness of this dilemma figures centrally in revisions

or emendations proposed by sympathetic critics of Habermas. Schnädelbach's resort to Wittgensteinian insights seeks to reintegrate ethical theory,
including discursive reasoning, into ordinary language frameworks. The
linguistic turn, in his view, militates against abstract universalism or a
radical decontextualization of norms since it "excludes the complete
representability of rationality in rules" (including rules for rule application). Similarly, relying at least in part on language theory, Albrecht
Wellmer has called into question the Kantian and Habermasian bifurcation of form and content, of normative rightness and the good life.
According to Wellmer, the rightness of norms cannot simply be predicated on formal-procedural grounds – since the former depends also on
the substantive quality of validating reasons. In his words: "The validity
of a grounded consensus or agreement derives from the quality or sound-
ness of the reasons on which it rests – not from the (procedural) fact that
all have accepted these reasons." Thus, in order to describe a norm or rule
as rationally valid one must "first know what are good reasons" – which,
in turn, depends on conceptions of goodness or the good life prevalent
in life-world contexts or ordinary language settings. This argument applies
even to agreements reached under conditions of a (procedurally defined
and counterfactual) "ideal speech situation" or "ideal communication
community." Accordingly, Wellmer concludes, normative standards cannot simply be gleaned from the formal structure of rational discourses,
but demand recourse to shared life-forms and to the "insight" and prudential "judgment" nurtured by such life-forms.[19]

III

The preceding comments were not meant simply to reaffirm Hegelian
motives, and certainly not to propagate a full-fledged Hegelianism.
Despite his dialectical subtlety, Hegel (like Kant) remained deeply
attached to Western metaphysical categories, including the founding
concepts of "logos" and "subjectivity" – in a manner which can no longer
be sustained (I believe) in our post-metaphysical period. Yet abandonment of these central categories does not necessarily entail rejection of
Hegel's basic ethical intentions, particularly of his notion of *Sittlichkeit* –
a point which has been recognized by many recent or contemporary
thinkers, including spokesmen of critical theory. In his emendation of
Habermasian discourse ethics, Wellmer invoked at least passingly the
memory of Adorno, namely, when alluding to the close linkage of reason
and sensibility, of cognition and aesthetics. This recollection strikes me
as eminently appropriate, given Adorno's life-long struggle to come to

terms with the legacies of both Kant and Hegel. His crowning opus, *Negative Dialectics*, contained complex chapters devoted to both philosophers, chapters seeking to vindicate both a genuine, though non-foundational concept of freedom and a historical dialectics stripped of positive synthesis or spiritual apotheosis. The chapter on "World Spirit and Natural History" chided Hegel for "detemporalizing" history and thereby truncating dialectics – while simultaneously applauding his attention to mediations operating in concrete life-contexts. For present purposes I want to glance briefly at Adorno's assessment of Kantian ethics, as outlined in the chapter titled "Freedom: Toward a Metacritique of Practical Reason."[20]

As Adorno observes in that chapter, Kantian ethics is predicated centrally on human freedom or the free spontaneity of human will, a spontaneity standing in sharp contrast to the determinism operating in nature and empirical reality. Given this starting point, this ethics – like later quasi-Kantian variations – exhibits a "two-world" theory, that is, a perspective revolving around noumenal–phenomenal, intelligible–sensible oppositions. In Adorno's words, Kant – following the thrust of Enlightenment thought – resolved the conflict between nature and spirit (or the "intelligible realm") in an antinomial or "dichotomous" fashion, namely, by shunning the concrete social-historical mediations of freedom and, more generally, the mediations of spirit through "otherness." In fact, mediation was deprecated as an intrusion of external constraints into freedom and thus as a mode of "heteronomy" – a view tending to internalize if not entirely privatize ethical freedom. In everyday moral experience, Adorno counters, multiple features of external, notably social reality "invade human decisions subsumed under the labels of 'will' and 'freedom'." As soon as the question of "free will' is contracted into the issue of noumenal decision, the question "succumbs to the fallacy of an absolutely pure being-in-itself"; but the supposedly noumenal subject is actually "mediated in itself by that from which it is segregated, namely, the correlation of all subjects." Abstractness and internalization of freedom had adverse effects on social and political reality, since the latter was seen as a realm of phenomenal givenness largely impervious to noumenal demands. Although directed against forms of oppression endemic to traditional regimes, Kantian theory unwittingly promoted new types of submission "harbored by the rationality principle itself." Internalization also affected the status of philosophy and its relation to empirical inquiry by reducing the former increasingly to abstract speculation while surrendering phenomenal reality to the imperatives of scientific research: "Kant banished the objects of research into the realm of unfreedom; positive science hence occupies a place beneath speculation or beneath the noumenal sphere. The flagging of speculative vigor and the development of specialized sciences have exacerbated the contrast to the utmost – a trend exacting the price of narrowmindedness from science, and that of noncommittal vacuity from philosophy."[21]

More importantly, the noumenal–phenomenal contrast was carried by Kant into the structure of the individual or human subject itself, in a manner which privileged or exalted noumenal reason or freedom over the inclinations of "inner nature." In modern times, the individual's rational core (the *ego cogitans*) was elevated to an agency of free initiative and mastery, while natural and social conditions were devalued to purely external constraints; given its internalized-noumenal character, however, agency was bound to be steadily frustrated by the latter. As Adorno writes: Individual identity or the *principium individuationis* to which rationality is tied "tends to insulate individuals from encompassing contexts and thus strengthens the flattering trust in the autarchy of the subject; under the label of freedom this autarchy is contrasted to the totality of all restrictive circumstances." While seemingly or fleetingly transcending the blind nexus of social relations, however, the individual's "windowless isolation" actually only corroborates the reproduction of that nexus as blind destiny. Adorno at this point turns to a Hegelian insight, namely, the notion of the necessary mediation of inside and outside, of identity and otherness. "As Hegel had shown in his *Phenomenology*," we read, "the subject acquires the ideas of freedom and unfreedom only through the encounter with the non-subjective and its constraining impact – ideas which then are transferred back into its own monadic structure."[22] Going beyond Hegel's formulation, Adorno adumbrates a dialectical or tensional view of freedom where the term designates both the possibility of rational agency *and* release from the confining dictates of such agency and rational identity structures; far from being simply the antipode of nature, reason here becomes embroiled with its own pre-rational (and pre-critical) substrate.

> The dawning sense of freedom feeds upon the memory of an archaic impulse not yet governed by a solid ego (or subjectivity). The more the ego curbs or controls the impulse, the more this archaic freedom will appear dubious or simply chaotic; yet, without recollection of this untamed impulse antedating the ego – an impulse later banished to the region of unfree bondage to nature – the idea of freedom could not be conceived, although that idea in turn ends up reinforcing the ego.[23]

Freedom thus is intrinsically rent by tension (or difference):

Only by acting as an ego, and not just reactively, can someone's action be termed free. But equally free can be called whatever is not yet tamed or controlled by the ego as source of determination – in other words, that region which, as in Kant's moral philosophy, strikes the ego as unfree and has indeed been unfree to this very day.[24]

In Adorno's account, the impulse of freedom – pre-rational though not irrational in origin – escapes the traditional bifurcations of mind and matter, reason and (external) nature. From the vantage of modern metaphysics, the impulse is a moment of lived concreteness transgressing its established categories – which is why Adorno calls it an "addendum" (*das Hinzutretende*). Disavowing the Cartesian dualism of *res cogitans* and *res extensa*, he writes, "the addendum is impulse, rudimentary trace of a stage or phase in which the distinction between extra-mental and intra-mental spheres was not yet fully consolidated" – although it cannot serve as "cognitive-ontological grounding." While not alien to reason or consciousness, the addendum is not synonymous or coextensive with the former but harbors a bodily or somatic quality – without lapsing into naturalist determinism. Simultaneously mental and somatic in character, we read, the impulse "pushes beyond the realm of consciousness to which it nonetheless belongs." In this manner, freedom's impulse penetrates into the domain of "lived experience," thereby acquiring or at least adumbrating a status which transcends "both blind (deterministic) nature and repressed nature" (controlled by reason); its guiding motive or longing – undeterred by logical casuistry – is the telos of a "reconciliation of spirit and nature." By penetrating into lived experience, the addendum also yields access to the field of social and moral praxis, a domain whose features and requirements can never be simply deduced from theoretical principles or axioms. Construed as a set of actions adequate to the idea of freedom, Adorno elaborates, "genuine praxis cannot do without theoretical reflection" (to avoid the lure of blind decisionism); yet this condition is not sufficient or exhaustive: "Praxis also needs something else, something bodily and non-identical with consciousness, something mediated through reason but qualitatively different from it." Social and moral praxis thus disrupts traditional metaphysical categories and dichotomies – to which it remains yoked in much of modern, including Kantian, philosophy: "By accepting only reason as motivating force of praxis, Kant remained under the spell of a pale theoreticism against which he then marshalled the primacy of practical reason as a supplement. This is what ails his entire moral philosophy."[25]

Admittedly, Adorno's arguments are directed against the noumenal character of Kantian morality, against what Habermas calls the "rigorism" of duty; yet, in many respects, his critique also reaches later neo-Kantian or quasi-Kantian variations. As indicated, Habermas's approach deviates from Kant's rigorism by his emphasis on argumentation about shared interests; likewise, the focus on subjective or inner consciousness is replaced by intersubjective deliberation. As also indicated, however, discourse ethics still pays tribute to central aspects of Kant's "two-world" perspective: namely, by segregating normative validity from practical interests or inclinations, formal rules from concrete applications, rational discourse from ordinary speech. In a particularly pronounced way, the continued impact of Kant's legacy surfaces in the emphasis on universalism or on principles construed as "general laws" of behavior, and in the distinction of principles from the good life. *Negative Dialectics* is eloquent in exposing the "law-character" of Kant's moral imperative and the close connection between lawfulness and obedience (or the criminalization of deviance). In exalting lawfulness, we read, Kant's doctrine of freedom is closely allied with legalism and criminal justice; in fact, "all the concepts whereby the *Critique of Practical Reason* proposes (in the name of freedom) to bridge the chasm between imperative and mankind – concepts like law, constraint, respect, duty – all these are repressive." Repression here is not the result of an arbitrary authoritarianism, but rather of cognitive rationality or universal reason itself in its opposition to the particularity of inclinations and to non-rational otherness. "Even prior to all social control," Adorno writes, "prior to all adjustment to systems of domination, the pure form of reason – the form of logical stringency – can be convicted of harboring unfreedom." From the beginning and even in the absence of repressive motives, rational thought "exerts a dominance which philosophy articulates in the concept of necessity." Modern rationalism projects the lawfulness of reason on to the objects and phenomena of the world, thereby subordinating them to a formal-logical principle, basically the principle of non-contradiction and logical identity. This formula is clearly operative in Kant's moral philosophy: "The unity governing his system is the concept of reason itself, and ultimately the logic of noncontradiction; nothing is added to this in Kant's theory of praxis."[26]

Countering the streamlining effect of legalism, *Negative Dialectics* seeks to rethink the notion of reason and its relation to non-reason. Without abandoning rational thought itself, the Kant chapter revokes the primacy of logic over the "diffuseness of nature," of rational unity over the "multiplicity of non-identity." This revocation affects the status of human selfhood or identity – including both the identity of individual agents and the transparent univocity of intersubjective consensus (or of an "ideal speech community"); in each case, what is excised by rational transparency is the diffuseness of external and inner nature. In Adorno's words: "Human beings become properly human only where they do not act or posit themselves as (self-identical) persons; the diffuseness of nature which transgresses such personhood resembles the lineaments of an intelligible creature, of a self delivered from the constraints of the ego." Properly human or a proper self would be someone who "by means of the strength deriving from identity would have cast off the encasing of identity." This casting off is not so much a denial as a further step in the process of human emancipation. While in early modernity emancipation meant the liberation of agents from heteronomous forces or constraints, the issue pending in our time is "the liberation of the subject from itself, as from a last myth." Properly conceived, utopia would be "the non-sacrificial non-identity of human subjects"; differently phrased: the reconciliation of "the rational subject with the non-ego" (of inner nature). The tensional character of freedom's impulse manifests itself here as the tensional intertwining of identity and non-identity, of sameness and otherness. As Adorno observes, at the end of the Kant chapter, this intertwining is thematized – but in a purely antinominal fashion – in Kant's moral philosophy. From a Kantian perspective, he notes, individuals are "free insofar as they are self-conscious and identical with themselves"; but simultaneously they are "unfree in this identity by being subjected to and perpetuating its compulsion." Conversely, human beings are "unfree as non-identical or diffuse nature"; yet in the same capacity they are also "free since their overpowering impulses will also rid them of identity's coercive character." Genuine freedom consists not in disrupting, but in soberly sustaining this tension: "The aporia derives from the fact that truth beyond compulsive identity would not simply be the latter's negation, but be mediated through it."[27]

Seen in the light of this mediated tension, ethics cannot simply be equated with formal deontology or a set of general rules, but must remain attentive to lived experience, more specifically, to the human quest for happiness or at least for the avoidance of unhappiness or suffering. As previously noted, Habermas's essay makes reference to the alleviation of suffering or of "damaged life" – but only as a marginal gloss not fully integrated in his argument; such alleviation takes center stage in *Negative Dialectics* and its conception of ethics. Attention to the "diffuseness of nature" and to nature's impulse implies a focus not simply on rational principles but on human sensibility and on concrete reactions to suffering and exploitation. On that level, moral questions are posed succinctly in statements like these: "No one shall be tortured; there shall be no concentration camps." The truth of such statements derives not from their logical correctness but rather from nature's impulse, from the subject's openness to the "non-ego" – including the suffering and torture of others. Such statements, Adorno insists, "must not be rationalized" because, treated as "abstract principles," they would promptly succumb to "the bad infinity of their rational deduction and validity." His critique of Kantian morality aims chiefly at the "transfer of logical consistency to human conduct" – where such logic turns quickly into an "organ of unfreedom." What is bypassed or negated by the endeavor of relentless rationalization, he notes, is the concrete "impulse immanent in moral conduct, namely, naked physical fear and the sense of solidarity with what Brecht called 'tormentable bodies' "; through this denial, the most urgent and pressing issues tend to become "contemplative" again, thus "mocking their very urgency." Prompted by this urgency, ethics cannot remain aloof from sensibility, from that "spontaneous reaction which, impatient with arguments, cannot tolerate the continuation of horror." As Adorno adds, anticipating more recent arguments by Foucault and others, ethics implies intrinsically this element of resistance or determinate negation; in fact, this counterpoint alone "is the stage of morality today" – which does not eliminate reflectiveness: "Consciousness will react spontaneously insofar as it recognizes evil as evil – without being content with mere cognition."[28]

Although not frequently discussed in the literature, Adorno's contributions to ethical thought have recently been explored by a number of writers, including Drucilla Cornell. In her essay titled "The Ethical Message of Negative Dialectics", Cornell focuses centrally on the issue of reconciliation (of spirit and nature) and its unorthodox Hegelian or post-Hegelian resonances. As she points out, Adorno's *Negative Dialectics* stands opposed to Kantian morality – but without on this score relinquishing the ethical domain of *Sittlichkeit*. "The emphasis on the natural desiring subject," she writes, "the dissolution of rigid ego dictates, the suspicion of the normalizing impulse in the call to do one's duty are anti-Kantian, to be sure, but these emphases do not make Adorno's message anti-ethical." In opposition to the rational ego and its bent to mastery (of self and others), Adorno's focus on nature's impulse – his "recollection of nature" – opens the path to a non-repressive or non-violative relationship with others beyond the pale both of consensual identification and of mutual rejection or indifference. This relationship, however, presupposes the ego's recollection of "inner nature": "The point made by Adorno is that without the recovery of a playful innocence through the re-connection with the other in oneself, one cannot become a human being capable of non-violative relations to the other." In articulating this perspective, Cornell observes, *Negative Dialectics* reveals its affinities with Hegelian *Sittlichkeit*, albeit in a thoroughly unorthodox or innovative fashion: Adorno "rebels against Hegel's ontological identification of meaning and being" or his privileging of identity over non-identity – while simultaneously embracing Hegel's indictment of Enlightenment rationalism and its rigid segregation of "mind and nature, body and soul." In this respect, Adorno's outlook can be called a "philosophy of redemption" wedded to a "dialectic of reconciliation" – although not a dialectic culminating in an affirmative apotheosis of spirit, but one pursuing the indirect or "negative" path of suffering which intimates obliquely the possibility of happiness (or the "good life"). Cornell cites in this connection this passage in *Negative Dialectics*, which in turn echoes a Nietzschean insight: "The bodily moment tells our reason that suffering should cease, that things should be different. Woe speaks: go (or go away)."[29]

NOTES

1 The notion that enlightenment means the awakening of mankind from a condition of self-induced immaturity was articulated by Kant in his "Beantwortung der Frage: Was ist Aufklärung?" (1784); see Immanuel Kant, *Ausgewählte Kleine Schriften* (Leipzig: Meiner, 1914), p. 1.

2 Max Horkheimer, "Traditional and Critical Theory" (with Postscript), in *Critical Theory: Selected Essays*, tr. Matthew J. O'Connell et al. (New York: Herder & Herder, 1972), pp. 207, 210, 230, 244–5 (translation slightly altered). Compare also the comment (p. 241) that critical theory strives for "a state of affairs devoid of exploitation and oppression, one where an all-embracing subject, namely self-conscious humanity, really exists and where it is possible to speak of a unified theory construction and a thinking transcending individuals."

3 Jürgen Habermas, *Knowledge and Human Interests*, tr. Jeremy J. Shapiro (Boston: Beacon Press, 1971), pp. 4–5; *Communication and the Evolution of Society*, tr. Thomas McCarthy (Boston: Beacon Press, 1979), pp. 22–3, 124–5. Regarding the affinity between Habermas's epistemology and Kant's legacy compare this comment (p. 22): "The transcendentally oriented pragmatism inaugurated by C. S. Peirce attempts to show that there is such a structural connection between experience and instrumental action; the hermeneutics stemming from Dilthey attempts – over against this a priori of experience – to do justice to an additional a priori of understanding or communicative action." Another essay in the same volume presents the development of modern philosophy as leading from substantive reason increasingly to rational formalism where formal procedures alone serve as constitutive grounds for validity claims (p. 184): "With Kant and Rousseau this development led to the conclusion that the formal principle of reason replaced material principles like Nature or God in practical questions, questions concerning the justification of norms and actions . . . Since ultimate

grounds can no longer be made plausible, *the formal conditions of justification themselves obtain legitimating force* . . . In transcendentally oriented theories, from Kant to Karl-Otto Apel, these conditions, as universal and unavoidable presuppositions of rational will-formation, are transposed either into the subject as such or into the ideal communication community." As a result, it is "the formal conditions of possible consensus formation, rather than ultimate grounds, which possess legitimating force."

4   Habermas, "Diskursethik – Notizen zu einem Begründungsprogramm", in *Moralbewusstsein und kommunikatives Handeln* (Frankfurt-Main: Suhrkamp, 1983), pp. 73, 89, 98–9, 103; for English version see "Discourse Ethics: Notes on a Program of Philosophical Justification", in *Moral Consciousness and Communicative Action*, tr. Christian Lenhardt and Shierry Weber Nicholson (Cambridge, MA: MIT Press, 1990), pp. 63, 78, 88–9, 93.

5   Habermas, "Moralität und Sittlichkeit: Treffen Hegels Einwände auch auf die Diskursethik zu?" in Wolfgang Kuhlmann, ed., *Moralität und Sittlichkeit: Das Problem Hegels und die Diskursethik* (Frankfurt-Main: Suhrkamp, 1986), pp. 16–37; for English version see "Morality and Ethical Life: Does Hegel's Critique of Kant Apply to Discourse Ethics?" in *Moral Consciousness and Communicative Action*, pp. 195–215. (In the above and subsequent citations I have changed the translation slightly for purposes of clarity.) For a parallel argument see Karl-Otto Apel, "Kant, Hegel und das aktuelle Problem der normativen Grundlagen von Moral und Recht", in Dieter Henrich, ed., *Kant oder Hegel? Über Formen der Begründung in der Philosophie* (Stuttgart: Klett-Cotta, 1983), pp. 597–624.

6   "Moralität und Sittlichkeit", pp. 17–19; "Morality and Ethical Life", pp. 196–8.

7   "Moralität und Sittlichkeit", pp. 20–22; "Morality and Ethical Life", pp. 199–201.

8   "Moralität und Sittlichkeit", pp. 25–6; "Morality and Ethical Life", pp. 204–5.

9   "Moralität und Sittlichkeit", pp. 26–7; "Morality and Ethical Life", pp. 205–6.

10 "Moralität und Sittlichkeit", pp. 28–9; "Morality and Ethical Life", pp. 207–8.

11 "Moralität und Sittlichkeit", pp. 29–31; "Morality and Ethical Life", pp. 208–9.

12 "Moralität und Sittlichkeit", pp. 31–32; "Morality and Ethical Life", pp. 210–11.

13 At the end of this essay, Habermas suggests that, in concrete moral-practical dilemmas, "historical and social sciences can be of greater help than philosophy"; he also refers to a statement by Horkheimer of 1933 according to which the materialist theory of society can remedy the "utopian character" of Kant's thought. See "Moralität und Sittlichkeit", p. 33; "Morality and Ethical Life", p. 211.

14 "Moralität und Sittlichkeit", pp. 22, 31; "Morality and Ethical Life",

pp. 201, 210. The charge of a sleight of hand was advanced in Hegel's *Natural Law* and is cited by Habermas himself (note 3).

15 "Moralität und Sittlichkeit", pp. 23–5; "Morality and Ethical Life", pp. 202–4. For a Kantian critique of discourse ethics along these lines see Otfried Höffe, "Kantian Skepticism Toward Transcendental Ethics of Communication", in Seyla Benhabib and Fred Dallmayr, eds, *The Communicative Ethics Controversy* (Cambridge, MA: MIT Press, 1990), pp. 193–219.

16 Habermas, "Moralität und Sittlichkeit", pp. 25–6; "Morality and Ethical Life", pp. 204–5. The reference to "damaged life" (and also to the "prohibition of images") seems to be an oblique allusion to Adorno – whom he has elsewhere castigated for his negativism or for ending in a cul-de-sac. Compare, e.g., Habermas, *The Theory of Communicative Action*, vol. 1: *Reason and the Rationalization of Society*,. Thomas McCarthy (Boston: Beacon Press, 1984), pp. 384–6; *The Philosophical Discourse of Modernity: Twelve Lectures*, tr. Frederick Lawrence (Cambridge, MA: MIT Press, 1987), pp. 119–20, 127–9.

17 Habermas, "Moralität und Sittlichkeit", pp. 26–7; "Morality and Ethical Life", pp. 205–6. Compare also Hans-Georg Gadamer, *Truth and Method*, 2nd rev. edn, tr. and rev. Joel Weinsheimer and Donald G. Marshall (New York: Crossroad, 1989), pp. 307–11; also Herbert Schnädelbach, "Remarks about Rationality and Language", in Benhabib and Dallmayr, *The Communicative Ethics Controversy*, pp. 270–92.

18 Habermas, "Moralität und Sittlichkeit", pp. 28–9; "Morality and Ethical Life", pp. 207–8. The deleterious effects of decontextualization or "demundanization" on moral and political life have been discussed, among others, by Hannah Arendt under the heading of "world alienation"; see *The Human Condition* (Garden City, NY: Doubleday Anchor Books, 1959), pp. 226–33. In her view, world alienation has ill effects particularly on prudential judgment (p. 187): "A noticeable decrease in common sense in any given community and a noticeable increase in superstition and gullibility are therefore almost infallible signs of alienation from the world." On the correlation between the progressive decay of common-sense judgment and the rise of "gullibility" or non-rational fideism compare also Alasdair MacIntyre, *Whose Justice? Which Rationality?* (Notre Dame: University of Notre Dame Press, 1988), pp. 3–6.

19 Schnädelbach, "Remarks about Rationality and Language", p. 280; Albrecht Wellmer, *Ethik und Dialog: Elemente des moralischen Urteils bei Kant und in der Diskursethik* (Frankfurt-Main: Suhrkamp, 1986), pp. 209–4.

20 Adorno, *Negative Dialectics*, tr. E. B. Ashton (New York: Seabury Press, 1973), pp. 211, 331–8. For references to Adorno see Wellmer, *Ethik und Dialog*, pp. 94–5, 165; compare also Wellmer's *Zur Dialektik von Moderne und Postmoderne: Vernunftkritik nach Adorno* (Frankfurt-Main: Suhrkamp, 1985).

21 *Negative Dialectics* pp. 212–14 (in these and subsequent citations I have

altered the translation for purposes of clarity).

22 *Negative Dialectics*, pp. 219–20.
23 *Negative Dialectics*, pp. 221–2.
24 *Negative Dialectics*, p. 222.
25 *Negative Dialectics*, pp. 228–9.
26 *Negative Dialectics*, pp. 232–4.
27 *Negative Dialectics*, pp. 256, 277, 281, 283, 299.
28 *Negative Dialectics*, pp. 285–6.
29 Drucilla Cornell, "The Ethical Message of Negative Dialectics", *Social Concept*, vol. 4 (1987), pp. 6–7, 22. As she adds (p. 9): "Reconciliation is the act of dis-union that allows things to exist in their difference and in their affinity. Adorno, then, is a philosopher of reconciliation in a very specific sense: his defense of a reconciled state is presented in the name of the plural and of the different . . . In his view, it is only by developing perspectives which illuminate our state of homelessness that we can begin to glimpse through the cracks and the crevices what it would be to be at home in the world. The redemptive perspectives displace and estrange the world so that we are revealed to be in exile. This exercise is not to teach us to forsake the world. Through the development of redemptive perspectives we can resist 'consummate negativity' without, on the other hand, perpetuating the myth of the ever-the-same" (or identity). The citation is from Adorno, *Negative Dialectics*, p. 203.

5

Habermas and Rationality

Reason and rationality are contested notions today; once construed as essential emblems of "man" and Western civilization, these notions have come to share in the latter's crisis or malaise. In the contemporary Western debate about culture and politics, Habermas occupies a relatively clear place: he is viewed as defender of reason or rationality against the forces of obscurantism, emotivism, and counter-enlightenment. The German cultural and intellectual scene, in particular, is marked today by a deep fissure of perspectives (sometimes epitomized by the term "*Tendenz-wende*"): a bifurcation pitting against each other the champions of reason, science, progress and modernity on the one hand, and devotees of common sense, practical wisdom and cultural particularism on the other. Occasionally the latter camp is augmented by a host of more novel critics of the Enlightenment legacy, including advocates of deconstruction, abnormal discourse and incommensurability. (In his more polemical moods, Habermas is liable to lump representatives of the second camp together under the label "young conservatives.") It is my impression or contention that this bifurcation is highly dubious and misleading and that discussions about rationality are not greatly advanced by a blind acceptance of customary categories or labels. My approach to Habermas in the following seeks to be immanent or internal to his position; my criticism – I need to state from the outset – will not derive from a perspective of irrationalism, emotivism or decisionism. Rather, I shall take seriously Habermas's claim to be a rationalist or defender of reason, and I want to probe the meaning of reason and rationality in his work.

Broadly phrased, my thesis is going to be that Habermas's notion of reason and rationality is a truncated version of reason, a version which owes much of its inspiration to neo-Kantian (and even neo-positivist) sources. His central category of "communicative rationality," in particular, can be seen as a curious amalgam of linguistic formalism and empirical or quasi-empirical knowledge. To this extent, I shall present Habermas as a "friendly" (or communicative) epistemologist, that is, as someone who wishes to combine scientific inquiry with communication (about objects, values, and even aesthetic experiences). Pushing the issue somewhat, I want to tease out lingering strands of positivism in his work – strands which, if combined with his stress on "normal" discourse, occasionally support tendencies toward conformism and normalization.[1] I want to add that, despite critical strictures of this kind, my approach to Habermas also remains "friendly" in a certain sense: I certainly find the conception of communicative rationality a vast improvement over a one-sided emphasis on technical or calculating reason and over popular neo-utilitarian models of rational choice.

My critique of Habermas relies to some extent on the classical German distinction between *Verstand* and *Vernunft* – but without embracing the totalizing aspirations of a Hegelian "world-spirit" or an all-encompassing knowledge. In my view, a chastised post-Hegelian outlook does not necessarily have to retreat into a neo-Kantian or neo-positivist formalism; in some measure it can still derive comfort from other traditions of "reason" – including the Socratic combination of knowledge and ignorance, or else Merleau-Ponty's conception of philosophy as a mode of "interrogation," a conception predicated on the view that the world itself "exists in an interrogative mode."[2] My presentation is going to proceed in three steps. I shall first examine Habermas's notion of rationality – especially communicative rationality – as it is portrayed in his *magnum opus, The Theory of Communicative Action*. Next, I shall turn to an essay written almost contemporaneously and which clarifies some of the points made in his *magnum opus*: the essay "Philosophy as Stand-In and Interpreter" (contained initially in *Moralbewusstsein und kommunikatives Handeln*). Thirdly, I shall try to place Habermas's outlook in the broader context of his other works in order finally to offer some critical assessments and suggestions for alternative ways of conceiving rationality and the unity of reason.

I

The issue of reason and rationality occupies a pivotal place in *The Theory of Communicative Action*; according to the study, the issue is the central theme both of philosophy and of sociological inquiry (properly understood). This claim is emphatically advanced in the opening chapter entitled "Approaches to the Problem of Rationality". In terms of the introductory pages, the "basic theme" of philosophy is and has always been "reason" (*Vernunft*).

> Since its beginnings, philosophy has endeavored to explain the world as a whole, that is, the unity in the multiplicity of appearances on the basis of principles to be found in reason . . . If there is anything common to philosophical theories, it is the intention of thinking being or the unity of the world by way of explicating reason's experience of itself.[3]

While thus acknowledging reason's pivotal place, Habermas immediately proceeds to qualify the scope of its ambitions; in his view, the holistic aspirations of traditional philosophy have become problematical in the modern age. "Philosophy today," he writes, "can no longer aim at the whole of the world, of nature, history and society in the sense of a totalizing knowledge." The collapse of holistic "worldviews" nurtured by philosophy is ascribed to the "factual progress of the empirical sciences" and to the "reflective consciousness" accompanying this progress. As a result of these developments philosophy is said to change into metatheory or "metaphilosophy" related to the "framework of scientific conventions"; differently phrased, philosophy turns into formal analysis, that is, the analysis of the "formal conditions of the rationality of cognition, of linguistic communication, and of action." The chief methodology of this analysis is said to be "rational reconstruction" devoted to the explication of "formal-pragmatic" premises and conditions (of possibility) of rational behavior. In this sense and with these specifications, philosophy in its "postmetaphysical, post-Hegelian currents" is claimed to move toward a "point of convergence in a *theory of rationality*."[4] As Habermas insists, this point of convergence leaves behind all ontological as well as transcendental-philosophical legacies:

> All attempts at discovering ultimate foundations – reflecting and preserving the intentions of *prima philosophia* – have failed. In this situation, a new constellation in the relation between philosophy and the sciences begins to emerge: as illustrated in the case of the philosophy and history of science, formal explication of the conditions of rationality and empirical analysis of the manifestation and historical evolution of rationality structures are peculiarly linked.[5]

Among contemporary social sciences, the discipline chiefly destined to explore this linkage, and the ramifications of rationality, from a concrete-empirical angle is the discipline of sociology. According to Habermas, the central theme of sociology is "the changes or transformations of social integration brought about in the structure of traditional European societies by the rise of the modern system of nation-states and by the differentiation of a market-regulated economy"; that is, its theme is the study of the development and "anomic" repercussions of "capitalist modernization." To the extent that it remained faithful to this task, sociology – "alone among social-scientific disciplines" – has retained its relation to "problems of society as a whole," and especially to the problem of societal rationality. Relying chiefly on Max Weber, Habermas distinguishes three main levels of sociological inquiry relating to societal rationality and progressive rationalization: a "metatheoretical" level concerned with the formulation of general frameworks for the analysis of the rationality of actions; a "methodological" level revolving around the rationality of social-scientific understanding; and an "empirical" level focused on actual transformations of societal structures, especially on the correlation of modernization and rationalization.[6] In Weber's work, these levels or dimensions of rationality are said to be combined not merely in an accidental but in a necessary fashion:

> I want to defend the thesis that Max Weber treats the historically and psychologically *contingent* question of Occidental rationalism – the question of the meaning of modernity and of the causes and side-effects of the capitalist modernization of society (as it first emerged in Europe) – for *compelling* reasons under the rubrics of rational action, rational life-styles, and rationalized worldviews. My thesis is that the interconnection of precisely three rationality themes contained in his work has a systematic status.[7]

Before proceeding to an examination of "rationality" as such, I want to draw attention to a few salient aspects of the preceding discussion. First of all, the emphasis on the "formal conditions of rationality" clearly carries a Kantian or neo-Kantian flavor; by restricting philosophy to this focus, Habermas places his approach squarely in line with inquiry into the "conditions of possibility" (of cognition, of action and the like). To be sure, the Kantian legacy is not fully preserved: whereas for Kant the "conditions of possibility" resided in the categories of pure consciousness, Habermas locates these conditions in the structure of language. Yet this shift is not without precedent and is in fact prefigured in neo-Kantian and later neo-positivist lines of argument. As will be recalled, neo-positivism – especially as articulated by the Vienna Circle – insisted on a strict division of labor between philosophy and science: a division which assigned to the former the task of furnishing a formal linguistic framework and to the latter the task of empirical or experimental research. This division of labor, one may note, did not do away with, but only slightly modified the Kantian subject–object polarity or the dualism between subjective categories and objective data – namely, by substituting for it the dualism between an intersubjective language (shared by a plurality of subjects) and the objective world. Regarding this correlation, a further aspect needs to be considered: the distinction between formal analysis and empirical science equals the distinction between form and content. The entire distinction, however, is simply introduced without philosophical or "critical" warrant. In fact, by equating philosophy with formal analysis Habermas has deprived himself of any further recourse – for, clearly, the distinction can be warranted neither by formal analysis nor by empirical research (since it is presupposed by both). From an Hegelian perspective, the distinction reflects the opposition between abstract concepts (of *Verstand*) and the immediately "given," an opposition which it is the task of philosophy to overcome.

Regarding the meaning of "rationality" itself, the introductory chapter offers a "preliminary definition" (which, in large measure, remains canonical throughout the rest of the study). "Whenever we use the term 'rational'," Habermas observes, "we imply a close relationship between rationality and knowledge [*Wissen*]. Our knowledge has a propositional structure: beliefs can be stated explicitly in the form of propositions." With these formulations, Habermas seems to place himself in an older tradition. For "knowledge [*Wissen*]" can be translated as "*episteme*," and the latter can be construed, with Plato, as participation in eternal ideas or else, with Husserl, as grasp of pure essences. Such construal, however, is precluded by the preceding identification of philosophy with formal metatheory or the "metaphilosophy" of science. In line with this identification, knowledge can only refer – at least in the prototypical cases – to empirical phenomena or data in the "objective world." Moreover, in light of the neo-Kantian subject–object division, knowledge can never designate a kind of "participation" in substantive ideas transcending subjects, but can only be the property and instrument of subjects (seen as agents endowed with various cognitive and linguistic competencies). Habermas explicitly embraces this conclusion when he writes that "rationality has to do less with the mere having of knowledge than with the question how linguistically and practically competent subjects *acquire and utilize knowledge*." Such utilization can occur through individuals directly or else through the medium of symbolic statements and social actions; but the latter are always the performative accomplishments of subjects: "persons who possess knowledge can be more or less rational, as can symbolic utterances as well as linguistic and non-linguistic, communicative or non-communicative actions embodying knowledge." As performances of subjects, utterances or actions involving a claim to knowledge can be criticized by other subjects and defended or vindicated by speakers and agents; in this sense, rationality means openness to argumentation. In Habermas's words: "Our considerations so far yield the conclusion that the rationality of an utterance is tied to the possibility of critique and justification. An utterance fulfills the demands of rationality if and insofar as it embodies fallible knowledge and therewith makes reference to the objective world (or world of empirical facts) and thus is amenable to objective assessment."[8]

Habermas's notion of rationality, it is true, is not restricted to references to the objective world but extends – through a kind of analogical transference – to other modes of knowledge or other forms of rational "validity claims." Even within the domain of empirical or descriptive knowledge, Habermas distinguishes two main cases: one in which knowledge is used purely instrumentally for the sake of a "successful intervention" in the world, and one in which knowledge claims are advanced for the sake of a discussion and clarification of empirical states of affairs. As he notes, the mode of utilization of knowledge is different in the two cases: in the first case the goal is "instrumental control,' in the second "communicative understanding and consensus [*Verständigung*]." This leads Habermas to the formulation of two basic types of rationality which he terms respectively "cognitive-instrumental rationality" and "communicative rationality" – the latter predicated (as he says) on "the basic experience of the freely uniting, consensus-producing power of argumentative speech."[9] As Habermas further elaborates, the second type is not narrowly tailored to empirical knowledge or to utilizations of knowledge guided by the standard of factual "truth." Relying on his formal-pragmatic analysis of language and its cognitive dimensions, he extends communicative rationality to a broad array of propositional (or quasi-propositional) statements and knowledge claims. Rational, he writes, we also call someone "who obeys an established norm and is able, when criticized, to justify his action by explicating a given situation in the light of legitimate expectations. We even call rational someone who truthfully utters a wish, a sentiment or a mood, shares a secret or confesses a deed," and who validates such disclosure by drawing the practical consequences in his behavior. In this sense, "norm-regulated actions" and "expressive self-presentations" raise knowledge claims which are comparable, by analogy, to the claim of empirical knowledge. Instead of appealing to the standard of truth, the speaker or agent in these instances "makes the claim that his behavior is 'right' in relation to a normative context recognized as legitimate, or else that the expressive utterance of an experience to which he has privileged access is truthful or sincere." In contrast to the reference to the "objective world" implicit in empirical statements, speakers and agents in these cases appeal to "something in the common social world or else something in the purely private, subjective world." "In summary one can say," Habermas states, "that norm-regulated actions, expressive self-presentations and evaluative expressions complement factual-constative speech acts in constituting a communicative practice which – against the backdrop of a shared life-world – aims at the production, maintenance and renewal of consensus, a consensus predicated on the intersubjective recognition of criticizable validity claims."[10]

Habermas's portrayal of rationality is clearly impressive in its coverage and intellectual verve; communicative rationality, in particular, appears as a sprawling edifice encompassing a great variety of cognitive and linguistic acts. Despite these merits, however, doubts quickly surface regarding precisely the rationality of the entire edifice. One issue concerns the broad distinction between instrumental and communicative rationality. As in the previous distinction between form and content, one can ask what mode of reasoning or rationality informs this differentiation itself – since it is clearly not covered by either the instrumental or the purely communicative type. A similar query pertains to the different forms of communicative rationality, their relationship with each other and with the "backdrop of a life-world." This issue emerges more clearly when rationality is linked with modernity – as is done by Habermas in his subsequent arguments. In comparing mythical and modern worldviews – the former marked by "closedness" and the latter by "openness" – Habermas finds the chief characteristic of modernity or modernization in the progressive differentiation and specialization of knowledge claims and corresponding modes of rationality. Relying on Gellner and others, he detects in the modern period "the increasing categorial separation between the objective, social and subjective worlds; the specialization of cognitive-instrumental, moral-practical, and expressive types of reasoning; and above all the differentiation of the aspects of validity relevant for these respective problems." This argument is further buttressed by recourse to cognitive psychology. From Piaget's perspective, cognitive development involves the "formation of an external and an internal universe," that is, a "progressive demarcation through the construction of a universe of objects and an inner universe of subjects"; simultaneously, these two universes are progressively segregated from the "reciprocal relation between a subject and other subjects," that is, from the domain of "normatively regulated interpersonal relations." Thus, Piaget offers a scheme for cognitive development in the broad sense, where development means "not merely the construction of an external universe, but the construction of a system of coordinates for the *simultaneous* demarcation of the objective and social worlds from the subjective world." Cognitive development, from this angle, signifies generally the differentiation and "decentering" of an initially unified or compact worldview.[11]

Against the background of these anthropological and psychological findings, Habermas sketches a theory of cultural development or modernization seen as progressive rationalization of worldviews and modes of life. At this point the concept of the "life-world" is specifically introduced, namely, as designation of a general cultural foil or practical horizon against which knowledge claims or types of rationality are progressively profiled. In mythical or primitive worldviews, knowledge claims (and rationality itself) were still entirely submerged in a taken for granted life-praxis. "To the extent that the life-world of a social group is interpreted through a mythical worldview," we read, "individual members are relieved of the burden of interpretation and also of the chance to produce a criti-cizable consensus"; the worldview at this juncture does not yet permit "a differentiation between the worlds of existing facts, of valid norms, and of subjective experiences capable of expression." Modernization, by contrast, involves the dissolution of this unquestioned life-praxis, the progressive specialization of rationality or knowledge claims, and thus the replacement of a "normatively ascribed consensus" by a "communica-tively achieved agreement." In Habermas's presentation, genuine modernization must display these prominent features (among others): (1) the cultural context "must furnish formal concepts for the objective, social, and subjective world; it must make room for differentiated validity claims (propositional truth, normative rightness, subjective truthfulness) and for a corresponding differentiation of basic attitudes (objectifying, norm-conformative, and expressive)"; (2) the cultural context or tradition must encourage "a reflective relation to itself; it must be so far stripped of its dogmatism that traditional interpretations can be questioned and be subjected to critical revision"; (3) the cultural context must further "con-strue the life-world in such a way that success-oriented (or instrumental) action can be freed from the imperatives of a communicatively renew-able consensus and thus at least partially uncoupled from communicative action."[12]

These arguments are again impressive for their élan and their unswerv-ing commitment to modern rationality; however, they literally bristle with unresolved questions and ambiguities precisely from the perspec-tive of a rational understanding. First of all, modernity is identified by Habermas with rationality or the progressive articulation of rational validity claims, while mythical or archaic worldviews are presented as pre- or non-rational. If this is so, however, the distinction between myth and modernity itself is not covered or warranted by any mode of reasoning available in Habermas's theoretical scheme. In fact, modernization or the emergence of reason out of unreason appears as a mysterious or else dogmatic event – in violation of reasonable expectations one might have of a "critical theory." A similar problem besets the status of the "life-world" and its relation to modernity. In Habermas's portrayal, the life-world appears as a non-rational matrix of habitual conventions and practices against which rational validity claims are progressively profiled in the course of modernization. If this is correct, however, both the concept of the life-world itself and its relation to modern rationality elude the confines of rational argument or validation in Habermas's sense. What emerges here is the lack of a mode of reasoning exceeding both empirical description and formal analysis – a mode implicitly presupposed but never thematized in Habermas's work. Habermas himself admits this troublesome state of affairs – but without drawing theoretical consequences from this admission:

> It would be senseless to assess a syndrome as a whole, that is, the *totality of a form of life*, from the perspective of individual rationality claims. If we do not want altogether to relinquish standards by which a life-form might be said to be more or less flawed, deformed, unhappy or alienated, then the only model we can perhaps use is that of sickness and health. We tacitly judge life-forms and life-histories according to standards of normality that do not permit an approximation to ideal limit values. Perhaps we should talk instead of a *balance between complementary moments*, an equilibrated interplay of cognitive, moral, and aesthetic-expressive dimensions.[13]

Habermas's admission at this point is disarming – although his appeal to "normality" (or normalization) appears problematical. However, the trouble goes deeper: instead of involving merely the fuzzy margins of his theory, it affects his categorial structure and the meaning of his categories. Rationality is initially introduced as a mode of knowledge(*Wissen*); in line with the "metatheoretical" (or metascientific) character of philosophical reasoning, knowledge refers initially to something in the external or empirical world, that is, the world external to reason. If this model is extended through analogy to the domains of ethics and personal expression, then a similar relationship must obtain, namely, between rational analysis and quasi-objective phenomena amenable to knowledge. This means that social norms or relations and even "inner nature" must be somehow externalized or objectified to become targets of rational knowledge possessed by a knowing subject. This assumption is confirmed by

Piaget when he speaks of an "inner universe of subjects" and of relations between "a subject and objects" and "a subject and subjects." In every case, thus, rationality involves a relation between a subject and objects (or quasi-objects). Since this subject–object relation, however, is presupposed by the very concept of rationality formulated by Habermas, it can no longer be rationally grounded or be the theme of independent rational inquiry – just as little as, given the premise of a purely formal (or procedural) rationality, the distinction between formal and substantive reason can be rationally explored or justified.

These considerations obviously conjure up the issue of the meaning and scope of reason. If rationality means formal rationality and rationalization increasing formalization, then modernization necessarily signals a widening gulf between the subject (as formal-rational analyst) and the (substantive) targets of his analysis. If, as Habermas further postulates, modernization means a progressive differentiation and segregation of "value spheres" or rationality domains, the widening is bound to affect not only the relation between the subject and its so-called "worlds", but also the relation among these worlds or rational "world-concepts." Against this background it is difficult to see how anything like a common bond should persist among subjects, or how and why they should concur on anything pertaining to a concrete world or subject matter (*Sache*). The bond cannot reside in formal rationality as such since it is supposed to be increasingly differentiated and segregated with time. Nor can the bond consist in "communication" per se because, as a rational category or rationality claim, communication refers only to the formal "comprehensibility" of language – which as a claim is demarcated from other claims. The bond can only be found in the communicative praxis of the life-world. But this praxis, as we have seen, is for Habermas basically non- or pre-rational; moreover, it is progressively undermined and dissolved by the advances of formal rationality. The notion of communicative (or practical) rationality, I conclude, can only be rescued or vindicated by stepping outside the confines of formal reasoning – that is, by stepping outside the basic parameters of Habermas's theoretical framework.[14]

II

Apart from its opening chapter, *The Theory of Communicative Action* refers only intermittently to reason or rationality – which complicates a coherent grasp of the theme. As it happens, Habermas on other occasions has focused on the issue in a more direct and detailed manner, pinpointing more clearly its significance in his overall scheme. His essay

"Philosophy as Stand-In and Interpreter" – written roughly at the same time
as the publication of his *magnum opus* – is particularly helpful and instructive in this respect. The essay starts from the present ferment or malaise
in philosophical thought, that is, from tendencies pointing in a radically
post-metaphysical, and even post-rational or post-philosophical, direction.
"The master-thinkers have become suspect," Habermas notes in the
opening paragraph. "This has been true for some time of Hegel . . . and
it is true periodically of Marx . . . Today even Kant succumbs to this verdict." According to the essay, Kant occupies a pivotal or paradigmatic
place in modern philosophy – which renders his eclipse today particularly
problematic and troublesome. Kant, we read, "has in fact introduced a
new mode of rational validation into philosophy," namely, by relating
philosophical reasoning to ongoing advances in the empirical sciences:
"Kant viewed the cognitive progress in the physics of his time as an
important fact – a fact of interest for the philosopher not simply as something empirically given but as confirmation of the possibilities of human
cognition." The question which Kant raised regarding Newtonian physics
pertained not to the level of causality but of cognitive possibility: "Kant
calls *transcendental* an inquiry aiming at the a priori conditions of the
possibility of experience." In Habermas's reading, such an inquiry is not
a purely logical-deductive exercise, but rather an effort at providing a
"non-empirical reconstruction" of the presupposed accomplishments of
a cognitive subject. "Transcendental validation," he writes, "thus does
not rest on the idea of a deduction from first principles, but rather on
our ability to grasp the non-substitutability of certain intuitively performed and rule-governed operations."[15]
    Notwithstanding his pivotal role, Kant has become suspect in our
time – precisely because of his celebration of distinct powers or preroga-
tives of philosophy. In Habermas's presentation, contemporary attacks
challenge primarily two claims of Kantian thought. The first has to do
with the "foundationalism of epistemology." "To the extent that it lays
claim to a knowledge *prior* to (empirical) knowledge," he observes,
"philosophy inserts between itself and the sciences an autonomous
domain over which it exerts dominion." To this degree, philosophy arro-
gates to itself the role of an "usher" (*Platzanweiser*) assigning to the
sciences their place and functions. In addition to its epistemological
ambitions, transcendental thought aims to offer a grounded critique (of
reason). "Jointly with the analysis of cognitive foundations," we read,
"the critique of pure reason endeavors to criticize the misuse of our
cognitive faculty which is tailored to phenomena. For the notion of a
'substantive' rationality bequeathed by the metaphysical tradition Kant
substitutes the concept of a differentiated reason whose unity retains only

a purely formal character." Despite his differentiation between pure, practical, and aesthetic reason, however, Kant assigned to philosophy the role of a supreme arbiter or "judge" (*Richter*) of reason adjudicating between the domains of science, ethics, and art. Referring to some "post-modern'" critics of transcendental thought (like Rorty), Habermas acknowledges the tenuous character of these claims and accordingly voices doubts that philosophy "really can fulfill the functions of usher and judge ascribed to it by the master-thinker Kant." While accepting these reservations, however, Habermas hesitates to follow the mentioned critics in a radically "post-rational" direction or to relinquish altogether the notion of philosophy as a "guardian of rationality" in a loose sense. Irrespective of idealist overtones or connotations Kant, in his view, retains a prototypical significance for all modern, including contemporary, thought. "Implicit in Kant's conception of a formal, internally differentiated reason," he states, "is a theory of modernity. The latter is marked by the abandonment of the 'substantive' rationality of inherited religious and metaphysical worldviews, on the one hand, and by its trust in a procedural rationality warranting our considered judgments . . . on the other." In light of this relevance of Kant's arguments for modern thought, Habermas raises the question whether such a theory of modernity really "should stand or fall with the foundationalist claims of epistemology?" The tenor of the essay points to a negative reply. As he notes, the essay seeks to vindicate the thesis "that, even after relinquishing the dubious roles of usher and judge, philosophy still can and should preserve its rationality claim in the more modest functions of stand-in [*Platzhalter*] and interpreter [*Interpret*]."[16]

Before actually elaborating on this thesis, the essay sketches in broad strokes the story of philosophical developments since Kant's time – a story which stretches from Hegel's reaction to Kant over immanent (but increasingly radicalized) critiques of both Kant and Hegel to the contemporary post-modern situation. I shall largely bypass this story, since very little of it is directly germane to the issue at hand. Regarding immanent reactions to Kant and Hegel, Habermas notes the progressive thinning out or evaporation of transcendental-logical and metaphysical premises: "Regardless of whether doubt centers on Kant's transcendental deduction or on Hegel's move to absolute knowledge, immanent critique assails in both cases the claim that either the categorical structure or the developmental pattern of the formation of human spirit can be shown to be necessary (or non-contingent)."[17] A more radical assault on the idealist legacy is found in pragmatist and hermeneutical approaches concentrating on the dimension of an experiential life-world or else on pre-rational common sense and everyday interaction. Ordinary life-praxis and interaction,

Habermas observes, "assume here an argumentative status deviating radically from that of self-reflection in the philosophy of consciousness: they have foundational relevance only insofar as with their help the desire for foundational grounding is rejected as spurious."[18] In Habermas's presentation, these approaches are gateways to a still more radical position: the post-modern "farewell to philosophy," manifest in three chief versions labelled "therapeutic," "heroic," and "salvaging" and associated, respectively, with the work of Wittgenstein, Heidegger, and Gadamer. Again, I shall bypass the details of this discussion as not particularly relevant (except to note a strong tendency toward simplification in Habermas's portrayal). The unifying feature of these post-modern perspectives is found in their common opposition to modern science, more specifically, in their effort to juxtapose to science a non-scientific or purely "edifying" philosophy:

> Post-structuralist, late-pragmatic, and neo-historicist perspectives incline toward a narrow, objectivist conception of science. In contrast to a type of knowledge loyal to the ideal of scientific objectivity, they want to make room primarily for an elucidating, awakening, and in any case non-objectifying mode of thinking, a thinking which renounces the standard of universal and criticizable validity claims . . . without renouncing the authority and superiority of philosophical insights."[19]

Following this critical review of post-modernism, Habermas returns to his initial concern: the proposal of retrieving, within limits, a rational role for philosophy in our post-metaphysical age. In contrast to post-modern anti-scientism, this proposal is predicated on a close conjunction or collaboration between philosophy and science. Pointing to social scientists like Weber, Mead, Piaget and Chomsky, Habermas finds their work marked by the effort to incorporate philosophical thought "within" science or at least within a specialized research project. Their writings, he notes, are illustrative for "a philosophically seminal idea *and* its combination with an empirically researchable, but universalist problematic."[20] In light of these precedents, the essay argues in favor of a new role of contemporary philosophy: namely, that of a "stand-in" for nascent, yet to be developed scientific theories. Against the background of recent trends, Habermas writes,

> it is not implausible to ask whether philosophy – in its relation to various sciences – might not exchange the untenable role of "usher" for that of a "stand-in" or "place-keeper" [*Platzhalter*] – a stand-in for empirical theories with strong universalist claims, such as have repeatedly been sketched by productive thinkers in specialized disciplines. This role applies

primarily to those "reconstructive" sciences which – relying on the pre-theoretical knowledge of competently judging, acting and speaking subjects as well as on inherited cultural forms of knowledge – seek to clarify the presumptively universal foundations of the rationality of experience and judgment, action and linguistic communication.[21]

As he adds, traditional transcendental or dialectical modes of argumentation can be helpful in this endeavor of rational reconstruction – provided they relinquish their purely philosophical pretensions: "They are tenable only on the level of reconstructive hypotheses suitable for further research in empirical contexts."[22]

As one may note, this new role of a stand-in is not far removed from neo-positivist construals of philosophy (in terms of empirical theory), nor from the "underlaborer" conception prevalent for some time in the analytical philosophy of science. Habermas, in fact, underscores this affinity by describing the philosopher explicitly as someone functioning as "an underlaborer [Zuarbeiter] for a theory of rationality" without raising "any foundational or comprehensive-absolutist claims." In its supportive or underlaboring capacity, philosophy draws its rationality clearly from its chosen target or object domain: the rationality of science; philosophical reasoning, to this extent, seems limited to providing a categorial structure or formal analysis of empirical phenomena.[23] Although strongly leaning toward an equation of philosophy with formal analysis, Habermas himself is reluctant to restrict philosophy entirely to the mentioned role. While being a suitable replacement for the task of ushering, the role of stand-in does not sufficiently answer to the need of adjudicating between different rationality domains as they have emerged in modernity. Given the increasing differentiation of these domains and given the obsolescence of philosophical arbitration (the philosopher's role as judge), Habermas asks, how can the notion of a "guardianship of rationality" still be maintained? His response is initially purely factual or empiricist in the sense of dismissing a rational grounding:

> The situation of culture as a whole or in its totality is no different from the situation of the sciences: culture does not need a rational grounding or approbation. Since the dawn of modernity in the eighteenth century, culture has produced those rationality structures which Weber, following Emil Lask, discovered and described as cultural "value spheres". Without the help of philosophy, modernity has engendered three separate rationality domains represented by modern science, by positive law and a secularized ethics (guided by principles), and by an increasingly autonomous art and institutionalized art criticism.[24]

The differentiation of value spheres is said to imply a progressive streamlining and formalization of thought. Thus, while modern science discards traditional worldviews and renounces the theoretical grasp of nature and history as a whole, modern cognitive ethics eliminates questions of the "good life," concentrating instead on strictly deontological, universalizable maxims (thereby substituting the "right" for the "good"). Modern autonomous art, finally, insists on the progressive distillation of aesthetic experience, with the result that "subjectivity is liberated from the conventions of everyday perception and purposive action." Given these pervasive developments, Habermas adds, the "sons and daughters of modernity" learn how to divide or differentiate their cultural tradition into the discrete rationality domains of truth, justice, and taste – without any rational or philosophical tutoring.[25]

Habermas does not rest his case at this point, however. Although rejecting the demand for a "grounding or justification" of modern trends, he recognizes the need for a "mediation" – a need previously fulfilled by the adjudicating role of philosophy. "How," Habermas asks, "can a reason divided into separate moments still preserve its unity within the various cultural domains; and how furthermore can the specialized spheres – increasingly ensconced in esoteric enclaves – still retain their nexus with a communicative life-praxis?" The problem of mediation applies first of all to relations within and among the separate value spheres of modernity. On this score, Habermas notes at least the sporadic emergence of various forms of blending or mutual intrusion – exemplified by hermeneutical and "non-objectifying" approaches in the social sciences, by realistic and "engagé" trends in modern art, and the like. More important is the problem of mediation between modern rationality structures and ordinary life-praxis. In this respect, philosophy seems to acquire a new holistic role replacing that of arbitration or adjudication: the role of interpreter. "The linkage with totality," we read, "might be recaptured by philosophy in its role as interpreter focused on the life-world. In this capacity, philosophy might at least assist in reactivating the interplay between the cognitive-instrumental, moral-practical, and aesthetic-expressive domains, an interplay that has been stalled like a tangled 'mobile'." As Habermas admits, the challenges faced by philosophy in this context are considerable; but he finds it possible and fruitful at least to pinpoint the task awaiting a philosophical inquiry ready to "relinquish the role of cultural judge for that of a mediating interpreter." In his formulation: "How can the spheres of science, ethics and art – presently encapsulated in specialized cultures – be opened up and, without violating their intrinsic rationality, be reconnected with the impoverished traditions of the life-world in such a way that the separated domains of reason can coalesce in a new balance in the communicative life-praxis?"[26]

Philosophy as a mediating interpreter: surely an attractive and impor-tant vision – but one unsupported, I am afraid, on Habermas's premises. Seen as a mode of reasoning, philosophy in its role of interpreter collides head on with its definition as formal analysis. The problem is obvious in the case of relations within or among modern value spheres. In order to perform its mediating services, philosophy in this case can draw suste-nance from none of the three modern rationality structures but must rely on resources outside these spheres. Habermas seems to acknowledge this dilemma when he writes that "the radically differentiated rationality aspects seem to point toward an integral unity – but a unity which can only be regained on this side of the specialized structures, that means, in everyday life and not on the other side: in the depths and abysses of the classical philosophy of reason." Yet how can the unity of reason – however reduced or minimalized – be accomplished in a domain presented as non- or pre-rational? Habermas's dualism (noted above) bet-ween reason and non-reason, or philosophy and non-philosophy, re-emerges and intrudes here to effectively block the envisaged mediation. The dilemma is further aggravated with regard to the more comprehen-sive reconciliation between life-praxis and modernity. In this respect, philosophical reasoning or inquiry has to find its bearings beyond the division between the (non-rational) life-world and modern rationality structures – in a region which transgresses Habermas's conception of rationality (as formal knowledge). Toward the end of his essay, Habermas seeks to mollify the dilemma by injecting some rational features into the life-world. "This communicative life-praxis," he states, "permits a com-munication governed by validity claims – and this as the only alternative to a more or less violent mutual manipulation." Absorbed into validity claims and their rationality spheres, however, the life-world loses precisely its capacity to be a resource for philosophical mediation. Strip-ped of rational features, on the other hand, its competence in this field is equally obscure. Suspended between life-world and formal analysis, philosophical interpretation – far from reactivating a stalled momentum – seems itself stranded.[27]

III

The dilemma of rationality in Habermas's framework is not peculiar to his recent writings but can be traced through some of his earlier publications as well. Thus, as is well known, his *Knowledge and Human Interests* dif-ferentiated between three types of cognitive interests (technical, practical, and emancipatory) and three corresponding forms of knowledge (empirical, hermeneutical, and critical); but the epistemological theory establishing these distinctions could not itself be collapsed into, or sustained by, any one of the three categories. Similarly, the division between "system" and "life-world" – first introduced in *Legitimation Crisis* – was clearly predicated neither on system-theoretical nor on purely phenomenological premises. For present purposes, I want to draw attention briefly to an essay which, in my view, sheds additional light both on the historical motivations and the epistemological leanings of Habermas's approach: the essay "Does Philosophy Still Have a Purpose?" (of 1971). Like the paper written a decade later, the essay started from the ferment in present-day philosophy, and more broadly from the far-reaching transformations and dislocations evident in philosophical thought since Hegel's time. While, in the wake of Hegel's opus, "great" or systematic philosophy came basically to an end – Habermas observed – today philosophizing represented by "great individual thinkers" (or master-thinkers) seems to share the same fate: "Even after relinquishing the systematic claim to a continuation of *philosophia perennis*, the type of philosophy propounded by influential teachers had persisted in the last century and a half; but now the signs are growing that this type of thought embodied in individual philosophers is disappearing." What seems to be steadily replacing the traditional contemplative type is philosophy seen as a mode of "research which collectively organizes scientific progress."[28]

For a long time and even until recently, it is true, German philosophy had managed to resist or elude the mentioned tendencies. According to Habermas, this resistance was due – among other factors – to the peculiar maladjustment of German life to Western cultural trends, a maladjustment deriving from Germany's delayed capitalist development, her belated emergence as a nation, and her general hesitation to catch up with modernity. As a result of this incongruence or "non-contemporaneity," he stated, German postwar philosophizing retained "an explosive critical potential, often at the price of analytical rigor"; none of the major schools of thought "conformed in their deepest intentions to the prevailing social and political order." In Habermas's words, what was lacking in most instances was "the serenity of a philosophy that is self-confidently ensconced in the *juste milieu*, that is synchronized with the progress of the epoch, or is satisfied with specialized research."[29] More recently, however, this maladjustment has begun to vanish, thus making room for a closer integration of German and Western culture. "Curiously prepared by the transformations of social structures under the Nazi regime," we read, "the Federal Republic during the post-war period of reconstruction has cancelled the non-contemporaneities of development:

under the auspices of an administratively regulated capitalism, this part
of Germany – for the first time in centuries – has become a contemporary
of Western Europe." Given this situation, German thought for the first
time is able to join Western philosophical trends which, since the dawn
of modernity, have pointed toward a close alliance of philosophy and
science (or philosophy and epistemology). While opposing a narrowly
positivistic mode of "scientism," the essay in the end pleaded in favor of
a conception of philosophy defined as a "non-scientistic" but science-
friendly mode of inquiry or research, that is, as philosophy or metatheory
of science (*Wissenschaftsphilosophie*). Only such an approach, Habermas
concluded, in which philosophical thought "communicates with the
sciences" can preserve the "fragile unity of reason" accomplished in rational
speech.[30]

Actually, the unity invoked in the essay was still more fragile and
tenuous than Habermas was willing to admit at the time. For how can a
scientific philosophy or a philosophical science provide a rational warrant
for science or epistemology – not to mention the range of non-scientific
modes of reasoning or argumentation? As previously indicated, the
tenuous unity has been further weakened in Habermas's more recent
publications – making room instead for segregated rationality spheres
(and their joint opposition to the life-world). Defined as formal analysis
and as a "stand-in" for scientific theories, philosophy on his own account
increasingly loses its ability to serve as a comprehensive "interpreter" or
mediator of diverse rationality claims. To this extent, the vaunted
rationality of modernity can be said to rest itself on non-rational presuppositions, in the sense that it cannot be rationally redeemed or sustained
in a comprehensive and non-circular (or non-tautological) manner. The
source of this dilemma – it seems to me – resides not in a partial or "selective" modernization, as Habermas suggests: that is, in the one-sided
emphasis on cognitive-scientific and instrumental rationality to the detriment of more "communicative" modes of reasoning; instead, the source
lies in the one-sided stress on formal rationality per se and in the equation
of philosophy with scientific theory (or metatheory). Along these lines, one
might speak of an "economy of reason" in human affairs: the more processes of thinking are formalized and rationalized, the more the presuppositions and concrete parameters of thought slip into non-rational
obscurity.

One way to highlight the drawbacks of Habermas's approach is by focusing on its link with instrumental reason. In *The Theory of Communicative
Action*, a categorial distinction is drawn between "cognitive-instrumental"
and "communicative" rationality; but the distinction is dubious given that
both are modes of formal reasoning. The trouble with formal rationality,

in turn, is not that it is only partially or selectively applied in modernity, but that it is inherently "possessive" and thus ultimately instrumental in character. This aspect is evident in Habermas's comments on the "having" and "utilization" of knowledge (cited above). Quite apart from these – possibly idiosyncratic – statements, however, the linkage with possession and instrumentalism results from the definition and intrinsic meaning of formal reason. Ever since Kant, the latter term has been employed to designate the inner structure of the human mind (or else the inner structure of language), a categorial matrix entirely unperturbed and uncontaminated by contingent, external or "substantive" features. Segregated from the variable content of the world (that is, from otherness), formal reason was seen as constituting the innermost endowment or possession of man, a faculty that most directly and universally "belongs" to man – in contrast to the alien and alienating forces of nature and history. Construed as generic possession of competent subjects, however, formal rationality necessarily distances the subject matter of knowledge to an external object-domain and thus to a target of utilization and possible control. The instrumental implications of this outlook were still clearly acknowledged in Weber's conception of "formal rationality" – a conception which Habermas recapitulates without comment: "If and to the extent that a domain of action is to be rationalized at all, advances in rationality are measured by the culture-invariant criteria of a successful control of processes in nature and society, processes encountered as something available in the objective world."[31]

Given these implications, the cure for instrumentalism must also be different from the one proposed by Habermas. Whereas, in his scheme, the antidote for our ills rests in a balancing of instrumental and communicative modes of thought – all equally formal and procedural in character – or else in a retreat to the (non-rational) life-world, the remedy in my view can only lie in an effort to replace or supplement formal analysis with "non-possessive" and "substantive" types of reasoning. This proposal, of course, calls for careful elaboration and exegesis. No doubt, in our post-Hegelian and post-metaphysical age, substantive reasoning can no longer denote any sort of rational triumphalism; under non-possessive auspices, philosophizing cannot mean the imposition of universal categories on a recalcitrant world, but at best the dispersal and dissemination of thought among the multitude of concrete phenomena. To this extent, Habermas is surely correct in observing that the unity of thought can be recovered only on "this side" of specialized rationality spheres and "not on the other side: in the depths and abysses of the classical philosophy of reason." Habermas's verdict seems to hold particularly for modern, Cartesian-type rationalism with its careful segregation of mind and world (although one should note that

Hegel's world-spirit was "absolute" by virtue not of its abstraction from, but its complex mediation with reality). Differently phrased: the sought after "unity of reason" cannot signify a unity or unification achieved within the confines of mind but only an openness of thought to the world – more precisely, reason's steadfast attentiveness to experience and its intimate linkage or interpenetration of reason and non-reason, meaning and non-meaning.

These considerations prompt a few additional comments on "substantive" reasoning and its relation to the life-world. In a post-metaphysical setting the former term, I believe, can no longer denote a traditional substantialism or essentialism – where thought is concerned with ontological "substances" or else mind itself is construed as a substance. Deviating from such traditional definitions, substantive reasoning here is meant to capture the concrete "embodiment" of reason or thought's involvement with its own "otherness." Instead of figuring as a noun, reasoning here is conceived as an activity occurring within a complex matrix – a matrix which is not of reason's making but by no means simply external or indifferent to reason. The latter aspect brings into view the difficult issue of the life-world. In Habermas's presentation, the life-world functions merely as the foil or backdrop for the differentiated rationality spheres emerging in modernity. While the life-world is progressively transformed and streamlined under the impact of rationalization, modern rationality itself (as formal analysis) remains basically immune from practical life-world influences. Differently put: While acting as teacher and task master, reason is not in turn perceived as a pupil exposed to the lessons and learning experiences of the life-world. To this extent, reason and life-world in Habermas's scheme are basically dichotomous or segregated – and this not only due to recent developmental anomalies (like the "uncoupling" of system and life-world).[32] In contrast to this segregation, I would prefer treating the life-world as a substantive experiential domain, a domain not only subject to the demands of reason, but one whose lessons reason has continuously to undergo in order to escape self-enclosure. Tied to life-world experience, reason is not merely an external yardstick but an intrinsic achievement – always fragile and ambivalent – of lived engagement and ongoing struggles for recognition.

Glimpses of substantive reasoning (in the sketched sense) can be found in the writings of the older Frankfurt School, especially in Adorno's later works. Thus, Adorno's *Negative Dialectics* outlines a correlation between reason and world which does no longer obey rationalist or traditional-metaphysical standards. "Everything mental or spiritual," we read there, "is a modified bodily impulse, and this modification in turn a qualitative change into something not merely empirically given . . . The supposed foundations of consciousness are emblems of difference or otherness: through the medium of pleasure and pain bodily experience penetrates into thought." The same post-metaphysical thrust also inspires Adorno's notion of "*mimesis*" or mimetic thinking – a notion unfairly and prematurely dismissed by Habermas as irrational mystification. As employed in *Negative Dialectics* and elsewhere, *mimesis* is not a synonym for archaic regression or an unreflective naturalism, but a term designating reason's effort to think beyond the confines of rational calculation and control – that is, to grasp and simultaneously preserve "non-identity." To this extent, the term stands for a radical openness and engagement, not for a naïve realism content with replicating the world. "Thought is not a copy of things," Adorno writes, in an intriguing variation on a Husserlian theme, "but aims at the things themselves" – which is impossible in a linear-intentional manner owing to the mutual implication of reason and world. In opening itself up to the lesson of things, substantive or mimetic thought captures one of the chief motivations of materialism (in its non-metaphysical sense). In the words of *Negative Dialectics*, the basic yearning of such a thinking "would be the resurrection of the flesh – a notion completely alien to idealism or the realm of absolute spirit."[33]

Adorno's argument finds numerous echoes and parallels in the work of a French phenomenological thinker who is sometimes treated as the prototypical philosopher of "embodied" or "incarnate reason": Maurice Merleau-Ponty. Efforts to explore the interlacing of reason and world form a central leitmotif linking Merleau-Ponty's early writings with his late "Working Notes." Thus, opposing the Cartesian dualism of mind and world, *Phenomenology of Perception* resolutely moved beyond the boundaries of the *cogito*. "For the other to be more than an empty word," we read, "it is necessary that my existence should never be reduced to my simple consciousness of existing, but that it should incorporate the awareness that *one* may have of it, and thus include my incarnation in some nature and the possibility, at least, of a historical situation." Once this embodiment is taken into account, however, the world is no longer simply an external target of rational calculation. Instead, reason – which in a first step discovered itself by excluding everything non-rational (or every content) – in a second step re-encounters within itself everything that had been excluded. "The world," Merleau-Ponty writes, "which I distinguished from myself as the totality of things or of processes linked by causal relationships, I rediscover 'in me' as the permanent horizon of all my *cogitationes* and as a dimension to which I am constantly relating." Given this interpenetration of thought and world, the latter cannot simply be external to reason but must harbor something like a call to reason or what Merleau-Ponty terms a "pre-existent *logos*" (or "wild *logos*"). As a corollary, philosophizing cannot mean the imposition of rationality on the world, but the more modest and arduous effort of "relearning to look at the world." A similar perspective re-emerges more than a decade later in Merleau-Ponty's comments on structural anthropology. Referring to the "symbolic function" as the "source of all reason and unreason," he observes that this function "must always be ahead of its object and finds reality only by anticipating it in imagination. Thus our task is to broaden our reasoning to make it capable of grasping what, in ourselves and in others, precedes and exceeds reason."[34]

The connection between reason and world was tightened further in Merleau-Ponty's last writings – to the point where it took the form of a reversible intertwining; at the same time, thinking was expelled still farther beyond the confines of the *cogito*. "We are not implicating in 'our experience' any reference to an *ego*," *The Visible and the Invisible* states. "We are interrogating our experience precisely in order to know how it opens us to what is not ourselves."[35] In order to accomplish this interrogation, philosophy – in Merleau-Ponty's view – had to renounce time-honored epistemological formulas and embark again on the labor of thinking, a labor obviated both by rationalism and irrationalism (or radical skepticism):

> If it is true that as soon as philosophy declares itself to be reflection or (rational) coincidence it prejudges what it will find, then once again it must recommence everything, reject the instruments reflection and intuition had provided themselves, and install itself in a locus where they have not yet been distinguished, in experiences that have not yet been "worked over", that offer us all at once, pell-mell, both "subject" and "object", both existence and essence, and hence give philosophy resources to redefine them.[36]

Seen as interrogation, philosophical inquiry ultimately embroils us in a "chiasm" or reversal – a kind of ontological vortex that "installs us far indeed from 'ourselves', in the other, in the things." To which the final "Working Notes" (written shortly before Merleau-Ponty's death) add:

> We do not begin *ab homine* as Descartes . . . we do not take nature in the sense of the scholastics . . . and we do not take *logos* and truth in the sense of "the Word" . . . The *visible* has to be described as something that is realized through man, but which is nowise anthropology . . . nature as the other side of man . . . *logos* also as what is realized in man, but nowise as his *property*.[37]

NOTES

1 For an example of this tendency see Jürgen Habermas, "Does Philosophy Still Have a Purpose?", in *Philosophical-Political Profiles*, tr. Frederick G. Lawrence (Cambridge, MA: MIT Press, 1983), pp. 1–19, and my comments below. I am familiar with Habermas's long-standing opposition to positivism (or his effort to supplement empirical science) and I realize that I am accentuating issues by seeking to "tease out" positivist strands. In this respect I am leaning toward the attitude of the "critical critic" delineated by Anthony Giddens (although in my case the critique is not devoid of "sympathy"); see Giddens, "Reason Without Revolution?", in Richard J. Bernstein, ed., *Habermas and Modernity* (Cambridge, MA: MIT Press, 1985), pp. 112ff.

2 See Maurice Merleau-Ponty, *The Visible and the Invisible*, ed. Claude Lefort, tr. Alphonso Lingis (Evanston: Northwestern University Press, 1968), p. 103.

3 Jürgen Habermas, *The Theory of Communicative Action*, vol. 1: *Reason and the Rationalization of Society*, tr. Thomas McCarthy (Boston: Beacon Press, 1984), p. 1. (In this and subsequent citations I have slightly altered the translation for purposes of clarity. Occasionally I have consulted more recent German editions of the work.)

4 *The Theory of Communicative Action*, vol. 1, pp. 1–2.

5 *The Theory of Communicative Action*, vol. 1, p. 2.

6 *The Theory of Communicative Action*, vol. 1, pp. 4–6.

7 *The Theory of Communicative Action*, vol. 1, p. 7.

8 *The Theory of Communicative Action*, vol. 1, pp. 8–9.

9 *The Theory of Communicative Action*, vol. 1, pp. 10–11. Habermas's fuller definition of the two types bears quoting (p. 10): "If we take our bearings from the non-communicative utilization of propositional knowledge in teleological actions, we opt in favor of a concept of *cognitive-instrumental rationality* which, via empiricism, has powerfully shaped the self-understanding of modernity . . . If, on the other hand, we take our departure from the communicative employment of propositional knowledge in speech acts, we opt in favor of a broader concept of rationality which derives from older notions of *logos*. This concept of *communicative rationality* carries with it connotations which ultimately derive from the basic experience of the freely uniting, consensus-producing power of argumentative speech in which different participants overcome their initial subjective views and, through the bond of rationally motivated convictions, grasp simultaneously the unity of the objective world and the intersubjectivity of their life-context."

10 *The Theory of Communicative Action*, vol. 1, pp. 15–17. As presented

in that volume (pp. 16–17), communicative rationality extends to the domain of "evaluative expressions" having to do chiefly with aesthetic experiences or judgments: speakers or agents are rational in this context if their utterances are such that "other members of their life-world could recognize in these descriptions their own reactions to similar situations."

11 *The Theory of Communicative Action*, vol. 1, pp. 62–4, 68–9. Paraphrasing Piaget, Habermas speaks of the decentering of an "egocentric" worldview. However, given the non-differentiation of the mythical outlook this terminology is very dubious; moreover, it is by no means clear why differentiation of the objective, social, and subjective worlds should not reflect an "egocentric" attitude. According to Habermas, a *contingent* defect of modernity during recent centuries has been the relative overemphasis on the objective world or the "external universe" – a defect which can be remedied, in his view, through the simultaneous cultivation of the broader spectrum of knowledge claims.

12 *The Theory of Communicative Action*, vol. 1, pp. 70–72. This freeing of instrumental action leads to the institutionalization of the subsystems of "a rational economy and a rational bureaucracy regulated by the media of money and power."

13 *The Theory of Communicative Action*, vol. 1, p. 73.

14 My point in the above comments is to note a lacuna; the concern is not properly or in the first instance with the restoration of the so-called "unity of reason" (construed in the sense of the rationalist or idealist tradition). Habermas's position with regard to this "unity" is deeply ambivalent. On the one hand, the segregation of rationality domains or modern "value spheres" is traceable to Kant's three Critiques (and thus has a common ground in modern subjectivity); on the other hand, the correlation of the spheres was simply presupposed but not thematized by Kant – a precedent followed by Habermas in large portions of his work. *The Philosophical Discourse of Modernity* clearly pinpoints the common source of the differentiated rationality domains in Kantian philosophy; the same study also shows that Hegel took his point of departure from the same segregated rationality spheres but in addition sought to explore the linkage left unthematized by Kant. See Habermas, *The Philosophical Discourse of Modernity: Twelve Lectures*, tr. Frederick Lawrence (Cambridge, MA: MIT Press, 1987), pp. 16–19. While claiming to follow in the footsteps of the Hegelian counterdiscourse, Habermas by and large brackets the notion of a "unity of reason." In *The Theory of Communicative Action* Lukács is chided for his Hegelianism and for having committed the "decisive error" of "locating the 'practical realization' of reason on a theoretical plane." Turning to Horkheimer and Adorno, however, Habermas at least obliquely invokes the Hegelian legacy. "The thesis developed in *Dialectic*

of Enlightenment," he states, "does not direct our thought to the path that is nearest at hand, a path which leads through the separate logics of the different spheres of rationality and through the processes of societal rationalization segregated according to universal validity claims, and which suggests a unity of rationality beneath the husk of an everyday praxis that has been simultaneously rationalized and reified." Given the non- or pre-rational character of everyday life-praxis, however, this invoked unity remains apocryphal. One cannot simultaneously define rationality as propositional knowledge *and* locate it in the everyday life-world. See *The Theory of Communicative Action*, vol. 1, pp. 363–4, 376, 382.

15   Habermas, "Philosophy as Stand-In and Interpreter", in *Moral Consciousness and Communicative Action*, tr. Christian Lenhardt and Shierry Weber Nicholson (Cambridge, MA: MIT Press, 1990), pp. 1–2. (In these and subsequent citations the translation has been slightly altered for purposes of clarity.) The essay was presented as a lecture at a Hegel congress in 1981 and appeared first as the opening chapter in Habermas, *Moralbewusstsein und kommunikatives Handeln* (Frankfurt-Main: Suhrkamp, 1983).

16   *Moral Consciousness and Communicative Action*, pp. 2–4.

17   *Moral Consciousness and Communicative Action*, p. 7. As example of a "minimalist" strategy combining some Kantian and Hegelian features, the essay singles out the "genetic structuralism" of Jean Piaget whose emphasis on "formal operations" is said to reflect Kantian teachings while his developmental scheme reflects Hegelian elements (p. 8).

18   *Moral Consciousness and Communicative Action*, pp. 9–10.

19   *Moral Consciousness and Communicative Action*, pp. 12–13. The critique of the various modes of "farewell" is continued and further elaborated in *The Philosophical Discourse of Modernity*. In my view, Habermas's treatment of these perspectives is in many respects highly questionable. Without entering into details, I merely note that the opposition between metascientific and edifying types of philosophy finds a parallel in Habermas's own bifurcation between formal rationality and non-rational action and especially between "system" and "life-world." For a critical review of *The Philosophical Discourse of Modernity* see my *Margins of Political Discourse* (New York: SUNY Press, 1989), pp. 39–72.

20   *Moral Consciousness and Communicative Action*, p. 15.

21   *Moral Consciousness and Communicative Action*, pp. 15–16.

22   *Moral Consciousness and Communicative Action*, p. 16.

23   *Moral Consciousness and Communicative Action*, p. 16. Regarding the "underlaborer" conception of philosophy see Peter Winch, *The Idea of a Social Science, and Its Relation to Philosophy* (London: Routledge & Kegan Paul, 1958), pp. 3–7.

24 *Moral Consciousness and Communicative Action*, p. 17.
25 *Moral Consciousness and Communicative Action*, p. 17.
26 *Moral Consciousness and Communicative Action*, pp. 17–19.
27 *Moral Consciousness and Communicative Action*, pp. 18–19. Regarding the problematic status of the "life-world" in Habermas's work compare my "Life-World and Communicative Action" in *Polis and Praxis: Exercises in Contemporary Political Theory* (Cambridge, MA: MIT Press, 1984), pp. 224–53.
28 Habermas, "Does Philosophy Still Have a Purpose?", pp. 1–2. (In these and subsequent citations I have slightly altered the translation for purposes of clarity.) The essay appeared first under the title "Wozu noch Philosophie?" in Habermas, *Philosophisch-politische Profile* (Frankfurt: Suhrkamp, 1971), pp. 11–36. For an earlier translation see "Why More Philosophy?", *Social Research*, vol. 38 (1971), pp. 633–54.
29 "Does Philosophy Still Have a Purpose?", pp. 5–6. While generally critical of Germany's retardation, the essay acknowledged its ambivalent effects regarding modernization: an ambivalence evident in the juncture of a heightened sensitivity for the ills of progress with the felt need to accelerate progress in order not to lag behind other nations or to lapse into archaic regression. Its "oblique stance" toward the process of modernization, Habermas stated (p. 7), rendered German thought "sensitive to both: to the loss of human substance exacted by the forcefully advancing rationalization of conditions in a society still submerged in traditional antagonisms; *and* to the necessity to accelerate this process in a retarded country in order to lessen the lingering barbarism of archaic life-forms profiled against the horizon of *possible* rationalization."
30 "Does Philosophy Still Have a Purpose?", pp. 8, 17–18.
31 *The Theory of Communicative Action*, vol. 1, p. 182. Compare in this context Ronald Beiner's distinction and juxtaposition of "formal" and "substantive" judgment in his *Political Judgment* (Chicago: University of Chicago Press, 1982), pp. 36–7, 44, 103–4. Beiner also speaks sensibly about the "overly rigid dichotomization of the cognitive and the non-cognitive" (or the rational and non-rational) in Kant's philosophy (p. 113): "For Kant, in any cognitive judgment the universal strictly determines subsumption of particulars. Conversely, any notion of judgment that seeks to allow some freedom or leeway in the subsumption of particulars must be non-cognitive." Regarding the prevalence of formal (or procedural) rationality in Habermas's work and its implications see also Giddens, "Reason Without Revolution?", p. 114.
32 The distinction between reason and life-world replicates basically the separation between "discourse" and ordinary communication, or between the "praxis of inquiry" and everyday "life-praxis," mandated in some of Habermas's earlier writings. As he wrote in his "Postscript" (of 1973) to *Knowledge and Human Interests*: "In everyday life-praxis, we

gain and exchange action-related experiences; statements made for the purpose of communicating experiences are themselves actions." By contrast, "given their communicative structure discourses are divorced from the constraints of action; nor do they provide room for processes of *generating* informations. Rather, discourses are immune from action and free from experience." See *Philosophy of the Social Sciences*, vol. 3 (1975), p. 181; also the "Introduction" to *Theory and Practice*, tr. John Viertel (Boston: Beacon Press, 1973), pp. 7–10, 16–19. The contrast between discourse and life-praxis (or between the "a priori of argumentation" and the "a priori of experience") was further fleshed out in Habermas, "Wahrheitstheorien," in Helmut Fahrenbach, ed., *Wirklichkeit und Reflexion* (Pfullingen: Neske, 1973), pp. 211–65. In a more recent text Habermas grants that practical discourses are "less" immune from action than theoretical discourses; but the sense of the "less" is not elaborated. He also maintains that practical life-forms need to accommodate themselves (*entgegenkommen*) to discursive rationality. See *Moral Consciousness and Communicative Action*, pp. 106, 109.

33 Theodor W. Adorno, *Negative Dialectics*, tr. E. B. Ashton (New York: Seabury Press, 1973), pp. 202, 205, 207. Treating *mimesis* as a purely aporetic idea, Habermas writes (*The Theory of Communicative Action*, vol. 1, p. 384): "Unlike Marcuse Adorno no longer strove to extricate himself from this aporia . . . *Negative Dialectics* is both an attempt to circumscribe what cannot be said discursively and a warning against seeking refuge in Hegel in this situation. *Aesthetic Theory* finally seals the surrender of cognitive competence to art in which the mimetic faculty gains objective form." As he adds a bit later (p. 391): "Adorno cannot elucidate the mimetic faculty by means of an abstract contrast to instrumental reason. The structures of reason to which Adorno only *alludes* become only accessible to analysis once the ideas of reconciliation and freedom are deciphered as codes for a form of intersubjectivity, however utopian it may be." According to Habermas, instrumentalism is overcome by a "change of paradigm" from individualism to intersubjective communication, that is, to a situation where reason is shared by a multitude of individuals. However, multiplication by itself does not alter the character of formal or possessive rationality.

34 Maurice Merleau-Ponty, *Phenomenology of Perception*, tr. Colin Smith (London: Routledge & Kegan Paul, 1962), pp. xii–xiii, xx (translation slightly altered); "From Mauss to Claude Lévi-Strauss" (1959), in *Signs*, tr. Richard C. McCleary (Evanston: Northwestern University Press, 1964), p. 122. On the notion of "incarnate reason" see the instructive volume *Leibhaftige Vernunft: Spuren von Merleau-Pontys Denken*, ed. Alexandre Métraux and Bernhard Waldenfels (Munich: Fink Verlag, 1986). In his essay on "Merleau-Ponty und die Postmodernität" contained in that volume, Gary B. Madison remarks

tellingly (p. 182): "What is important for us today is the fact that his [Merleau-Ponty's] properly *postmodern* conception of reason has nothing in common with a *postmodernist* rejection of reason . . . Merleau-Ponty's questioning and dislodging of traditional modern rationalism involves by no means an abandonment of reason or rationality but rather the attempt to develop a new conception of reason, namely, *une raison élargie*."

35 Merleau-Ponty, *The Visible and the Invisible*, pp. 159–60.

36 *The Visible and the Invisible*, p. 130.

37 *The Visible and the Invisible*, p. 274. The "substantive" mode of reasoning invoked above has a close affinity with the notion of "responsive rationality" as articulated by Bernhard Waldenfels in *Ordnung im Zwielicht* (Frankfurt-Main: Suhrkamp, 1987), p. 178. There are also resonances with Heidegger's notion of *Andenken* and with Eric Voegelin's view of reason as an occurrence within "being" (which is never able to exhaust the latter). See Martin Heidegger, *What is Called Thinking?*, tr. J. Glenn Gray (New York: Harper & Row, 1968); Voegelin, "On the Theory of Consciousness", in *Anamnesis*, tr. and ed. Gerhart Niemeyer (Notre Dame: University of Notre Dame Press, 1978), pp. 14–35. Regarding Voegelin and Waldenfels compare my *Margins of Political Discourse*, pp. 73–94, 95–115. One should also note that, of late, Habermas has mellowed somewhat toward the notion of "thinking"; see especially his *Nachmetaphysisches Denken* (Frankfurt-Main: Suhrkamp, 1988).

6

Heidegger and Marxism

To affirm even rapture like a thing . . .

Rilke

In a spirited address to the Society for Phenomenology and Existential Philosophy in 1982, Thomas Sheehan emphasized the need to find "Heidegger's Marx" in a manner akin to the familiar Hegel–Marx sequence.[1] Sentiments along these lines are not infrequently voiced these days, and are commonly traceable to a claimed aloofness or lack of practicality in Heidegger's thought – a defect supposedly remedied through a renewed "Marxist turn." Despite an undeniable remoteness of some Heideggerian formulations, however, several caveats are immediately in order. First of all, Heidegger obviously is not Hegel; whatever improvements seem desirable thus cannot be obtained through a simple repetition of the original Marx. Also, while sympathetic at some level to Hegelian dialectics, Heidegger never embraced an "idealist" system – with the result that post-Heideggerians cannot readily imitate the formula of putting things "right side up" or "back on their feet." Most importantly, the notion of a Heidegger–Marx sequence is unhistorical (and un-Heideggerian) in a glaring sense: it neglects or downplays the rootedness of Marxism in nineteenth-century thought and thus the need of its continuing critical assessment in light of more recent philosophical (including post-Marxist) perspectives. By encouraging this neglect, the suggested sequence wittingly or unwittingly enhances doctrinaire-ideological commitments – and in the end the "sclerosis" of Marxist thought rightly bemoaned by Sartre.[2]

The present chapter seeks to promote a cautious and non-doctrinaire rapprochement, by relying on a number of relevant insights or arguments present in Heidegger's philosophy. While not immune from further development, these arguments (it seems to me) need to be taken seriously on their own terms – prior to, or as a condition for, any possible "Marxist turn." By referring to "relevant" arguments I do not, or not in the first instance, mean Heidegger's overt statements about Marxism – although some of them have received broad publicity and deserve to be mentioned at least briefly. Thus, in the "Letter on Humanism" Heidegger comments, among other things, on the Marxist conception of labor and technology. In order to enter into a "productive dialogue with Marxism," he writes, it is necessary

> to free oneself from naive notions about materialism, as well as from the cheap refutations directed against it. The essence of materialism consists not in the assertion that everything is simply matter but rather in a metaphysical determination according to which every being appears as the material of labor. Now, the modern-metaphysical nature of labor is anticipated in Hegel's *Phenomenology of Spirit* as the self-propelled process of unconditional production, that is, as the objectification of reality through man experienced as subjectivity. The essence of materialism is concealed in the essence of technology, about which much has been written but with little reflection.[3]

While closely linking materialism and technical production, Heidegger in another context stresses Marxism's necessarily truncated understanding of this linkage. Regarding the possibility of grasping the "essence of technology" he remarked in 1970: "In my view this cannot happen as long as one remains philosophically on the level of the subject–object correlation – which means that on Marxist premises the essence of technology cannot be understood."[4]

Although important and rich with implications, statements of this kind are too scattered and fragmentary (I believe) to permit a coherent assessment of Heideggerian philosophy and its relevance to Marxist and post-Marxist thought. To facilitate the proposed rapprochement, a broader type of inquiry seems to me required: one which examines this philosophy in its extensive sweep, including facets not overtly or directly related to Marxism or to social-political issues as such. In the following I intend to focus on four major thematic domains or problem areas: first, the notion of Marxism as a "dialectical" or else a "historical materialism"; secondly, the Marxist conception of "labor" and "production"; thirdly, the relationship between "base" and "superstructure," especially to the extent that this correlation implies a causal determinism; and lastly, the thesis of the "withering away" of the State and of class domination in favor of the inauguration of a "classless" society or the so-called "reign of freedom."[5]

I

According to a handy formula, officially sanctioned at one time in socialist countries, Marxism can be defined as a "dialectical materialism" (abbreviated as "diamat"). At least since the days of Lukács, dispute has raged over the respective advantages and disadvantages of the expressions "dialectical" and "historical materialism" – with the first phrase carrying universal-cosmological and the second more restricted or "humanist" connotations. For present purposes my concern is not with settling this dispute but only with a clarification of terminology. Turning to the noun of the official formula, it is obvious that the term "materialism" is rife with philosophical quandaries and difficulties. According to the First Thesis on Feuerbach, the defect of traditional "materialism" resided in its objectivism, that is, in its tendency to construe "the thing, reality" only "in the form of the object" and not as "human sensuous activity or praxis." Heidegger's cited formulation (in the "Letter on Humanism") finds the core of materialism not in "the assertion that everything is simply matter" but rather in the "metaphysical determination according to which every being appears as the material of labor." Neither of these comments, however, fully elucidates the status of "matter" and thus of materialism. While Marx's Thesis leaves opaque the relationship between "thing" and "activity," Heidegger's statement – despite the shift to technology – still presents "every being as material" and thus ultimately as matter in the process of instrumental production. Moreover, as can hardly be doubted, the linkage between materialism and objectified or "reified" matter has played a prominent role in the history of Marxism, particularly during the sway of scientism under the aegis of the Second and Third International. Echoing the complaints of many observers (including "critical" Marxists), Lukács at one point speaks of a "vulgar Marxism" which not only shares but pushes to the limit the proclivity of bourgeois sciences toward objectification of the world.[6]

   In view of this historical background and the persistent lure of reification, a renewed philosophical investigation of such terms as "matter" or "thing" appears urgently desirable. As is well known, Heidegger's philosophy has made this theme a domain of continuing inquiry and concern; in fact, efforts to recast the traditional notion of the "thing" can be seen as an Ariadne thread linking different phases of his work. During the early phase the "thing" – styled as "being-at-hand" – was still loosely inserted into the framework of empiricist epistemology: one of the chief aims of *Being and Time* (1927) was the endeavor to differentiate human existence or *Dasein* from both "being-at-hand" and "being-to-hand," that is, from the domains of objects and practical utensils. The subsequent decade, however, saw resolute strides beyond the confines of a purely anti-positivist dichotomy or trichotomy. An important role in this development must be accorded to the essay on "The Origin of the Work of Art" (1936). The first part of the essay was specifically entitled "Thing and Work" and discussed three traditional conceptions: first, the thing as substance endowed with properties (or "accidents"); secondly, the thing as the unity emerging from sense impressions; and lastly, the thing as formed matter. According to Heidegger, all three conceptions were deficient and basically unable to yield access to the "thing." The definition of the thing as substance-plus-accidents was misleading precisely because of its deceptive simplicity: "This current thing-concept, to be sure, always and everywhere seems to fit everything; nevertheless, its grasp does not reach the thing in its own being but rather attacks or assaults it."[7] Similar objections applied to the sensualist approach.

> The now mentioned thing-concept implies not so much an assault upon the thing as rather the inordinate attempt to bring it into the greatest possible proximity to us; but a thing never obtains that closeness as long as we identify its "thingly" feature with sense impressions. Whereas the first interpretation keeps the thing, as it were, at arm's length from us, thus placing it too far off, the second makes it impinge too directly upon us; in both versions the thing vanishes.[8]

Regarding the third definition the essay portrayed "form" and "matter" (or content) as "the most hackneyed concepts under which anything and everything may be subsumed" – as the history of metaphysics demonstrates: "Thus the construal of thinghood as form–matter correlation – in either its medieval or Kantian-transcendental guise – has become customary and self-evident; but this does not make it any less than the other interpretations an encroachment or assault upon the thing-being of the thing."[9]

From Heidegger's perspective the task was not to blend into a reified world by abandoning reflection, but rather to rethink, or initiate a new reflection on, the nature of thinghood. In the pursuit of this aim, he wrote, "only one element is needful: namely, by bracketing all the preconceptions and encroachments of the above modes of thought, to leave or respect the thing in its thing-being." This appears to be a relatively simple and uncomplicated prescription; for what could be "easier than to let a thing be just the being it is?" Yet, appearances in this case are deceptive: "Or does this turn out to be the most difficult of tasks, particularly if such an endeavor – to let a being be as it is – represents the opposite of the indifference that merely turns its back upon beings?"[10] As the essay pointed out, the difficulty was not fortuitous but resulted from the topic under inquiry – the intrinsic elusiveness of thinghood:

> The inobtrusive thing evades the grasp of thought most stubbornly. Or could it be that precisely this reticence of the mere thing, this unhurried self-sufficiency, belongs to the very nature of the thing? In this case, must not the alien and uncommunicative feature in the nature of the thing become familiar or accustomed to a reflective thought that attempts to think the thing?[11]

Beyond these and similar queries, however, the discussed essay did not fully pursue the investigation of thinghood: given the essay's focus on art-works, things were relevant only indirectly through their incorporation into "works" – an incorporation reflected in the correlation between "world" and "earth" or between open meaning-horizons and thing-like enclosure. In the words of the essay's concluding section: "What, in an objectified work, looks like thinghood in the sense of traditional thing-concepts, is actually the earth-quality of the work . . . The central guidepost for the interpretation of the thing-being of things must focus on their belonging to, or embeddedness in, the earth."[12]

Further and more concerted advances toward a rethinking of the topic can be found in Heidegger's postwar writings – for example, in the essays entitled "The Thing" (1950) and "Building Dwelling Thinking" (1951). The former essay resumes or recapitulates the critique of traditional thing-concepts, concentrating particularly on the identification of things with "beings-at-hand" and "beings-to-hand," that is, with reified objects and practical utensils. Closely connected with the focus on utensils and instrumental production, in Heidegger's view, is the subsumption of things under categories like form, model, or "idea"; overtly or covertly, he notes, these categories reflect the artisan's outlook: "But what (for instance) a vessel of a certain shape *is* as this jug, what and how the jug *is* as this jug-thing – this is something we can never learn, let alone think properly, by looking at the appearance of *idea*" (after the manner of Plato and his followers). While broadly aimed at Western metaphysics, the critique of objectivism or objectification is directed more specifically against modern science and its pretense to have unlocked the riddle of thinghood through its analysis of matter and material (or atomic) particles. "Science," Heidegger retorts, "always encounters only what *its* kind of representation has admitted beforehand as a possible object for science . . . Thus, science reduces the jug-thing to a nonentity by not granting to things their genuine reality." Though compelling in its own sphere, that of objects, scientific analysis for Heidegger has "annihilated things as things long before the atom bomb exploded. That explosion is only the grossest of all gross confirmations of the long-standing annihilation of the thing: confirmation that the thing as a thing remains nil."[13]

Heidegger's essay treats the thing neither as an object, nor as a fabricated utensil, nor even directly as matter, but rather initially as something elusive and inconspicuous. In the case of the jug, for example, he detects thinghood first of all in its "emptiness," its capacity to receive and hold liquid. "The emptiness or void," we read, "is what performs the vessel's task of holding. Thus, the empty space, this nothingness in the jug, reveals what the jug *is* as the holding vessel . . . The vessel's thing-being does not lie at all in the material of which it consists, but in the void that holds." In Heidegger's usage, the term "holding" has the double meaning of receiving or taking and keeping and retaining; their unity, however, is determined by the purpose of the jug, namely, "the outpouring (of liquid) for which the jug is fitted as a jug." Outpouring in turn is a manner of giving (note the affinity in German between "*Ausschenken*" and "*Schenken*"). Thus, the essay can say that "the nature of the holding void is gathered in the giving" or in the "poured gift." More generally, Heidegger detects the essence of the thing in a kind of "gathering" or "assembly" – a view gaining etymological support from Old High German: "Our language denotes what a gathering is by an ancient word; that word is: thing" (or "*dinc*"). Against this background it becomes, at least linguistically, feasible to assert that "the thing things" in the sense that "thinging gathers." It is in specifying further the character of this gathering that Heidegger introduces one of the central concepts of his later thought: the so-called "fourfold" (*das Geviert*). The liquid in the jug, for instance, may be water or wine; in both, however, a certain gathering is at work. For in the water of the spring "dwells the liaison or marriage of sky and earth; it also dwells in the wine yielded by the fruit of the vine, the fruit in which the earth's nourishment and the sky's sun are wedded to one another." Simultaneously, the jug's liquid may be a thirst-quenching drink or else a religiously consecrated libation. In this manner the jug gathers or assembles the "unity of the four": "The giving involved in outpouring is a gift because it assembles and holds together earth and heaven, mortals and immortals." Heidegger at this point also designates the mentioned fourfold as "world," adding: "If we let the thing happen in its 'thinging' [or gathering] out of the 'worlding' world, then we think of the thing as thing." Similarly the essay "Building Dwelling Thinking" portrays a bridge as a thing in the sense of a particular mode of gathering: "The bridge gathers in *its own way* earth and sky, mortals and immortals . . . The bridge then is a thing –

and it is such *as* the gathering of the mentioned fourfold."[14]

As it seems to me, Heidegger's elaborations on thinghood cast a new (and non-objectivist) light on the concept of matter and thus on the Marxist notion of materialism.[15] A similar ferment or fermenting effect is contained in his views on "dialectics" (and its role in "dialectical" materialism). As is well known, Heidegger's arguments on this topic – and more generally his attitude toward the Hegelian legacy – are surrounded by considerable controversy. As in the case of Kant and Schelling, Heidegger's opus at many points shows a keen attentiveness to Hegel's philosophy – while simultaneously distancing itself from the latter's idealist metaphysics. Without trying to do justice to this complex relationship I limit myself here to a few central points. Heidegger's favorable disposition toward dialectics – or a certain kind of dialectics – is evident in his lectures on *Schelling's Treatise on the Essence of Human Freedom* (1936). Commenting on the general meaning of the term, the lectures describe dialectics as the transcendence of "ordinary common sense," an outlook which refuses to grasp that something "is what it is, a distinct being, only in differentiation from something else." As Heidegger observes, there cannot be "a genuine philosophy as long as this immaturity or blindness is not overcome. The overcoming of common sense is the first step into philosophy." From this perspective, he adds, all the "decisive statements in philosophy" are ultimately dialectical – provided the term is understood in the "broad but basic" sense that something "can be grasped in its essence only in its mediation through something else." Dialectical in this fashion, for example, is Parmenides' phrase according to which "thinking and being" are the same (the same precisely in their difference); in a like manner dialectical are Plato's claim that "nonbeing is being," or Hegel's thesis that "I am the thing and the thing is me," or finally Heidegger's own assertion that "being" is or implies "nothingness."[16]

The same lectures, however, also caution immediately against a scholasticism or dogmatic fixation of dialectics. Severed from the mentioned initial step beyond *doxa*, they note, dialectics turns

> from a genuine means of philosophical insight into its corruption. From the fact that the essence of being is "dialectical" in the specified sense it does *not* necessarily follow that the proper method of philosophy must in every case be dialectics; rather, where the latter is treated and used only superficially as a technique of thought, it becomes a seduction and a source of embarrassment.[17]

Heidegger's critique of a canonical dialectics, incidentally, extends even to some of its uses in German idealist philosophy. Commenting on Schelling's philosophical system – in a manner which seems equally applicable to Hegel – he asserts that as long as this system exists only "in thought" or in the mind unmediated by being, then being "as the 'otherness' of the system remains excluded from it – with the result that the system in its totalizing ambition is no longer truly system." Statements of this kind clearly point beyond traditional formulas of dialectics as they have been absorbed in Marxism and neo-Marxism, including the tripartition of thesis–antithesis–synthesis and the focus on conceptual "totality" or "totalization." More sharply put, the statements (I believe) can be seen as part of Heidegger's endeavour to sublate (*aufheben*) traditional dialectics in the direction of a post- or "hyperdialectical" kind of dialectics.[18]

The move toward post-dialectics is paralleled in Heidegger's work by a post-historicist treatment of history and temporality. Contrary to widespread allegations (especially on the part of rationalist critics) history or "historicity" in his treatment is by no means synonymous with "historicism," nor with the notion of a linear teleology. The endeavor to demarcate his position from historicism is a frequent theme in his writings. Thus, one of his seminars on Schelling (1941) insists that thinking must be radical and original enough "so as not to lose itself in past epochs in order to distill from them lessons for our time and to adapt them to present needs. The former distillation or calculation is the essence of 'historicism', the latter adaptation is what we mean by 'actualism'; both belong together." Genuine historicity from Heidegger's perspective is not simply a string of events but a dimension permeated by an ontological "mission" or destiny (*Geschick*), that is, by the interplay of disclosure and concealment of being. In the assessment of a competent observer, this interplay is not compatible with a linear teleology in the sense of a "historical continuum" – including the continuum typically postulated by adherents of "historical" materialism.[19] The denial of teleology does not reduce history to a chaotic assembly of facts nor to a story of progressive decline; rather, what the move entails is a complex combination of unity and diversity, continuity and discontinuity – a conception echoed in the arguments of several contemporary thinkers. For present purposes I merely allude to Michel Foucault in whose work history and its status occupies a prominent place. As he writes in *Language, Counter-Memory, Practice*:

An entire historical tradition (theological and rationalistic) aims at dissolving the singular event into an ideal continuity – as a teleological movement or a natural process. "Actual" or concrete history, however, deals with events in terms of unique characteristics and acute manifestations . . . We want historians to confirm our belief that the present rests upon profound

intentions and immutable necessities. But the true historical sense confirms our existence among countless lost events, without fixed coordinates
or points of reference.[20]

II

I turn now to the second thematic context: that of "labor" and "production." As indicated, Heidegger's "Letter on Humanism" finds the core
of Marxism in the proposition that all reality is ultimately "the material
of labor" – where labor signifies a "self-propelled process of unconditional production" or fabrication which culminates in modern technology.
As a counterpoint to this focus on fabrication Heidegger's philosophy
articulates not only the avenue of "recollective thinking," but also the
alternative of a non-instrumental type of action – a type which, deviating
from both individual and collective (or intersubjective) designs, can best
be described as an "ontological" or ontologically motivated praxis. The
change in the meaning of action is accompanied by a corresponding transformation of the notion of "production" or "mode of production," in the
sense that the accent is shifted from an economic-instrumental process
to a broader ontological kind of production, that is, to an endeavor of
"bringing forth" (*poiesis*) or "putting to work" the disclosure of being.
   The mentioned changes were only loosely sketched but not really developed in *Being and Time* and other works of Heidegger's early phase. In
Being and Time the theme of "action" or "praxis" was discussed primarily
in connection with the topic of "resoluteness" (*Entschlossenheit*) – but
without any ambition to formulate a coherent view of the theme.[21] The
elaboration of a non-instrumental and non-subjective notion of praxis
occurred primarily during the following decade. The essay on "The
Origin of the Work of Art" finds the source of art-works – and of works
in general – in the happening or disclosure of being, and the core of
creative production (*Schaffen*) in the instantiation or implementation of
this disclosure. As Heidegger points out, a "work" is always something
"worked up" or creatively produced, with the result that an investigation
of the status of works necessarily implies an inquiry into the nature of
creative production. "We think of creation as a displaying or bringing
forth," he notes. "But such a 'bringing forth' is also involved in the making of equipment or utensils," that is, in fabrication. Thus, the question
arises: "What is the criterion distinguishing 'bringing forth' as creation
from 'bringing forth' in the mode of fabrication?" According to the essay,
the demarcation resides basically in the distinction between "work" and
"equipment" (*Zeug*): "The nature of creation is determined by the nature

of the work. Even though the work's createdness is linked to its creation, nevertheless both createdness and creation must be defined in terms of the work-being of the work." For Heidegger, however, works involve a disclosure of the "truth of being," and correspondingly creation or the genesis of works denotes "a mode of the becoming and happening of truth." More pointedly phrased: "Where bringing forth explicitly yields the openness of being or truth, that which is brought forth is a work. This kind of bringing forth is the emblem of creative production [*Schaffen*]."[22]

Corroborating and amplifying this central criterion, the essay pinpoints the distinction between creation and fabrication also in several other ways; one of these has to do with the correlation of "world" and "earth." Whereas, in the case of works, the earth is an integral partner in the interplay with the meaning-horizons of the world, fabrication merely manipulates and exploits the earth and its products. "Truth (of being)," we read, "occurs only as the conflict between disclosure and concealment in the interplay of world and earth. Truth wants to be established or 'put to work' in this conflict between world and earth."[23] The demarcation from utensils resides basically in the status assigned to the earth in its various forms:

> In the creation of works, the conflict or rift must be implanted into the earth; the latter must itself be displayed and used as the domain of reticent self-enclosure. However, this use does not misuse or "use up" the earth as a mere stuff or material, but rather emancipates it to perform its integral role. Such usage of the earth means "working" with it.[24]

By contrast, fabrication of utensils never implies directly a "happening of truth"; rather, production in this case is finished when some material has been made "ready for use," at which point the material is "used up in its utility." Another means of differentiating the two modes of behavior concentrates on the function of purposive planning and means–ends calculations. In Heidegger's perspective, creative production is not simply a purposive activity rooted in authorial designs.

> The emergence of createdness from the work does not mean that the work is to publicize its author, that is, its having being created by a great artist . . . It is not the "*N.N. fecit*" that is to be made known; but rather the simple "*factum est*" is to be openly displayed in the work: more precisely, the fact that unconcealment of being has happened here and is constantly happening anew.[25]

Particularly in discussing the work-character of poetry Heidegger denounces the pretensions of subjective "creativity" or personal genius, pretensions characteristic of modern aesthetics. "Modern subjectivism", he writes, "immediately misconstrues creation by portraying it as the genial act of the sovereign subject."[26]

The mentioned differentiation is further buttressed in another work of the same period: the lectures on *Schelling's Treatise on the Essence of Human Freedom*. Juxtaposing creative production (*Schaffen*) to fabrication or instrumental "making," the lectures bemoan the confusion generally surrounding the character of production and creation: "Either one conceives creation as the fabrication by an artisan who makes or constructs things (as utensils) . . . or else one views things purely as targets of theoretical analysis and tries to determine how, under such auspices, they are independent from the observing subject as objects." Countering these interpretations Heidegger affirms – echoing in large measure Schelling's teachings: "The being of things is a becoming; therefore, createdness does not signify being fabricated, but rather participating in creation as an ongoing becoming." Enhancing the contrast to fabrication, another passage remarks: "What vitiates the conception of creative production as a making is the fact that such production does not serially juxtapose a producer on the one hand and a product on the other; rather, the creative agency in the creative process is itself transformed into a created work in which it remains continually present."[27]

To round out discussion of this theme I turn briefly to some of Heidegger's postwar writings. Particularly well known in this context is the "Letter on Humanism" and its somewhat provocative opening lines: "We are still far from pondering the nature of action carefully enough. We view action only as causing an effect; the actuality of the effect is estimated in terms of its utility. But the essence of action is accomplishment" (or bringing forth fully, *Vollbringen*). According to the Letter, genuine action is by no means synonymous with fabrication or purposive-instrumental designs. Rather: "To accomplish means to unfold something into the fullness of its essence, to lead it forth into this fullness – *producere*. Therefore only what already is can really be accomplished; but what 'is' above all is being."[28] The same Letter establishes a close linkage between accomplishment – seen as an "ontological" mode of praxis – with recollective or commemorative thinking (*Andenken*), a thinking sharply differentiated both from objectifying theoretical analysis and from subjective-intentional activity. Such thinking, we read,

> exceeds all theoretical observation because it tends to the light or clearing in which observation as *theoria* becomes possible in the first place . . . In this manner thinking is a doing – but a doing that surpasses all (subjective)

praxis. Thinking transgresses such action and fabrication not through the grandeur of its achievement nor through its effective repercussions, but through the modesty of its inconsequential accomplishment.[29]

The essay entitled "The Question Concerning Technology", written almost a decade later, portrays accomplishment more explicitly as a "bringing forth" or "pro-duction" which, in turn, is interpreted in the ontological light of the Greek term "*poiesis.*" "It is of crucial importance," Heidegger writes, "that we think 'bringing-forth' in its full scope and at the same time in the sense in which the Greeks thought it," namely, as *poiesis*. The central feature of *poiesis*, however, is the embeddedness of this kind of praxis in the happening and disclosure of being: "Bringing-forth brings out of concealment into unconcealment. Thus, bringing-forth happens only insofar as something concealed comes or emerges into unconcealment; this latter emergence is the basic mark of what we call disclosure (of being)."[30]

III

The third thematic area revolves around the relation between "base" and "superstructure," a relation commonly construed by Marxists in terms of a causal determinism (irrespective of whether the base is said to be determining in the first, second, or last instance). In this respect attention must initially be given to Heidegger's critique of causality seen as a metaphysical principle – a critique which is a recurrent topic in many of his works. In the words of a lecture series of 1930: "In the customary understanding of being – both in common opinion and in traditional metaphysics – causality functions as the basic category of the being of reality" (or beings-at-hand). This role surfaces even in Kant's various formulations of the nature of human freedom where every time "the problem is placed under the aegis of the category of causality" (a special, "noumenal" causality, to be sure), without this category itself being subjected to a "radical inquiry into its ontological premises."[31] A more thoroughgoing examination of causality is contained in a lecture series of the postwar period entitled *Der Satz vom Grund* (1955–6). The series characterizes Kant in essence as a philosopher of causality who identified cause or "ground" (*Grund*) basically with transcendental or *a priori* "conditions of possibility":

The phrase regarding "a priori conditions of possibility" is the *leitmotiv* which permeates Kant's entire opus . . . These a priori conditions of possibility furnish the grounding matrix which circumscribes and offers a full delimitation of the essence of nature and freedom. What is disguised behind the formula "a priori conditions of possibility" is the operation of sufficient reason, of the *ratio sufficiens*, which as *ratio* coincides with pure reason.[32]

According to Heidegger, however, Kant's conception of sufficient reason is part and parcel of objectifying theoretical analysis and thus of traditional metaphysics; his transcendental method "marks the immanence of subjectivity, that is, the kind of theorizing in which objects find their sufficient reason or ground as objects of representational thought."[33]

The chief aim of the cited lecture series is to translate the "Satz vom Grund" or principle of sufficient reason from the idiom of causality or causal determinism into a different idiom or (musical) "key." "What is involved in the notion of a change of key," we read, "is the cross-over from the 'Satz vom Grund' construed as a principle about ontic beings to the same phrase seen as a statement about being. Cast in a both recollective and anticipative light the phrase indicates a 'Satz' in the sense of a leap." The main consequence of the mentioned cross-over or leap is the transposition of thinking from a calculative-explanatory level to a more meditative-ontological plane, a plane yielding access to the intimate linkage between being and "ground." As Heidegger states: "In tuning in to the second or new key, we no longer place being under ontic-empirical auspices but rather conceive it as being and as ground: that is, not as *ratio*, nor as cause, nor even as reason or principle of (sufficient) reason, but as a gathering mode of disclosure." As used in the lectures, one should note, the term "ground" is not synonymous with foundation or foundational support – which would reduce it to a derivative and explicable phenomenon; devoid of antecedent scaffolds, ground actually coincides with "groundlessness" or abyss (*Ab-grund*), although not in the sense of a simple vacuum: "To the extent that being means grounding, and only to that extent, can one say that it is groundless." In a different formulation, the cross-over into the new key signifies a change from the causal-explanatory genre of "because" to the epic-narrative genre of "since." "'Because' and 'since' have different connotations," we are told. "'Because' and 'why' [*warum*] are terms dominating the question of sufficient reason; 'since' [*weil*], by contrast, responds by pointing to the ground. 'Because' inquires about reason, while 'since' furnishes a grounding."[34]

Does the shift to the new key or to the narrative genre still permit us to speak of a correlation between "base" and "superstructure"? In my view, the vocabulary can loosely be maintained – provided the constituent elements are wrenched out of the framework of a causal determinism (as well as a reciprocal functional dependence). In several of his writings, Heidegger offers suggestive clues pointing toward a different type of mutual relationship; one example is the discussion of the interplay between "world" and "earth" in "The Origin of the Work of Art". According to the essay, this interplay involves not so much an ontic-empirical juxtaposition as rather a qualitative-ontological contest or "strife"; the distinctive achievement of art-works (and of works in general) is their ability not simply to terminate but to sustain the strife and ultimately to reconcile the contesting partners in a heterogeneous harmony. World, the essay states, "is not the mere collection of countable or uncountable, familiar and unfamiliar existing things"; rather, the term denotes the non-subjective horizon of experience, the "self-disclosing openness of the broad paths of the simple and essential decisions in the destiny of a historical people." By contrast, earth is "the reticent, unhurried display of a mode of permanent self-seclusion or sheltering." Thus, "world and earth are essentially different from one another and yet are never separated: world grounds itself on the earth, while earth juts through the world." The antagonism between world and earth results not from willful designs but from basic ontological dispositions: "In resting upon the earth, world strives to surmount it; as disclosing openness, it cannot endure anything secluded. On the other hand, earth in its mode of sheltering tends to embrace and harbor the world in its own ambiance." In Heidegger's presentation, the relationship eludes the scheme of causal or functional dependence – because neither partner is a sufficient reason for the existence of the other; nor can the interplay be adequately grasped in traditional-dialectical categories – since earth is not the "antithesis" of world nor their eventual reconciliation a mere conceptual "synthesis" (but rather a concrete "work"): "The work-being of the work consists in the enactment of the strife between world and earth. It is because the strife achieves its culmination in the simplicity of mutual intimacy that this enactment yields the unity of the work . . . The serene repose of a work at peace with itself reflects the intimacy of the strife."[35]

Another example of a non-causal, ontological relationship can be found in the lectures on *Schelling's Treatise on the Essence of Human Freedom*. Elaborating on Schelling's general metaphysical perspective, Heidegger in these lectures comments on the paired categories of "ground" and "existence" – and proceeds to reformulate their connection along the lines of an ontological "difference" or "juncture of being" (*Seynsfuge*). "Ground" in this context basically denotes a dynamically revised version of "earth" (in the sense just outlined), while "existence" is a synonym for open meaning-horizons or else for a "clearing" (*Lichtung*) in the midst of a dense forest or underbrush. "Ground," the lectures state, "is what sustains self-disclosing appearance and maintains it in its grasp. Existence, on the other hand, is self-transcendence and manifestation – a movement which is based on the ground and explicitly confirms the latter as *its* ground. Ground and existence belong together; only their linkage renders possible their separation and strife – which in turn yields a higher harmony."[36] As in the case of the pairing of "world" and "earth," the linkage between "ground" and "existence" has the character neither of a causal or functional dependence nor of a dialectical-logical antithesis; as participants in the "unfolding" of being (as seen by Schelling), the two terms are paired rather in the mode of an "intertwining" or ontological "difference" – where the role of both partners is predicated on a reciprocal "letting be."

> The ground's gravity is what weighs down and contracts and, in this contraction, withdraws itself. By contrast, light is the clearing, a translucent effusiveness and self-dispersal. However, light only lights or clears up what is in itself opaque, twisted, and covered in darkness; thus, light is predicated on non-light as its ground from which it proceeds in order to manifest itself as light.[37]

IV

I come now to the fourth and final thematic area I wish to discuss here: the thesis of the "withering away" of the State and of the replacement of all modes of domination by a "classless" society and an impending "reign of freedom." As is well known, Marxism maintains a strongly critical stance toward the "State"; at least since Lenin (but not exclusively in Leninist thought) the State is construed as an instrument of class domination – a construal applicable even to the aftermath of the "revolution," that is, to the period of the "dictatorship of the proletariat"; only the transition to full-fledged "communism" is said to usher in the dismantling or withering away of the State and the unlimited sway of human freedom.[38] What surfaces behind these tenets (it seems fair to point out) is a basically "negative" conception not only of the State but of political power and of politics in general – a conception according to which "power" invariably coincides with exploitation and repression and thus stands in antithesis to "freedom" by which it is finally conquered. Scant attention to contemporary theorizing suffices, however, to show the restrictiveness of this outlook. Thus, in a string of publications (from *The*

Human Condition over *On Revolution* to *On Violence*), Hannah Arendt has pointed to the positive or constructive aspects of politial "power" as differentiated from repressive "violence"; a more thoroughgoing attack on the repressive model – the identification of power with repression "from above" – has been launched by Michel Foucault in some of his later works.[39] As it seems to me, similar arguments, though advanced on a more philosophical-ontological level, can also be found in Heidegger's writings – as particularly Hermann Mörchen has shown in his study entitled *Power and Domination in the Thought of Heidegger and Adorno*.

In Mörchen's view, the issue of power is not merely "a special topic but rather a central, though hitherto virtually neglected ingredient in Heidegger's thought." Starting from *Being and Time*, Heidegger's entire opus is said to be permeated by a persistent "critique of domination" – a critique which, though directed against repressive constraints, does not simply negate power understood as an enabling potency or empowerment. In *Being and Time* the critical thrust is aimed chiefly at empiricist reification: more specifically at the predominance of objectified "beings-at-hand" to the detriment of the enabling role of being. As an antidote to this predominance – which is closely linked with the "dictatorship" of "the They" (*das Man*) and the "spell" of chatter – the study mobilizes the counterforce of "conscience" as well as the category of "care" or "solicitude" which is claimed to "govern" human *Dasein*. In the domain of human intersubjectivity (*Mitsein*), *Being and Time* juxtaposes a repressive type of care, called "meddling-domineering solicitude," to a more generous and enabling mode styled as "anticipative-emancipatory" care. In the first case, Heidegger notes, the fellow being is reduced to a "dependent and dominated individual," even though domination "may be silent or covert and undetected by its victim." By contrast, the second type does not so much meddle or interfere in the other's life as it seeks to anticipate his "existential possibility of being – with the aim not of relieving him of care but of properly handing it over to him." This latter type – which, Heidegger adds, is "genuine care in that it involves the other's existence and not merely a particular topic of worry" – basically helps the fellow being "to acquire self-transparency and thus to become *free* for the solicitation of care."[40]

The notion of the "counterforce" of conscience and care, it is important to note, points to an ontological kind of potency which, as endowment of being, is not simply available to human manipulation and thus may also be described (in human terms) as a mode of powerlessness or "non-power" (*Ohnmacht*). This linkage of power and non-power surfaces again clearly in Heidegger's critical "reception" of the Nietzschean legacy –

which occurred or gathered momentum particularly during the time of the Nazi regime. As has frequently been observed, Heidegger's attitude toward Nietzsche is basically double-edged: on the one hand, his writings criticize Nietzsche's concept of the "will to power" as an exercise in metaphysics or a metaphysically inspired "will to will"; on the other hand, the same writings protect Nietzsche against biological reductionism and fascist abuse. According to Heidegger, Nietzsche's concept of the "will to power" must be construed not biologically or racially but rather "ontologically"; above all, it furnishes no warrant for fascist brutality or indulgence in violence. "Such interpretations of the 'will to power' in which romanticism and meanness coalesce," he asserts, "basically corrupt the meaning of the key notion of Nietzsche's metaphysics." From Heidegger's perspective, what is at issue in Nietzsche's formula is a distinctive metaphysical construal of being, or of the totality of beings, in light of the guiding category of "will" or "willing."[41] In terms of the Nietzsche lectures (of 1936-7), the formula basically indicates the substantive content of being, just as the concept of "eternal recurrence" pinpoints the mode or manner of being's self-enactment and manifestation:

> As label for the central character of all beings, the phrase "will to power" responds to the question regarding the nature of being. From time immemorial this question is *the* guiding question of philosophy. The phrase "will to power" thus necessarily figures in the title of the chief opus of a thinker who claims that being as such is essentially will to power.[42]

While locating Nietzsche's formula on a properly philosophical plane, Heidegger simultaneously attacks both the focus on will and its metaphysical moorings; as he tries to show, Western metaphysics – and particularly a metaphysics of will – invariably reflects a neglect or oblivion of being (*Seinsvergessenheit*): "Everywhere and always we find manipulative designs – disguised as orderly-prudent management – bent on elevating ontic things to the highest rank while casting being aside." As a remedy or counter-strategy he counsels renewed attentiveness to being and thereby the recovery of an ontological potency which eludes purely human control. "The highest decision which can be reached and which forms the basis of all history," the Nietzsche lectures affirm, "is the decision between the predominance of (ontic) beings and the rule of being." As Mörchen elaborates, Heidegger's notion of ontological "rule" or "power" is intimately linked with his critique of domination – a domination reflected in the thrust of Western metaphysics and especially in the formula of the "will to power." Under etymological auspices,

Heidegger's view of "power" (*Macht*) is said to derive not from manipulation or fabrication (*Machen*) but rather from such terms like potency (*Vermögen*) and enabling possibility (*Möglichkeit*) – terms which adumbrate the dimension of a generative but peculiarly powerless power. "This type of power," Mörchen comments, "is radically different from the usual kind, compared with which it might be called powerlessness or non-power. For, ontological meaning or disclosure is not posited by human will; rather, it is experienced in the attitude of 'not-willing'" or the mode of "serenity" [*Gelassenheit*].[43]

In Heidegger's postwar writings, the dual theme of repressive domination and generative potency recurs in the opposition between "*das Gestell*" and "*das Geviert*" and also in the confrontation between man as "lord" and as "shepherd of being." In commenting on modern technology, Heidegger portrays "*das Gestell*" as a peculiar kind of ontological dominance: a kind accentuating concealment and alienation – but without constituting an inexorable fate; precisely in expanding its global sway, technology is said to generate salvaging resources and thus ultimately to contribute to its own supersession. Mörchen alerts to this oblique "dialectic" by focusing on the aspect of power. "Although devoid of overt power or dominion," he writes, "the 'overcoming' of the *Gestell* uncovers in the latter a hidden or latent potency which, in the midst of technological domination, turns against it." A similar dialectic is also operative in the relationship between human lordship and guardianship as outlined in the "Letter on Humanism". As the Letter observes in a well-known passage: "Man is not the lord of beings; rather, man is the shepherd of being." With this "demotion" from lordship, Heidegger adds, man is in no way diminished or deprived; on the contrary, "he gains by attaining to the truth of being." Metaphorically stated, man "gains the essential poverty of the shepherd, whose dignity consists in being summoned to the task of preserving the truth of being."[44]

Heidegger's views on power and potency are relevant also to the anticipation of the future, "classless" society (or, in classical terms, the attainment of the "good life"). As results from the preceding arguments, the transition to this goal, in his judgment, cannot simply be equivalent to the shift from power and domination to a condition of pure powerlessness or non-power; in particular the so-called "reign of freedom" cannot rashly be divorced from the moorings of ontological potency, but rather requires these moorings as an enabling condition of its possibility. Differently phrased: liberation or emancipation cannot simply be a human "project" subject to manipulative designs, but must be embedded in a generative or enabling process – in such a manner that freedom and power mutually condition and sustain each other. These

observations also have repercussions on the Marxist model of intersubjectivity, to the extent that "communism" denotes a shared way of life
and "classless society" a non-repressive type of human "community."
Heidegger's writings entirely reject the equation of intersubjectivity or
"co-being" with a merger of wills or a homogeneous collectivity; just as
Dasein cannot be reduced to individual subjectivity, community life
from his perspective cannot be identified with a higher type of subjectivism or a "subjectivity-writ-large." As the "Letter on Humanism" asserts
(with a clear edge against dominant ideologies of our age):

> Every nationalism is metaphysically an anthropocentrism and as such sub-
> jectivism. But nationalism is not transcended through a mere interna-
> tionalism; it is rather only expanded and elevated into a system.
> Nationalism is as little elevated to, and submerged in, *"humanitas"* by
> internationalism as individualism is by an ahistorical collectivism; the lat-
> ter is only the subjectivity of men in their totality or of man writ-large.[45]

Moving beyond a purely critical stance, other passages of the period
spell out in greater detail Heidegger's conception of genuine community,
a conception (I believe) Marxists might fruitfully wish to ponder. As
emerges from these passages, co-being for Heidegger is essentially
predicated on mutual recognition – but a recognition which, transcending the narrowly "cognitive" level, involves a reciprocal "letting be" or
acknowledgment of ontological capabilities. Such acknowledgment of
reciprocal potential, moreover, is closely associated with a genuine sympathy or liking (in line with the etymological connection between
"Vermögen" and *"Mögen"*). "We really are capable of doing only what
we are inclined to do, that is, what we care for by letting it be," a lecture
of 1952 notes. "And again, we truly incline toward something only when
it in turn inclines toward us, toward our essential being, by caring for
it. Through this inclination or liking our being is summoned or called
upon."[46] In a similar vein (but with more direct reference to intersubjectivity) the "Letter on Humanism" states:

> To care for a "thing" or a "person" in their essence means: to love or favor
> them. More radically construed, such favoring means to bestow being as
> a gift. Favoring [*Mögen*] of this kind is the proper essence of enabling
> potency [*Vermögen*], a potency which not only can achieve this or that,
> but can let something unfold in its original potential, that is, let it be.
> It is by virtue of the potency of such liking that something is genuinely
> able to be.[47]

NOTES

1 Thomas Sheehan, "Heidegger and Derrida", in Hugh J. Silverman and Don Ihde, eds, *Hermeneutics and Deconstruction* (Albany: SUNY Press, 1985), pp. 201–18. Sheehan portrayed Jacques Derrida as Heidegger's Feuerbach.

2 Jean-Paul Sartre, *Search for a Method*, tr. Hazel Barnes (New York: Knopf, 1963), p. 29. In the same context, Sartre deplored Marxists' unwillingness to learn further or rethink their position (p. 38): "Yes, Lukács has the instruments to understand Heidegger, but he will not understand him; for Lukács would have to *read* him, to grasp the meaning of the sentences one by one. And there is no longer any Marxist, to my knowledge, who is capable of doing this."

3 Martin Heidegger, "Letter on Humanism", in David F. Krell, ed., *Martin Heidegger: Basic Writings* (New York: Harper & Row, 1977), p. 220. The same Letter also speaks of Marx's attentiveness to human alienation (p. 219): "What Marx recognized in an essential and significant sense (though one derived from Hegel) as the estrangement or alienation of man has its roots in the homelessness of modern man . . . Since Marx by experiencing estrangement penetrates into an essential dimension of history, the Marxist view of history is superior to that of other historical accounts."

4 Richard Wisser, ed., *Martin Heidegger in Gespräch* (Freiburg-Munich: Alber, 1970), p. 74. The same volume also contains comments on Marx's "Eleventh Thesis on Feuerbach", to the effect "that a world-change presupposes a change of the understanding or conception of the world and that a world-conception can be gained only through an adequate interpretation of the world" (p. 68). In probing the relationship between Heidegger and Marx, Schweickart presents the Eleventh Thesis as both the supreme value and the truth-criterion of Marxism; styled as the principle of "liberatory praxis," the Thesis is also used as a yardstick against which to measure Heidegger's philosophy – but without sufficient elaboration of the meaning of "liberation" (or freedom) and of "praxis." See David Schweickart, "Heidegger and Marx: A Framework for Dialogue", in Thomas Sheehan, ed., *Heidegger: The Man and the Thinker* (Chicago: Precedent Publ. Co., 1981), pp. 229–43.

5 I do not mean to suggest that Heidegger has been alone in critically addressing or reassessing these topics – only that his comments carry a particular kind of philosophical stringency Nor do I mean to imply that the four chosen topics are the only prominent themes in Marxist theory; other issues (such as the problem of "surplus value") might be singled out, but Heidegger's contribution on this score would seem more elusive.

6 Georg Lukács, *History and Class Consciousness: Studies in Marxist Dialectics*, tr. Rodney Livingstone (Cambridge, MA: MIT Press, 1971), p. 32.

7 Heidegger, "The Origin of the Work of Art", in *Poetry, Language,*

Thought, tr. Albert Hofstadter (New York: Harper & Row, 1971), p. 25. (In this and subsequent citations the translation has been slightly altered for the sake of clarity.)

8   "The Origin of the Work of Art", p. 26.

9   "The Origin of the Work of Art", pp. 27, 30.

10   "The Origin of the Work of Art", p. 31.

11   "The Origin of the Work of Art", pp. 31–2.

12   "The Origin of the Work of Art", p. 69.

13   Heidegger, "The Thing", in *Poetry, Language, Thought*, pp. 168–70. As he adds (p. 170): "That annihilation is so frightening because it carries with it a twofold delusion: first, the notion that science is superior to all other experience in grasping the real in its reality; and second, the illusion that, notwithstanding the scientific investigation of reality, things could still remain things."

14   Heidegger, "The Thing", pp. 153, 169, 172–4; "Building Dwelling Thinking" in *Poetry, Language, Thought*, p. 181. The particularity of the bridge-thing is said to consist in the fact that "it gathers the fourfold in such a way that it provides a site or place for it . . . By this site are determined the localities and pathways through which a space is opened up." For a more detailed treatment compare Walter Biemel, "The Development of Heidegger's Concept of the Thing", *Southwestern Journal of Philosophy*, vol. 11 (Fall 1980), pp. 47–64.

15   This is recognized by Alfred Schmidt when he writes: "If domination of nature is to be curtailed and if human history is to cease being merely a prolonged struggle for survival (natural history), we need a new kind of thinking which allows things to have their own say." See Schmidt, "Herrschaft des Subjekts: Über Heideggers Marx-Interpretation", in *Martin Heidegger: Fragen an sein Werk; Ein Symposion* (Stuttgart: Reclam, 1977), p. 65. In a similar vein Reinhart Maurer comments that only "the non-reified thing permits non-reified relations between human beings." *Revolution und Kehre, Studien zum Problem gesellschaftlicher Naturbeherrschung* (Frankfurt: Suhrkamp, 1975), p. 49.

16   Heidegger, *Schellings Abhandlung Über das Wesen der menschlichen Freiheit (1809)*, ed. Hildegard Feick (Tübingen: Niemeyer, 1971), pp. 95, 98–9.

17   *Schellings Abhandlung*, p. 99.

18   *Schellings Abhandlung*, p. 194. On the notion of "hyperdialectics" compare Maurice Merleau-Ponty, *The Visible and the Invisible*, ed. Claude Lefort, tr. Alphonso Lingis (Evanston: Northwestern University Press, 1968), p. 94.

19   Heidegger, *Schellings Abhandlung*, p. 203; Schmidt, "Herrschaft des Subjekts", p. 64.

20   Michel Foucault, *Language, Counter-Memory, Practice*, ed. Donald F. Bouchard, tr. Bouchard and Sherry Simon (Oxford: Blackwell, 1977), pp. 154–5 (translation slightly altered).

21 See Heidegger, *Sein und Zeit* (11th edn; Tübingen: Niemeyer, 1967), esp. paragraphs 60 and 69. The attempt to derive some kind of action theory from *Being and Time* has been undertaken nonetheless by Gerold Prauss in *Denken und Handeln in Heideggers "Sein und Zeit"* (Freiburg-Munich: Alber, 1977).
22 Heidegger, "The Origin of the Work of Art", pp. 58, 60, 62.
23 "The Origin of the Work of Art", p. 62.
24 "The Origin of the Work of Art", p. 64.
25 "The Origin of the Work of Art", p. 65.
26 "The Origin of the Work of Art", p. 76. The critique of subjectivist aesthetics is pursued at greater length in Hans-Georg Gadamer, *Truth and Method* (2nd rev. edn, tr. and rev. Joel Weinsheimer and Donald G. Marshall (New York: Crossroad, 1989), pp. 42–100.
27 Heidegger, *Schellings Abhandlung*, pp. 157–8, 163.
28 Heidegger, "Letter on Humanism", p. 193.
29 "Letter on Humanism", p. 239.
30 Heidegger, "The Question Concerning Technology" in Krell, ed., *Martin Heidegger: Basic Writings*, pp. 293–4. As Maurer comments (correctly, I think): "Thinking is in itself a mode of doing because it 'lets be', suspending at least temporarily the will to power. But its greatest practical significance resides not in a mere omission but rather in its intimate proximity to being." See *Revolution und Kehre*, p. 47. For a critique of economism or a narrowly economic notion of production compare also Jean Baudrillard, *The Mirror of Production*, tr. Mark Poster (St Louis: Telos Press, 1975).
31 Heidegger, *Vom Wesen der menschlichen Freiheit: Einleitung in die Philosophie* (Frankfurt: Klostermann, 1982), pp. 300, 302.
32 Heidegger, *Der Satz vom Grund* (Pfullingen: Neske, 1957), pp. 125–6.
33 *Der Satz vom Grund*, p. 134.
34 *Der Satz vom Grund*, pp. 70, 151, 184–5.
35 "The Origin of the Work of Art", pp. 44, 48–50.
36 *Schellings Abhandlung*, p. 137.
37 *Schellings Abhandlung*, p. 138. In my synopsis above I use Merleau-Ponty's notion of "intertwining" (or "chiasm") to elucidate the point of Heidegger's and Schelling's arguments; see *The Visible and the Invisible*, pp. 130–55.
38 I do not wish to enter here into the controversy whether class domination is a structural feature of the capitalist mode of production or whether it reflects the interests and inclinations of a ruling class. For some recent literature on the Marxist theory of the State compare Ralph Miliband, *The State in Capitalist Society* (London: Weidenfeld and Nicolson, 1969); Nicos Poulantzas, *Political Power and Social Classes* (London: New Left Books, 1973); J. Holloway and S. Picciotto, eds, *State and Capital: A Marxist Debate* (London: E. Arnold, 1978).
39 See Hannah Arendt, *The Human Condition* (Chicago: University of Chicago Press, 1958); *On Revolution* (New York: Viking Press, 1963); *On Violence* (New York: Harcourt, Brace & World, 1970); also Michel

Foucault, *Discipline and Punish: The Birth of the Prison*, tr. Alan Sheridan (New York: Vintage Books, 1979); *The History of Sexuality*, vol. 1: *An Introduction*, tr. Robert Hurley (New York: Vintage Books, 1980). Regarding Foucault compare Charles Taylor, "Foucault on Freedom and Truth", *Political Theory*, vol. 12 (May 1984), pp. 152–83.

40 Heidegger, *Sein und Zeit*, paragraphs 26–7, 35; Hermann Mörchen, *Macht und Herrschaft im Denken von Heidegger und Adorno* (Stuttgart: Klett-Cotta, 1980), pp. 24–7, 29–30.

41 Heidegger, *Nietzsche*, vol. 3, tr. Joan Stambaugh, David F. Krell, Frank A. Capuzzi, ed. David F. Krell (New York: Harper & Row, 1987), pp. 170, 193, 231; see also Mörchen, *Macht und Herrschaft*, pp. 50–51, 54–7.

42 Heidegger, *Nietzsche*, vol. 1, tr. David F. Krell (New York: Harper & Row, 1979), p. 4.

43 Heidegger, *Nietzsche*, vol. 3, pp. 4–5, 181; Mörchen, *Macht und Herrschaft*, pp. 69, 93–4.

44 Heidegger, "Letter on Humanism", p. 221 (translation slightly altered); Mörchen, *Macht und Herrschaft*, p. 81.

45 "Letter on Humanism", p. 221. For a more detailed discussion of Heidegger's views on intersubjectivity or "co-being" see my *Twilight of Subjectivity: Contributions to a Post-Individualist Theory of Politics* (Amherst: University of Massachusetts Press, 1981), pp. 64–71.

46 Heidegger, ˙Was heisst Denken?", in *Vorträge und Aufsätze* (3rd edn; Pfullingen: Neske, 1967), pt. 2, p. 3.

47 "Letter on Humanism", p. 196.

7

Psychoanalysis and Critical Theory: A Lacanian Perspective

As I understand it, the term "political psychology" seeks to capture the correlation of psyche and polis; instead of simply reducing one dimension to the other, it aims to highlight the peculiar interlacing between psychic drives and social contexts, between inner human "nature" and public institutions or norms. The same ambition, it appears, lies at the heart of psychoanalysis – despite a shift of accent from manifest behavior to latent or covert motivations. Ever since *Civilization and its Discontents*, a central preoccupation of Freud's heirs has been the linkage of instinctual impulses and social constraints, of unconscious "libido" and publicly sanctioned rules. To be sure, psychoanalytic theory does not offer a compact consensus on these matters. In fact, Freudianism in our century has splintered into an array of competing schools – all of them providing a distinct slant on the mentioned correlation. During recent decades, antagonism has prevailed chiefly between spokesmen of libidinal or "id" psychology, on the one hand, and champions of "ego" and "superego" psychology (and facets of "object relations" theory), on the other. In large measure, the conflict centers around the definition of human "nature": with proponents of the two schools stressing unconscious, inner-psychic and moral or interpersonal components respectively.[1] The conflict carries over into conceptions of psychic illness and therapy. While "id" psychologists seek to rescue the individual from the traumatizing or destabilizing effects of society, their opponents see the main goal of therapy in the effort to reintegrate the patient into the world of social norms and public meanings.

It cannot be my task here to sort out the many disputes raging between

This essay was initially presented at the annual meeting of the International Society of Political Psychology in San Francisco in July 1987.

Freud's heirs – a task exceeding not only the confines of one chapter but also the limits of my professional competence. Instead, adopting a more restricted focus, I intend to concentrate on the status and changing fortunes of psychoanalysis in the context of the Frankfurt School. Even within that context I shall not offer a detailed historical narrative but rather highlight salient views of some prominent spokesmen of "critical theory" (notably Adorno, Marcuse, and Habermas). My overall concern here, I should add, is not so much historical or descriptive as theoretical in character – the latter term embracing the fields of both psychoanalytic theory and political theory (and their mutual connection). A crucial, but largely unresolved issue in much psychoanalytic literature involves the relation of "inner" and "outer" domains. Frequently, the libidinal unconscious is treated as a completely internal or privatized sphere, as an "innate" endowment of individuals segregated from interpersonal contacts or social rules. Yet, how plausible is this conception – given that libidinal nature basically precedes or antedates the process of individuation and thus the emergence of subject–object and inner–outer dualisms? A corollary of this issue is the nexus of reason and libido, especially to the extent that the two are construed as polar antipodes. For how can reason (and normative rules) be viewed as entirely alien or external to libidinal nature – without degenerating quickly into unnatural or counter-natural constraints? Conversely, how can libido be entirely privatized and recalcitrant to rules (no matter how embryonic) – without negating the centrality and civilizing effect of language in human life?

Issues of this kind are prominently displayed in the writings of the Frankfurt School. My thesis is that the accent of the school has shifted over time from a relatively "orthodox" Freudianism, stressing libido and instinctual frustrations, to a position more akin to ego- and superego psychology, that is, to an emphasis on normatively regulated interpersonal relations. In the case of Habermas who epitomizes this trend, the change is buttressed by a presumed "paradigm shift" in contemporary thought – namely, the move from an individualist philosophy relying on reflection and "inner" nature to a linguistically informed outlook focusing on interpersonal communication. Although not entirely in agreement with the libidinal stance of the older Frankfurt School, I am troubled by Habermas's progressive weakening of the Freudian legacy and its virtual replacement by theories of cognitive and moral development (patterned on Piaget and Kohlberg). As an antidote to Habermas's approach I shall invoke the neo-orthodoxy of Jacques Lacan whose work instantiates the paradigm shift or "linguistic turn" postulated by Habermas, but without in any way abandoning the insights of Freudian "id" psychology. Accordingly, the middle section of the chapter offers a synopsis of central Lacanian themes or teachings, together with a critical application of these themes to Habermasian developmentalism. In the concluding section I turn to one of Freud's crucial precursors, Friedrich Nietzsche, in an attempt to illustrate the implications of the preceding discussion – namely, by sketching a Lacanian or quasi-Lacanian reading of *The Birth of Tragedy*.

I

A review of the Frankfurt School's treatment of psychoanalysis may usefully – though not lightly – begin with Theodor Adorno. The beginning is appropriate in view of Adorno's grasp of the broad range and tensional character of Freud's legacy; it is also difficult since it means starting *in medias res* and because he was perhaps the most complex, occasionally enigmatic representative of the school. Adorno's involvement with psychoanalysis dates back to an early essay on the "unconscious" and, more importantly, to the first phase of his association with the Frankfurt Institute (during the 1940s) when he actively participated in various social-psychological research projects dealing with prejudice, authoritarianism, and the like. The type of psychoanalysis which Adorno, together with most other members of the institute, embraced at the time was libidinal or "id" psychology, that is, a more or less orthodox version of the Freudian theory of instincts, but *minus* the death instinct. From the vantage of this theory, human behavior – at least in its psycho-biological depth structure – was seen as outgrowth of unconscious libidinal drives or energies, drives which are only precariously channeled by a supervening rational ego and modified or constrained by societal norms internalized in the "superego." The attractiveness of this outlook for critical theory resided in its radical anti-idealism, that is, in its refusal to dissolve the unconscious in rational transparency and to blend psychoanalysis into *Geisteswissenschaft*. In political terms, the Freudian stance entailed that deep-seated drives could be invoked as potential antipodes or countervailing challenges to existing social norms and thus as sources of resistance to societal manipulation. As Adorno wrote in an essay of 1946 which sharply attacked revisionist tendencies to water down or emasculate Freudian libido theory: "Concretely, the denunciation of Freud's so-called instinctivism amounts to the denial that culture, by enforcing restrictions on libidinal and particularly on destructive drives, is instrumental in bringing about repressions, guilt feelings, and need for self-punishment."[2]

As espoused by Adorno at the time, Freudianism thus involved a profound antagonism between drives and social rules or, loosely, between inner and outer domains. To this extent, his outlook clearly showed the imprint of *Civilization and its Discontents* with its bold thematization of the conflict between societal progress and instinctual frustration, between reason and "inner" nature. According to Adorno, this conflict reached its apex in the contemporary period of organized or late capitalism with its large-scale and systematic manipulation of human lives; at this stage, any notion of a harmony or congruence between society and individual happiness was in his view preposterous. As he observed in his "The Revised Psychoanalysis" (of 1946), the merit of Freud consisted precisely in his decision to leave the contradictions between "human nature" and society unresolved, in his refusal "to pretend a systematic harmony when the subject itself is torn."[3] To be sure, in the modern age the restrictions on instinctual nature were not simply externally imposed, but in some measure the result of individual self-restraint. For the sake of advancing his economic interests as well as his religious aspirations, the modern rational subject adopted initially a system of instinctual repression or non-gratification – a system which, in part, forms the basis of the capitalist mode of production. In more general terms, the modern ego – construed along Cartesian lines – was bound to confront the surrounding world as an arena of external objects amenable to control and exploitation, that is, amenable to the dictates of scientific and "instrumental" reason. In the course of time, however, this extension of control carried a price: namely, the progressive subjugation of human inner nature, in the sense that this nature was increasingly alienated from the subject (and thus turned into an internal "foreign territory"). Moreover, the development of organized capitalism steadily transferred the seat of control from the rational ego to anonymous social institutions, to systemic societal forces sedimented in the superego. Thus, the autonomous individual ultimately became the victim of his own designs: the victim of the unleashing of instrumental reason.

In dramatic form, the sketched development constitutes the central theme of *Dialectic of Enlightenment* (of 1947), authored jointly by Max Horkheimer and Adorno. Going back to the roots of Western civilization, the study offers a cost-benefit analysis of Western rationalism and rationalization: an analysis carefully weighing the undeniable advances in scientific knowledge and technological prowess against the losses in terms of human integrity and harmony with inner and outer nature. Streamlined under the auspices of instrumental reason, the authors noted, modern civilization tends to make "the domination of outer and inner nature the absolute goal of life"; rationalization accordingly becomes the motor of a "savage [*verwildert*] self-affirmation or self-maintenance." Although at first launched by the rational ego, the assault on nature progressively rebounds against the individual – in a manner

which links the story of rationalization with the "history of subjectivity."[4] In the authors' words:

> At the moment when man undercuts awareness of his own "nature" (i.e.,
> of himself *as* nature), all purposes of survival – including social progress,
> the cultivation of material and intellectual capacities, and even con-
> sciousness itself – become null and void . . . The domination of man over
> himself which establishes his ego or selfhood means at the same time
> potentially the destruction of the subject in whose service it occurs; for,
> the dominated and repressed substance – dissolved for the sake of
> survival – is nothing but life itself whose maintenance survival is meant
> to promote, that is, the very thing which is supposed to be preserved.[5]

As antidote to progressive self-destruction or self-mutilation accomplished via instrumental survival, *Dialectic of Enlightenment* appealed
to a critical mode of thinking transgressing the bounds of instrumental
reason: a kind of recollective thought in which reason remembers its
rootedness in nature, thus enlightening itself about its own dialectic.
"Through such recollection of nature in the subject," we read, "a recollection containing within itself the ignored truth of all culture, enlightenment is basically opposed to domination."[6]

Recollection of this kind, and its promise of a "reconciliation with
nature," became the consuming focus of Adorno's later thought and
works. Without relinquishing the claims of reason or rationality, his
Negative Dialectics appealed to the rational ego to open itself to radical
"otherness" beyond the confines of instrumental control – to a domain
of "non-identity" transcending rational thought and comprising both
inner and outer nature. Similarly, his *Aesthetic Theory* adumbrated a
mode of creative behavior which – far from subjugating or manipulating
the world – seeks to preserve and recreate "objects" by inserting them in
a series of novel constellations. The chief means of reconciliation in these
works was the endeavor of *"mimesis"* or mimetic rapprochement – a term
denoting neither mere external adaptation nor subjective projection or
invention.[7] Despite its intriguing and immensely suggestive power, one
should note the tensional and deeply antinomial, if not paradoxical,
character of Adorno's later thought: described as an "impulse" and thus
located outside rational cognition, *mimesis* was supposed to serve as a
bridge between consciousness and the unconscious, between reason and
nature; in psychological terms, the category functioned both as an internal or inner-psychic capacity ("impulse") and as a magnet catapulting the
subject toward "otherness." On a more general plane, the same tension
pervades Adorno's conception of "non-identity" or his notion of ego–
other relations. For how can reason or the ego possibly be reconciled and

even correlated with a domain which is defined as radically non-identical or "other" than the rational ego? Does such reconciliation not presuppose a common bond – perhaps something like the bond of "being" or of an ontological happening – which undergirds both consciousness and libido, both reason and non-reason in their mutual difference?[8]

The theme of "reconciliation with nature" was not the exclusive preserve of Adorno but was shared by other members of the early Frankfurt School, most prominently by Herbert Marcuse. Like Adorno, Marcuse relied with slight modifications on orthodox psychoanalysis, that is, on Freudian "id" psychology or libido theory. In his more optimistic moods, he tended to place his hopes for reconciliation entirely in the human instinctual structure – the pent-up potential of "Eros" – while relegating reason and societal norms to a derivative and relatively subordinate status. Whereas Adorno preferred to uphold the stark antinomy of reason and nature, Marcuse at crucial junctures was inclined to suspend or at least relax this tension in favor of libidinal drives defined as man's "inner" or pre-social nature and as harbingers of a transformed or liberated future society. To be sure, this tendency was not uniformly maintained and was subject to dramatic oscillations – to moments when libidinal hopes seemed crushed by the weight of societal, technological domination. In a sense, Adorno's tension thus resurfaces in Marcuse's intellectual biography, as illustrated, for example, in the alternation between the gloomy *One-Dimensional Man* (of 1964) and the more ebullient *Essay on Liberation* (of 1969).[9]

As in the case of Adorno, Marcuse's involvement with psychoanalysis goes back to the early years of his institutional affiliation, to the period when Frankfurt theorists – under Horkheimer's leadership – sought to define the program or basic tenets of the institute under the label of "critical theory." While participating actively in this endeavor, Marcuse from the start gave to critical theory a less social-scientific and more psychological or emotive slant – a slant manifest in the combination of Hegel, Marx, and Freud. In this combination, while Hegel provided basic philosophical premises and Marx concrete social-economic parameters, the importance of Freud consisted in furnishing the actual goal and substantive context of human liberation or emancipation. In Marcuse's portrayal, this goal was human "happiness" defined as instinctual fulfillment or the fulfillment of the demands of inner human nature. Whenever the structure of a given society – particularly the structure of modern capitalist society – conflicted with the striving for human happiness, the structure stood condemned in the eyes of critical theory and had to be changed or amended. As Marcuse wrote in an essay of 1937, entitled "Philosophy and Critical Theory": "Two aspects above all link

(Marxist) materialism with the correct or proper theory of society: the concern with human happiness and the conviction that such happiness can only be achieved through a transformation of the material conditions of human life."[10] Thus, when capitalist society imposed on its members severe deprivations in terms of unemployment or military service (entailing the possible loss of life or limb), the basic principle animating this society was defective and illegitimate and needed to give way to a social formation more conducive to human need satisfaction and self-development.

Regarding Marcuse's psychoanalytic approach, the most important and revealing work is undoubtedly his *Eros and Civilization* (of 1955). Harking back, even in its title, to Freud's *Civilization and its Discontents*, the study depicted modern social developments in terms of a complex balance sheet of human gains and losses. On the one hand, autonomous ego structures and cognitive enlightenment could only emerge as a result of instinctual frustration and of a certain emancipation from inner nature and its guiding "pleasure principle." On the other hand, individual and social rationalization has come to rebound against the ego by extending the control over external nature to individual and social life, thus subjugating libidinal drives increasingly to a rigid "reality principle" wedded to instrumental reason and competitive performance or achievement. While, up to this point, Marcuse's narrative largely coincided with Freud's account, the study proceeded to propose a dramatic dénouement of developmental conflicts and paradoxes – a dénouement which radically departed from Freud's ingrained pessimism. The proposal consisted in the convergence or simultaneity of further rationalization *and* libidinal gratification – a notion predicated on the assumption that economic abundance, accomplished through technological advances, would permit the reduction of societal "surplus repression" and thus the reinvigoration of man's libidinal or erotic potential. Although still channeled by efforts of self-sublimation, this resurgence of the "pleasure principle," in Marcuse's view, would not be limited to the libidinal or unconscious domain, but permeate ego and superego structures as well. In line with an "eroticization of the whole human being," the same resurgence would also promote a strengthening of phantasy and recollection in human thought, thus curbing the predominance of instrumental reason.[11]

Marcuse's hope for a revival of libidinal energies was not limited to the cited study but resurfaced also in his later works – after the more subdued and austere interlude of *One-Dimensional Man*. Thus, his *Essay on Liberation* pinned the expectation of further human emancipation on the potency of frustrated or repressed cultural and aesthetic needs – needs ignored by contemporary capitalist society preoccupied exclusively with vulgar consumption rather than the quality of life. Similarly, his *Counter-revolution and Revolt* (1972) detected, even in the face of the pervasive cooptation of the working class and the "technostructure of exploitation" muffling dissent, the potential of social transformation rooted in unfulfilled moral and aesthetic needs, in demands for a qualitatively enriched life-style and for participation in public life. Challenging the conservative and reactionary tendencies of those times, Marcuse wrote: "A potential mass base of social change finds its diffuse, prepolitical expression in the work attitudes and protests which threaten to undermine the operational requirements and values of capitalism."[12] The question Marcuse failed to address in this as well as in his previous writings was how "inner nature" could be liberated in the prevailing industrial technological setting, more precisely: how the unleashing of libidinal drives could be deliberately promoted or engineered without subjecting libido even more fully to the dictates of instrumental reason from which liberation was sought? A closely related question was how, without some radical transformation, technological man was still supposed to have access to the buried or eroded domains of Eros and sensuality.

To some extent, attentiveness to such questions – especially that of the inner–outer issue – forms the dividing line between the older and the younger generation of Frankfurt theorists. The work of Jürgen Habermas, above all, approaches human and social emancipation not so much from the angle of inner-psychic drives as from the perspective of social coordination and interpersonal correlation. While Marcuse took his bearings from "id" psychology and a strongly internalized conception of libido, Habermas, even when invoking Freudian teachings, resolutely shifted the accent to the level of ego and superego structures, that is, the level of human rationality and normatively guided communication. To be sure, the difference of focus emerged at first haltingly, and only slowly assumed the character of a stark contrast or opposition. A measure of intergenerational consensus or continuity was still evident in some of Habermas's early writings. Thus, his *Knowledge and Human Interests* (1968) assigned to the Freudian model not merely a marginal but a crucial and constitutive role: namely, the role of functioning as epistemological paradigm for critical theory or for a critical social science wedded to the "critique of ideology." In Habermas's portrayal, the model could fulfill this function because of its peculiar blending of explanatory and interpretive methodologies. While natural or empirical science is restricted to the causal explanation of (unconscious) natural processes, and while the human sciences, following Dilthey, seek to "understand" cultural or symbolic meanings, critical social science pursued a more ambitious task: that of analyzing structural social deformations in the hope of promoting more equitable and intelligible social arrangements. Although limited to individual experiences, Freudian psychoanalysis followed a similar path by seeking to unravel not only intentional meanings but rather subconscious inhibitions and "systematically distorted" modes of self-understanding. In Habermas's words: "Psychoanalytic inquiry is not directed at meaning structures on the level of conscious intentions; its critical labor removes not merely accidental lapses . . . The symbolic structures that psychoanalysis seeks to grasp are corrupted by the impact of internal constraints; mutilations (of meaning) have meaning *as such*."[13]

Although reflecting a methodological blend, psychoanalysis in Habermas's view in the end accorded pre-eminence to intelligible meaning. It is true that in its effort to overcome inner constraints and inhibitions, Freudian theory offered both a structural model of the psyche and a number of explanatory hypotheses pinpointing the causes of psychic traumas. In Habermas's account, however, such devices were at best a means, but in no way the end or goal of psychoanalysis: as reflected in the interaction between analyst and patient, this goal consisted in the recovery of unimpaired ego and superego structures through therapeutic exchanges. Once an explanatory proposal was accepted by the patient as fitting his or her case, the deformation of inner nature was assumed to be removed in favor of self-understanding and a restored ego-identity. As endorsed in *Knowledge and Human Interests* Freudianism thus carried a pale and distinctly reflective cast: in comparison with Adorno's stark antinomial conception, therapy in Habermas's construal seemed capable of dissolving the conflict between libido and societal norms (including linguistic norms) and thus of "sublating" inner nature into reflective rationality. Building on this construal, Habermas's subsequent writings further mitigated libidinal factors and the impact of psycho-analysis in general by subordinating the latter progressively to formal-pragmatic and "reconstructive" modes of analysis. As a corollary of this shift, Habermas explicitly limited the role of psychoanalysis to individual experience and private "self-reflection," while affiliating critical social inquiry more closely than before with general societal and linguistic structures and with the basic "rationality claims" embedded in such structures. Differently phrased: while psychoanalysis was confined to the domain of "particularity" and individual abnormality, social or sociological theory was tied to the "rational reconstruction" of the universal features of human interaction, including the normative and normal components of social life. On the level of a "universal pragmatics" of language, inner-psychic life figured basically as one ingredient in an interlocking set of validity claims inherent in social communication: namely, as anchor of the claim to "truthfulness" or personal sincerity juxtaposed to the standards of truth, rightness, and comprehensibility.[14]

In Habermas's presentation, the modified outlook reflected or implemented a deep-seated "paradigm change" in a contemporary thought: the change from a focus on self-reflection to concern with language and interpersonal communication. The same shift, in his view, resolved or rendered moot the issue of a "reconciliation" between society and libido, between reason and nature, the theme so central to the first generation of Frankfurt theorists. This claim is by no means marginal or incidental; it forms the topic of an extensive polemic against Adorno and Marcuse in Habermas's recent work. As *The Theory of Communicative Action* bluntly states: "A philosophy which retreats behind the arena of discursive reasoning toward a 'recollection of nature' pays for the suggestive power of its endeavor with the renunciation of theoretical knowledge."[15] The contrast with the earlier generation is particularly pronounced regarding "external" nature – where Habermas endorses adamantly the project of instrumental control as the goal of science and technology. With regard to inner psychic nature, Habermas's ethical writings occasionally suggest a willingness to compromise, that is, to incorporate an element of libidinal "happiness" into discursive ethical standards or formal-rational validity claims. The theoretical fragility or incongruence of this compromise, however, has been widely noted by a number of critics, above all by Joel Whitebook. In his essay on "Reason and Happiness", Whitebook points to "certain tensions and ambiguities" in Habermas's analysis which suggest that "the demand for happiness cannot be adequately accommodated within a formalistic approach as he conceives it." The reason for this fact resides in Habermas's basic sociological or social-psychological orientation, his preponderant concern with ego and superego structures. While conceding that the extent to which inner nature can be socialized remains "an historically open question," Whitebook comments: "It does not follow, however, from the linguisticality of society and the linguisticality of the socialization process that a pre-established harmony exists between society and inner nature . . . The possibility of a completely public language is not entailed by the demonstration of the impossibility of a totally private language." And he adds: "I am afraid that Habermas's linguistic reinterpretation of Freud has the effect of, as it were, destroying certain of Freud's central intentions in order to save them . . . The requirements of his communicatively conceived methodological program cause Habermas to violate a cardinal tenet of Freudian psychoanalysis, namely, the reality and independence of the body as formulated in the theory of the drives."[16]

II

Whitebook's comments, one should note, were not meant as a defense of traditional Freudian school doctrines. In fact, his essay chides both generations of Frankfurt theorists for adhering too closely to elements of Freud's structural model. Both Marcuse and Habermas are said to reach a theoretical impasse, though for radically different reasons: "Marcuse drawing on 'id' psychology, presupposes an absolute opposition – a preestablished disharmony – between the instinctual substratum, which is the seat of happiness, and the repressive ego. He calls for a revolt of the instincts as the only way of meeting the demands of happiness." By contrast, Habermas "like the ego psychologists" errs in the "opposite direction: Because of the thrust of his linguistic approach, he fails to capture the sense of an 'inner foreign territory' which is the hallmark of Freudian thought; in principle, everything is potentially transparent." By emphasizing opposed components of the psyche, both thinkers, according to Whitebook, are tempted to embrace utopian social schemes: schemes predicated in one case on the "eroticization" of the total personality and, in the other, on the prospect of a rational, discursively transparent society: "With both Marcuse and Habermas, utopianism results from the failure to grasp theoretically the dialectic of harmony and disharmony between human rationality and its instinctual substratum."[17]

Although largely correct in its diagnosis, Whitebook's essay is unfortunately much less helpful regarding remedies or possible alternative ways of formulating the Freudian legacy.[18] A main reason for this gap, it seems to me, resides in Whitebook's continued endorsement of some traditional conundrums: above all the inner–outer bifurcation. Clearly, as long as libidinal nature or the "natural" dimension in humans is viewed as strictly internal, privatized and irrational, human libido necessarily calls for as its complement and corrective the domain of public, rational relationships. Undeniably, the older Frankfurt School and especially Marcuse attributed to the unconscious a predominantly internal, "monological" and thus non-relational character. Accordingly and almost predictably, Habermas's antidote to this approach consists in his so-called "linguistic turn," that is, in his decision to insert libido into the context of normative-societal rules; a turn, by the way, which does not by itself obviate the inner–outer distinction. But how, prior to the emergence of ego and superego structures, can libido possibly be the inner property or faculty of individual agents? Another related conundrum concerns the issue of linguisticality. Whitebook tends to concede the domain of language or linguisticality to Habermas's focus on interpersonal relations, while seeking to defend the strictly non-linguistic character of the unconscious. But this concession, in my view, is unwarranted. For why should language be restricted to a Habermasian range of discursive-rational communication? Why should language – as a replica of the psyche – not also be granted its "unconscious," as well as its dimension of silence and amorphous creativity?

To approach these conundrums from a different angle, I draw upon selective parts of the work of Jacques Lacan and his interpretation of Freud. One intriguing and attractive aspect of Lacan's work is his own "linguistic turn," that is, his semiotic, post-Saussurean construal of psychoanalysis that culminated in the well-known phrase that the unconscious is "structured like a language." Contrary to facile misreadings, this phrase does not attribute to the unconscious a rational-discursive quality, which would be a nonsensical notion, but rather highlights its non-subjective or decentered character, the fact that, like a language, libido is not the private possession or medium of individual agents. Far from pressing psychoanalysis into a narrow syntactical or discursive strait-jacket, Lacan's approach opens Freudianism to the multidimensionality of language, to the intermingling of discursive and non-discursive, rational and non-rational strata. The same multidimensionality is also evident in another trademark of Lacanian theory: the juxtaposition of the "Imaginary" and the "Symbolic." In sharp contrast to customary inner-outer or private–public dichotomies, Lacan views the pre-discursive not as the locus of inner-psychic whim but as the domain of imagination, of an amorphous-creative potency and inventiveness. In adopting this view, his approach returns to an insight already thematized by Vico but later buried under the weight of rationalization: the notion that the precursor of discourse is not mere babbling or "distorted communication" but rather poetry or poetic speech. Supervening on such speech, the "Symbolic" heralds the rise of rational-discursive or rule-governed language, a development carrying in its wake both the formation of ego-identity and the alienation of the ego from "its" unconscious. Supplementing the two linguistic layers in Lacan's scheme is the realm of the "Real," a term denoting radical "otherness" or the sphere of non-identity never completely absorbed n language or thought.[19]

These comments call for amplification. In Lacanian theory, the Imaginary performs not only a different function from the Symbolic, but also indicates an earlier but never abandoned layer in the process of psychogenesis or human maturation. The most prominent threshold in the formation of this layer is said to be the "mirror stage," that is, the stage of infancy between six and eighteen months in which the child first recognizes his or her own image in the mirror without the aid of self-reflection or a developed ego-structure. Basically, the mirror stage inaugurates a phase of multiple bodily images, of an indiscriminate mêlée of visual impressions and counter-impressions which are not yet tied to ego–alter or subject–object categories. Following Charlotte Bühler, Lacan speaks at this point of a "normal transitivism" between agents or between actions and reactions, adding: "The child who hits says he has been hit, the child who sees another child fall begins to cry. Similarly, it is by way of identification with the other that the infant lives the entire spectrum of reactions from ostentation to generosity."[20] As portrayed by Fredric Jameson whose useful synopsis I follow in part, the mirror phase corresponds essentially to "that pre-individualistic, pre-mimetic, pre-point-of-view stage in aesthetic organization which is generally designated as 'play' " and whose distinctive work lies "in the frequent shifts of the subject from one fixed position to another, in a kind of optional multiplicity of insertions" of the agent into a broder fabric. As a pre-individual stage, this phase of infancy is not simply an "inner" preserve, nor is it discursively rational in a proper sense since it is unavailable to inspection by a detached spectator. To quote Jameson again, the Imaginary opens up a space of experience which is "not yet organized around the individuation of my own personal body, or differentiated hierarchically according to the perspectives of my own central point of view" and which, instead, "swarms with bodies and forms intuited in a different way, whose fundamental property is, it would seem, to be visible without their visibility being the result of the act of any particular observer . . . In this," he adds, "– the indifferentiation of their *esse* from a *percipi* which does not know a *percipiens* – these bodies of the Imaginary exemplify the very logic of mirror images."[21]

Indifferentiation in this case, however, does not mean a complete amalgamation of perspectives or a harmonious symbiosis. While it is pre-individual, mirror perception heralds the beginning of a self–other distinction, although on a purely immediate, dyadic and non-reflective level. According to Lacan, the perceiving infant discovers in objects and fellow humans an image of himself or herself; but this discovery has itself an imaginary or phantastic character and does not promote stable relationships. While conducive in large measure to a stance of narcissism, the mirror stage thus harbors also its own peculiar mode of nondescript conflict and antagonism, but a conflict which does not obey fixed rules or lines of demarcation. In Jameson's words, the Imaginary level is pregnant with a polymorphous kind of aggressivity which results "from that indistinct rivalry between self and other in a period that precedes the very elaboration of a self or the construction of an ego"; far from cancelling the "normal transitivism" between agents, aggressivity at this point manifests a "situational experience of otherness as pure relationship, as struggle, violence, and antagonism, in which the child can occupy either term indifferently, or indeed, as in transitivism, both at once." These experiences of empathy and rivalry, of imaginary identification and conflict also provide initial clues for later moral distinctions and ethical valorizations of human conduct. To this extent, the Imaginary level reflects a concretely lived "ethos" which can function as a storehouse of normative precepts. Thus, it is possible to describe the Imaginary as the scene of "that primordial rivalry and transitivistic substitution of imagoes, that indistinction of primary narcissism and aggressivity, from which our later conceptions of good and evil derive."[22]

In Lacan's theory, the Imaginary functions as a backdrop, and as a necessary and ineradicable backdrop, to the Symbolic order which is the level of rule-governed, syntactical and discursive language. As he writes, highlighting the crucial importance of this sequence: the moment when "the child is born into language is also that in which 'desire becomes human'."[23] For Lacan, the move to discursive language is by no means arbitrary or fortuitous, but rather an integral part of the infant's "humanization." Nevertheless, in contrast to the harmonizing claims of ego and superego psychology (as well as theories of communicative rationality), the move is not seen as an unmitigated advance, nor does it result in stable interactions. By being "born into language," the child acquires an ego and a sense of self-identity – mainly by relying on personal pronouns which enable the child to differentiate between "I" and others or between "mine" and "yours." However, pronouns do not provide a secure identity; in linguistic theory they are known as "shifters" because they can be appropriated indiscriminately by speakers and agents – with the result that subjectivity is simultaneously constituted and dispersed or discarded. Moreover, discursive language does not establish a stable reference to the world but only an indirect or "symbolic" linkage. According to Saussure, words or "signifiers" do not directly or unequivocally relate to objects; rather, the function of signification is to point circuitously to missing or absent objects. This point is accentuated by Lacan into an intimate connection between symbolization and absence or non-identity. In the words of Jacqueline Rose:

> Symbolization starts when the child gets its first sense that something could be missing; words stand for objects, because they only have to be spoken at the moment when the first object is lost. For Lacan, the subject can only operate within language by constantly repeating that moment of fundamental and irreducible division. The subject is therefore constituted in language *as* this division or splitting (Freud's *Ichspaltung*, or splitting of the ego).[24]

In Lacan's view, the most fundamental division or splitting pertains not so much to signifiers and their objects but to the relation of the subject to itself. Following Freud, Lacan sees the formation of the ego also as the scene of a "primal repression," in the sense that the emergence of ego-identity drives underground the teeming ambivalence of experiences thematized on the Imaginary level, thus giving rise to the unconscious as the nether side of the ego. With this development, the subject is cut adrift from its own amorphous moorings and henceforth exposed to the stark duality of consciousness and the unconscious, of reason and "nature," an exposure which Lacan describes as a "lack of being" (*manque à être*), a lack nurturing a profound yearning or "desire" whose fulfillment is forever barred or forestalled (at the level of the subject). The chief barrier to such fulfillment is rule-governed, syntactical language itself, that is, the Symbolic order as an order of normative prohibition – as the "No" and "Name of the Father" (*le nom [non] du père*) forever militating against the amorphous union or reunion of child and image and, especially, of child and mother. In terms of psychogenesis, the Symbolic order links up with the Freudian themes of the "Oedipal complex" and of castration – themes which in turn are at the root of sexual differentiation and identification. As Jameson writes, in an instructive passage:

> The very cornerstone of Freud's conception of the psyche, the Oedipus complex, is transliterated by Lacan into a linguistic phenomenon which he designates as the discovery by the subject of the Name-of-the-Father, and which consists, in other words, in the transformation of an Imaginary relationship to that particular imago which is the physical parent into the new and menacing abstraction of the parental role as the possessor of the mother and the place of the Law.[25]

Without going into further details I want to lift up some features which seem particularly relevant in the present context. An important aspect of Lacan's "linguistic turn" is the rejection of the internalization or privatization of the psyche and its attendant inner–outer, private–public dichotomies. On both the Imaginary and the Symbolic levels, the subject, while not abolished, is radically dislocated or decentered, either by participating in a mêlée of interactions or by being basically split or divided against itself. Therefore, in contrast to Marcuse (and other Freudo-Marxists), relief from societal pressures cannot simply be expected from a revitalization of "inner nature" or libidinal energies.[26] Even less can psychic or social harmony be found through an emphatic cultivation of syntactical-rational discourse in the Habermasian sense, given that discursive rationality or the Symbolic order is precisely the site of psychic alienation and of the reason–nature conflict. The contrast between Lacan and Habermas's critical theory has frequently been noted by commentators, on both sides of this theoretical divide. Pleading the former's case, Norbert Haas in a translation of *Écrits* voiced strong reservations regarding a reflective-discursive construal of psychic events. "The ideal dialogue situation which is the heritage of the historical Enlightenment," he wrote, "can be distilled from the processes of the psychoanalytic situation only on the basis of deformations. We read of 'intact language games' (Lorenzer), of 'symmetrical communication' and 'non-repressive discourse' (Habermas)." However, in Lacan one finds that "there is no language game untouched by the unconscious, no communication which is not asymmetrical in relation to the being of the communicant, no discourse in which there is no repression. Lacan is an ontologist only in the sense that he believes the being of subjects dominates their consciousness." Similar sentiments were expressed by Rainer Nägele who observed that "if in Habermas's work reflection appears as a kind of metapower which sublates all other powers, experience nevertheless teaches that being is always prior to reflection."[27]

As indicated, however, Lacan's critique of a discursive "culturalism" does not vindicate an archaic naturalism. Wedded to a strongly tensional or conflictual view of the psyche – reminiscent in many ways of Adorno–Lacanian theory militates both against a simple "return" to nature and against a singleminded embrace of rational or rationalized culture: the first alternative, in his view, is regressive by cancelling the "humanizing" achievements of symbolic language; the second alternative is repressive by neglecting the counter-natural constraints thematized in Freud's notion of "primal repression." Entangled in the nature–culture dilemma, Lacanianism at this point seems to offer a counsel of despair – but only at a first glance. The structural tension discovered by Freud and reaffirmed by Lacan does not produce a psychic stalemate but rather a creative-dynamic potential or unrest. Once inducted into the Symbolic order, the subject's "lack of being" generates a persistent yearning which permanently transgresses natural-biological and discursive resources. Unable to be stilled by purely natural or else discursive means, fulfillment of "desire" – beyond the satisfaction of wants – takes on the character of a trans-natural *"jouissance"* or an ontological *"promesse de bonheur"* (although this aspect is relatively under-thematized by Lacan). Pursuing its path beyond or outside regression and repression such fulfillment can take place only in the domain of art viewed as the reconciliation of reason and nature or the recovery of nature on a higher plane. In social and political terms the same promise is manifest in those moments or interludes when ill will and resentment are temporarily suspended in favor of generous playfulness. Such moments may well be the unrelinquishable kernel of the classical notion of the "good life."[28]

III

To illustrate the implications of the preceding discussion, I want to move from the level of psychoanalytic theorizing to that of aesthetics – more specifically, to a well-known text about aesthetics: Nietzsche's *The Birth of Tragedy*. The choice of the text does not seem to be far-fetched, given the fact that Nietzsche was in many respects Freud's precursor, anticipating often in uncanny ways the latter's psychoanalytic insights. The psychic split mentioned above – the drama of "civilization and its discontents" – surfaces in Nietzsche's text as the conflict between Dionysos and Apollo or between the Dionysian and Apollonian dimensions of experience. "Much will be gained for aesthetics," the opening paragraph asserts, "once we have succeeded in apprehending directly (rather than merely intuiting) that art owes its continuous evolution to the Apollonian–Dionysian duality, even as the propagation of the species depends on the duality of the sexes, their constant conflicts and periodic acts of reconciliation." While reflecting deep-seated principles, the two Greek deities, Apollo and Dionysos, represented for Nietzsche concrete "embodiments" of divergent energies or creative tendencies, energies giving rise respectively to the "plastic, Apollonian arts" and the "non-visual art of music inspired by Dionysos." According to the text, the development of the arts involved over long stretches the juxtaposition and "fierce opposition" of the two creative tendencies, "each by its taunts forcing the other to more energetic production, both perpetuating in a discordant concord that *agon* which the term 'art' but feeble designates – until at last, by the thaumaturgy of an Hellenic act of will, the pair accepted the yoke of marriage and, in this manner, begot Attic tragedy which exhibits the salient features of both parents."[29]

Profiled against the background of classicist interpretations of Greek art, the most innovative and disturbing discovery of *The Birth of Tragedy*, the one articulated most vividly , was the realm or reign of Dionysos. In Nietzsche's portrayal, Dionysos holds sway in a world of untamed intoxication and rapture, a world not yet streamlined through civil discourse: "Dionysian stirrings arise either through the influence of those narcotic potions of which all primitive races speak in their hymns, or through the powerful approach of spring which penetrates with joy the whole frame of nature. So stirred, the individual forgets himself completely." As the last phrase indicates, Dionysos does not rule over subjects or individuals; in Lacanian language, his realm is the domain of Imaginary and pre-Imaginary experience, a domain subsequently exiled into the unconscious under the aegis of the ego. Moreover, Dionysos' reign disregards not only ego–alter demarcations but also the boundaries between humans and nature: "Not only does the bond between man and man come to be forged once again by the magic of the Dionysian rite, but nature itself, long alienated or subjugated, rises again to celebrate the reconciliation with her prodigal son, man. The earth offers its gifts voluntarily, and the savage beasts of mountain and desert approach in peace." Even long-standing social hierarchy and discrimination is suspended by the impact of Dionysian rapture and amorphous non-differentiation: "Now the slave emerges as a freeman; all the rigid, hostile walls which either necessity or despotism has erected between men are shattered." What results from the destruction of these walls is a kind of "oceanic feeling," a sense of mutual implication and substitutability – a condition in which man "becomes not only reconciled to his fellow but actually at one with him, as though the veil of Maya had been torn apart and there remained only shreds floating before the vision of mystical Oneness."[30]

As Nietzsche goes on to argue, the Greek version of Dionysian rapture must be distinguished from the still wilder celebrations of Dionysos by barbarian peoples. While Greek culture from the beginning was tempered by the subdued light of Apollonian constraint, barbarian rituals or festivals were a stark mixture of Eros and destruction. "All the savage urges of the mind were unleashed on those occasions," Nietzsche writes, "until they reached that paroxysm of lust and cruelty which has always struck me as the 'witches' cauldron' *par excellence*." Even in the milder Greek setting, Dionysian revelry still was marked by a "peculiar blending of emotions" – a basic "ambiguity if you will" – harking back to those days "when the infliction of pain was experienced as joy while a sense of supreme triumph elicited cries of anguish from the heart." In Lacanian terms, the Greek version of Dionysos carried overtones not only of the Imaginary mélange of narcissism and aggressivity but also hints of an incipient "lack of being," a lack inaugurated by civilized life. "In every exuberant joy," we read, "there now is heard an undertone of terror, or else a wistful lament over an irrecoverable loss. It is as though in these Greek festivals a sentimental trait of nature were coming to the fore, as though nature were bemoaning the fact of her fragmentation, her decomposition into separate individuals." At its peak, Nietzsche reiterates, the unleashing of Dionysian energies issues in an obliteration of boundaries, in a state of amorphous non-differentiation: "In the Dionysian dithyramb man is incited to strain his faculties of imagination to the utmost. Something quite unheard of is now clamoring to be heard: the desire to tear asunder the veil of Maya, to sink back into the original oneness of nature; the desire to express the very essence of nature symbolically."[31]

In contrast to Dionysian frenzy, Apollo in Greek culture is the representative of light or enlightenment, or rather of a mild light suffused with dream and illusion. As Nietzsche points out, Apollo is etymologically "the 'lucent' one, the god of light" and thus exudes a luminous quality. Endowed with a "sunlike" eye, he brings light where otherwise there is darkness or rapture; he is able to establish distinctions and boundaries, and to weigh or balance judiciously diverse elements. Following a clue contained in Schopenhauer's *The World as Will and Representation*, Nietzsche links Apollo with individualism or the rise of the subject and thus with a cornerstone of discursive civilization: "One might say that the unshakable confidence in that principle [i.e., of individual selfhood] has received its most magnificent expression in Apollo, and that Apollo himself may be regarded as the marvelous divine image of the *principium individuationis*, whose looks and gestures radiate the full delight, wisdom, and beauty of 'illusion'." The process of individuation encourages self-reflection and rational insight, including reflection on the limits of individual life. From an Apollonian perspective, Nietzsche comments, "there is one norm only: the individual – or, more precisely, the observance of the limits of the individual: *sophrosyne*. As a moral deity Apollo demands self-control from his people and, in order to observe such self-control, a knowledge of self; and so we find that the aesthetic postulate of beauty is accompanied by the imperatives, 'Know thyself' and 'Nothing too much'."[32] Self-knowledge, however, is not unproblematic and exacts a price: rigorously pursued individuation entails division and thus incipient modes of mastery or domination. In a striking passage, *The Birth of Tragedy* anticipates aspects of Lacan's "law" or "name of the father," albeit in a mythological setting. Pointing to the place of Apollo among the Olympian gods and the latter's role in Greek culture, the text observes:

At first the eye is struck by the marvelous shapes of the Olympian gods who stand upon its pediments and whose exploits, in shining bas-relief, adorn its friezes. The fact that among them we find Apollo as one god among many, making no claim to a privileged position, should not mislead us: the same drive that found its most complete representation in Apollo generated the whole Olympian world, and in this sense we may consider Appollo the father of that world.[33]

To be sure, Apollo was still the symbol of creative-artistic energies and not merely the representative of discursive knowledge and civilized rationality. According to Nietzsche, such rationality arose only in the twilight or aftermath of Greek culture and found its chief incarnation in Socrates – the great exemplar of the purely "theoretical man," that is, the man wedded to the belief that "reason might plumb the farthest abysses of being and even *correct* it."[34] In the heyday of Greek culture, on the other hand, Apollonian beauty was still in creative tension with, and intimately related to, Dionysian turbulence, just as the Olympians were linked with the Titans. In Nietzsche's words, although Apollo may be the "apotheosis of the *principium individuationis*," he is also the figure in whom "the eternal goal of the original Oneness, namely its redemption through illusion, accomplishes itself. With august gesture the god shows us how there is need for a whole world of torment in order for the individual to produce the redemptive vision and to sit quietly in his rocking rowboat in mid-sea, absorbed in contemplation." Contrary to modern conceptions of classical "naïveté" or simplicity, Greek culture was from the beginning rent by a profound tension: the calm reign of Apollo was established on the volcano of Dionysian torment and excess: "Whenever we encounter 'naiveté' in art, we are face to face with the ripest fruit of Apollonian culture – which must always triumph first over titans, kill monsters, and overcome the somber contemplation of actuality, the intense susceptibility to suffering, by means of illusions strenuously and zestfully entertained."[35]

This combination reached its highest and most captivating expression in Greek or Attic tragedy. In Nietzsche's portrayal, Attic tragedy was an intricate blending of Dionysian and Apollonian energies – the former represented chiefly in the lyrical or dithyrambic chorus, the latter in the measured flow of the dramatic action. Together with Schiller he views the introduction of the chorus as the "decisive step" in the birth of tragedy; the chant of the chorus, he notes, erects a "living wall against the onset of reality because it depicts reality more truthfully and more completely than does civilized man, who ordinary considers himself the only reality." The reality evoked by the chorus is the pre-civil teeming non-division, the world between humankind and nature symbolized by the Dionysian satyr. To this extent, the chorus of early tragedy was a "projected image of Dionysian man," and the satyr quality of the chorus a "vision of the Dionysian multitude" or the throng of Dionysian revelers. The measured lines of the "dramatis personae," on the other hand, are emblems of Apollonian reflection and distinctness – but a distinctness which is never (at least not until Euripides) severed from its dithyrambic moorings. Thus, Nietzsche writes, "we have come to interpret Greek tragedy as a Dionysian chorus which again and again discharges itself in Apollonian images. Those choric portions with which the tragedy is interlaced constitute, as it were, the matrix of the *dialogue*, that is to say, of the entire stage-world of the actual drama." Differently phrased, the choric matrix or substratum permeates or "irradiates" through its consecutive interventions the entire action on stage, transforming the latter from an epic spectacle into a symbolic rite or festival. To this extent, Greek tragedy presented a vision which, on the one hand, was "completely of the nature of Apollonian dream-illusion and therefore epic," but on the other hand, "as the manifestation of a Dionysian state" tended toward "the shattering of the individual and his fusion with the original Oneness." Thus, ancient tragedy was "an Apollonian embodiment of Dionysian insights and powers, and for that reason separated by a tremendous gulf from the epic."[36]

To Nietzsche *The Birth of Tragedy* was not merely an antiquarian exercise, but carried broader diagnostic and therapeutic significance. The tensional correlation of Dionysos and Apollo appeared to him not simply as an isolated or curious historical phenomenon, but as a continuing possibility and challenge – even in our completely changed modern conditions. As epitomized in Greek tragedy, high art involved not merely regression or a relapse into the frenzy of subconscious drives; nor could art be streamlined into rational insight – the abstract "Socratism" of discursive civilization. Without instinctual energies, it is true, art could never flourish; to this extent, the Dionysian element "proves itself to be the eternal and original power of art, since it calls into being the entire world of phenomena." Yet, for this power to be compatible with civilization, a "new transfiguring light" is needed to transform Dionysian chaos and to "hold in life the stream of individual forms" – which is the contribution of Apollo. Extracted from its narrowly aesthetic context, Nietzsche's therapeutic counsel thus is not simply a return to nature nor the abandonment of nature in favor of reason, but rather a reconciliation achieved on a higher level (though not without trauma or dislocation). "Art," he writes, "is not an imitation of nature but its metaphysical supplement, raised up beside it in order to overcome it. Insofar as tragic myth belongs to art, it fully shares its transcendent intentions." In Nietzsche's view, this supplementation can still provide a guidepost in our highly rationalized age and civilized way of life. "We must hold fast to our luminous guides, the Greeks," he pleads. "It is from them that we have borrowed, for the purification of our aesthetic notion, the twin divine images, each of whom governs his own realm and whose commerce and mutual enhancement we have been able to guess at through the medium of Greek tragedy."[37]

These comments lead me back to the beginning of the present chapter where I addressed the issue of Freudianism or of the status of Freud's legacy today. As I indicated, this legacy in recent decades has been deeply divided among competing factions or doctrines, and particularly between two opposing orientations: traditional Freudians stressing the primacy of the libidinal unconscious, on the one hand, and more "revisionist" schools accentuating the role of ego and superego, and hence of moral and societal rules, on the other. This division, I suggested, has troubling effects on the conception of "human nature" as well as on the character of therapy. Does Freudian theory, I asked, support a rigid inner–outer dichotomy, by identifying human nature with inner-psychic drives while relegating society and rational norms to an external environment? By the same token: does therapy aim at the healing and restoration of instinctual drives – or does it seek to reintegrate the patient into the world of norms and public meaning (rescuing him from inner traumas)? In its first section, this chapter explored these questions in the context of the Frankfurt School, focusing on the reception of psychonalysis by critical theorists. As I tried to demonstrate, the noted dilemmas and bifurcations largely persisted in that context. In Adorno's writings, instinct and reason, libido and social rules tended to confront each other in an aporetic or antinomial fashion. Attempts to resolve the conflict were undertaken by other critical theorists – but at the price of truncating the tensional richness of Freud's model: While Marcuse subordinated social rules to the reinvigoration of inner-psychic drives, particularly the "eroticization" of human life, Habermas tends to treat the libidinal unconscious as only a deviation from, or prelude to, societal rationality. As this point the essay turned to the writings of Lacan, in an effort to disclose a different theoretical possibility. Lacan's "linguistic turn," I sought to show, undercuts the inner privatization of libido and its opposition to social-linguistic norms. More importantly, bypassing dualism as well as coincidence, his correlation of the "Imaginary" and the "Symbolic" points in the direction of a complex intertwining of nature and culture, psyche and society – akin to Nietzsche's entwining of Dionysos and Apollo. This aspect has been ably expressed by Ragland-Sullivan whose comments I invoke by way of conclusion. Lacan, she writes, problematized psychoanalysis by taking seriously the tensions in Freud's model. In doing so, "he showed that there are no clear-cut polarities between subject and object, inside and outside, self and other, conscious and unconscious. He also complicated philosophy by making others – human interdependence – the sole proving ground in human causality, and unconscious intentionality the motive force."[38]

NOTES

1 The status of "object relations" theory in the above conflict is difficult to pinpoint due to its complexity and many nuances. Recently Fred Alford has marshalled the resources of that theory (with a focus on Melanie Klein and her successors) for a critical assessment of the contributions of the Frankfurt School. While Alford tends to stress the ego- or subject-pole of "object relations," I find the approach more congenial when that pole is de-emphasized. See C. Fred Alford, "Habermas, Post-Freudian Psychoanalysis and the End of the Individual", *Theory, Culture and Society*, vol. 4 (1987), pp. 3–29; and his *Narcissism: Socrates, the Frankfurt School, and Psychoanalytic Theory* (New Haven: Yale University Press, 1988). Compare also Jay Greenberg and Stephen Mitchell, *Object Relations in Psychoanalytic Theory* (Cambridge, MA: Harvard University Press, 1983).

2 Theodor W. Adorno, "Social Science and Sociological Tendencies in Psychoanalysis" (unpublished), cited in Martin Jay, *The Dialectical Imagination* (Boston: Little, Brown & Co., 1973), p. 104.

3 Adorno, "Die revidierte Psychoanalyse", in Adorno, *Gesammelte Werke*, ed. Rolf Tiedemann, vol. 8 (Frankfurt-Main: Suhrkamp, 1972), p. 40.

4 Max Horkheimer and Theodor W. Adorno, *Dialectic of Enlightenment*, tr. John Cumming (New York: Seabury Press, 1972), pp. 31–2.

5 *Dialectic of Enlightenment*, pp. 54–5.

6 *Dialectic of Enlightenment*, p. 40.

7 See Adorno, *Negative Dialectics*, tr. E. B. Ashton (New York: Seabury Press, 1973), and *Aesthetic Theory*, tr. Christian Lenhardt (London: Routledge & Kegan Paul, 1984). For a discussion of *mimesis* compare Martin Jay, *Adorno* (Cambridge, MA: Harvard University Press, 1984), pp. 155–8.

8 The antinomial character of Adorno's thought in this field is evident from a memorandum of 1944 pinpointing methodological maxims: "We do not call the influence of socio-economic factors psychological since they are more or less on a rational level . . . The term psychological should be reserved for those traits which are *prima facie* irrational. This dichotomy means that we do not approve of a socio-psychological approach à la Fromm, but rather think in terms of rational and irrational motivations which are essentially to be kept apart." Cited in Jay, *The Dialectical Imagination*, pp. 229–30.

9 See Herbert Marcuse, *One-Dimensional Man: Studies in the Ideology of Advanced Industrial Society* (Boston: Beacon Press, 1964), and *An Essay on Liberation* (Boston: Beacon Press, 1969).

10 Marcuse, "Philosophy and Critical Theory", in *Negations: Essays in Critical Theory*, tr. Jeremy J. Shapiro (Boston: Beacon Press, 1968), p. 135 (translation slightly altered).

11 Marcuse, *Eros and Civilization* (Boston: Beacon Press, 1955). For a sensitive synopsis of some of the main arguments of the study see Jay, *The Dialectical*

Imagination, pp. 107–12. Regarding the difference of Marcuse from his former Frankfurt colleagues Jay writes (p. 107): "Unlike Horkheimer and Adorno, who used Freud's insights into the profound contradictions of modern man to support their arguments about non-identity, Marcuse found in Freud, and the later, meta-psychological Freud to boot, a prophet of identity and reconciliation."

12   Marcuse, *Counterrevolution and Revolt* (Boston: Beacon Press, 1972), p. 23.

13   Jürgen Habermas, *Knowledge and Human Interests*, tr. Jeremy J. Shapiro (Boston: Beacon Press, 1971), pp. 216–17.

14   Compare Habermas, "What is Universal Pragmatics?" in *Communication and the Evolution of Society*, tr. Thomas McCarthy (Boston: Beacon Press, 1979), pp. 1–68. In terms of speech-act theory, subjective experience in Habermas's scheme provides the ground for "expressive" or self-representative speech acts, just as in the field of sociological action theory, subjectivity serves as springboard for "dramaturgical" action geared toward self-display in front of an audience. In every instance, thus, psychic life is integrated into a fabric of complementary and mutually supportive categories: in the case of validity claims, into the structure of "communicative rationality," and in the case of action types, into the framework of communicative action and interaction. Among the types of "reconstructive" analysis Habermas pays tribute particularly to Chomsky's generative grammar, Piaget's theory of cognitive development, and Kohlberg's model of stages of moral maturation.

15   Habermas, *The Theory of Communicative Action*, vol. 1: *Reason and the Rationalization of Society*, tr. Thomas McCarthy (Boston: Beacon Press, 1984), p. 385. The case against the older Frankfurt School is broadly developed on pp. 366–90.

16   Joel Whitebook, "Reason and Happiness: Some Psychoanalytic Themes in Critical Theory", in Richard J. Bernstein, ed., *Habermas and Modernity* (Cambridge, MA: MIT Press, 1985), pp. 154–5. Compare also his comments (p. 155): "Where the philosophers of the consciousness had difficulty reaching extra-mental existence from within the closed circle of subjectivity, Habermas has difficulty contacting extralinguistic reality from within the equally closed circle of intersubjectivity." Habermas's compromise with hedonism occurs chiefly on the highest (seventh) stage of moral development where discursive reasoning is given the task of interpreting private needs.

17   Whitebook, "Reason and Happiness", p. 157. His observations seem less applicable, in my view, to Adorno whose ambition was precisely to maintain the mentioned "dialectic of harmony and disharmony."

18   The essay does contain, however, numerous suggestive or tantalizing passages, for instance the following (pp. 145–6): "While we are indeed accustomed to thinking of the ego as anti-instinctual, I would like to suggest that, insofar as the ego possesses a synthetic function, and insofar as *Eros* is defined as the drive to establish and preserve 'ever greater unities', we

can locate something like *Eros* in the ego itself."
19 For helpful introductions to Lacan's thought see Anthony G. Wilden, *The Language of the Self* (Baltimore: Johns Hopkins University Press, 1968); Anika Rifflet-Lemaire, *Jacques Lacan* (Brussels: Dessart, 1970); John P. Muller and William J. Richardson, *Lacan and Language: A Reader's Guide to Écrits* (New York: International Universities Press, 1982); Jane Gallop, *Reading Lacan* (Ithaca, NY: Cornell University Press, 1985); Ellie Ragland-Sullivan, *Jacques Lacan and the Philosophy of Psychoanalysis* (Urbana: University of Illinois Press, 1986); and Shoshana Felman, *Jacques Lacan and the Adventure of Insight: Psychoanalysis in Contemporary Culture* (Cambridge, MA: Harvard University Press, 1987). These comments by Felman strike me as particularly insightful (p. 57): "As for the theory of psychoanalysis, its originality for Lacan consists not so much in Freud's discovery of the unconscious . . . as in Freud's discovery of the unprecedented fact that *the unconscious speaks* . . . The unconscious is therefore no longer – as it has traditionally been conceived – the simple outside of the conscious, but rather a division, *Spaltung*, cleft within consciousness itself." In relying on Lacan I do not mean to endorse all his teachings – for the simple reason that I cannot claim to understand all of them fully.
20 Jacques Lacan, *Écrits* (Paris: Seuil, 1966), p. 113.
21 Fredric Jameson, "Imaginary and Symbolic in Lacan: Marxism, Psychoanalytic Criticism, and the Problem of the Subject", in *Yale French Studies*, No. 55/56 (1977), pp. 354–5.
22 Jameson, "Imaginary and Symbolic in Lacan", pp. 356–7.
23 Lacan, *Écrits: A Selection*, tr. Alan Sheridan (New York: Norton, 1977), p. 103.
24 Jacqueline Rose, "Introduction – II", in Juliet Mitchell and Rose, eds, *Feminine Sexuality: Jacques Lacan and the école freudienne* (New York: Norton, 1985), p. 31. Rose (pp. 31–2, note 2) also points to Lacan's concern with "the structure of metaphor (or substitution) which lies at the root of, and is endlessly repeated within, subjectivity in its relation to the unconscious. It is in this sense also that Lacan's emphasis on language should be differentiated from what he defined as 'culturalism', that is, from any conception of language as a social phenomenon which does not take into account its fundamental instability (language as constantly placing, and *displacing*, the subject)."
25 Jameson, "Imaginary and Symbolic in Lacan", p. 359. Jameson (p. 363) also quotes Rifflet-Lemaire to the effect that "the subject mediated by language is irremediably divided because it has been excluded from the symbolic chain (the lateral relations of signifiers among themselves) at the very moment at which it became 'represented' in it."
26 This stricture also seems to apply to the Deleuze–Guattari endorsement of schizophrenia and their celebration of archaic, pre-verbal layers of the psyche; see Gilles Deleuze and Felix Guattari, *Anti-Oedipus*, tr. Robert

Hanley, Mark Selen and Helen Cane (New York: Viking Press, 1982). Regarding Lacan's linguistic turn and his critique of a subjectivist humanism compare also the comments by Juliet Mitchell: "The humanistic conception of mankind assumes that the subject exists from the beginning. At least by implication ego psychologists, object-relations theorists and Kleinians base themselves on the same premise. For this reason, Lacan considers that in the last analysis, they are more ideologues than theorists of psychoanalysis . . . Lacan dedicated himself to reorienting psychoanalysis to its task of deciphering the ways in which the human subject is constructed – how it comes into being – out of the small human animal. It is because of this aim that Lacan offered psychoanalytic theory the new science of linguistics which he developed and altered in relation to the concept of subjectivity." See Mitchell and Rose, *Feminine Sexuality*, pp. 4–5.

27 Jacques Lacan, *Schriften II*, ed. Norbert Haas (Freiburg: Olten, 1975), p. 26; Rainer Nägele, "Freud, Habermas and the Dialectic of Enlightenment: On Real and Ideal Discourses", *New German Critique*, No. 22 (1981), p. 43. Compare also Nägele, "The Provocation of Jacques Lacan: An Attempt at a Theoretical Topography apropos a Book about Lacan", *New German Critique*, No. 16 (1979), pp. 8–9. On the other side of the fence see, e.g., Peter C. Hohendahl, "Habermas and His Critics", *New German Critique*, No. 16 (1979), pp. 89–118.

28 I realize that the above comments are not fully supported by Lacan's writings. However, the themes have been developed or at least sketched by some of Lacan's critical students or readers. Compare Luce Irigaray, *This Sex Which Is Not One*, tr. Catherine Porter with Carolyn Burke (Ithaca, NY: Cornell University Press, 1985); Julia Kristeva, *Desire in Language*, tr. Thomas Gara, Alice Jardine and Leon S. Roudier (New York: Columbia University Press, 1980) and *Revolution in Poetic Language*, tr. Margaret Waller (New York: Columbia University Press, 1984). Jameson points vaguely in the above direction when he writes that "at a time when the primacy of language and the Symbolic Order is widely understood – or at least widely asserted – it is rather in the underestimation of the Imaginary and the problem of the insertion of the subject that the 'un-hiddenness of truth' (Heidegger) may now be sought." See "Imaginary and Symbolic in Lacan", p. 383.

29 Friedrich Nietzsche, *The Birth of Tragedy*, in *The Birth of Tragedy and The Genealogy of Morals*, tr. Francis Golffing (Garden City, NY: Doubleday Anchor Books, 1956), p. 19 (translation slightly altered for purposes of clarity). In invoking Dionysos and Apollo, Nietzsche explicitly rejects customary inner–outer dichotomies or the distinction between "subjective" and "objective" art. Challenging the Kantian and post-Kantian aesthetics of taste he writes (p. 37): "All that more recent aesthetics has been able to add by way of interpretation is that here the 'objective' artist is confronted by the 'subjective' artist. We find this interpretation of little use, since to us the subjective artist is simply the bad artist and since we demand above

all, in every genre and range of art, a triumph over subjectivity, deliverance from the self, the silencing of every personal will and desire." Compare also these comments on lyrical poetry (pp. 38–9): "The 'I' here sounds out of the depth of being; what recent writers on aesthetics call 'subjectivity' is a mere figment . . . Being the active center of that world he (the poet) may boldly speak in the first person, only his 'I' is not that of the actual waking man, but the 'I' dwelling, truly and eternally, in the ground of being."

30 *The Birth of Tragedy*, pp. 22–3.

31 *The Birth of Tragedy*, pp. 25–7. A little later Nietzsche adds (p. 32): "The more I have come to realize in nature those omnipotent formative tendencies and, with them, an intense longing for illusion, the more I feel inclined to the hypothesis that the original Oneness, the ground of being, eversuffering and contradictory, time and again has need of rapt vision and delightful illusion to redeem itself."

32 *The Birth of Tragedy*, pp. 21–2, 34.

33 *The Birth of Tragedy*, p. 28.

34 *The Birth of Tragedy*, pp. 92–3. Somewhat later (p. 137), Nietzsche attacks "a Socratism bent on the extermination of myth. Man today, stripped of myth, stands famished among all his pasts and must dig frantically for roots, be it among the most remote antiquities. What does our great historical hunger signify, our clutching about us of countless other cultures, our consuming desire for knowledge, if not the loss of myth, of a mythic home, the mythic womb?" Nietzsche's ambivalence regarding Socrates is well known. Elsewhere (e.g., p. 90) he calls for an "artistic Socrates," that is, a balance of knowledge and art, reason and nature.

35 *The Birth of Tragedy*, pp. 31, 33–4.

36 *The Birth of Tragedy*, pp. 49, 53–4, 56–7. Compare also this comment (p. 58): "Thus we may recognize a drastic stylistic opposition: language, color, pace, dynamics of speech are polarized into the Dionysian poetry of the chorus, on the one hand, and the Apollonian dream world of the scene on the other."

37 *The Birth of Tragedy*, pp. 138, 142, 145.

38 Ragland-Sullivan, *Jacques Lacan and the Philosophy of Psychoanalysis*, p. 65.

8

Heidegger and Psychotherapy

Explore transformation throughout . . .

Rilke

The relation between Heidegger and psychology has long been a neglected theme. Outside narrowly professional circles – particularly the school of *Daseinsanalyse* inaugurated by Binswanger – the implications of Heidegger's thought for psychology and psychotherapy have tended to be de-emphasized if not entirely discounted. One reason for the neglect has been the scarcity of relevant source materials in this field. During the last few years this situation has dramatically changed, mainly due to the publication of the so-called *Zollikon Seminars* (*Zollikoner Seminare*) in 1987.[1] Edited by the Swiss psychiatrist Medard Boss, the book records in detail, sometimes verbatim, Heidegger's intensive engagement or interaction with a group of medically trained psychiatrists in Zurich, an interaction occurring in periodic seminar meetings stretching over a period of about a decade (from 1959 to 1969). In addition to protocols of these seminar meetings, the volume contains the gist of extensive discussions between Boss and Heidegger on a variety of relevant topics, together with excerpts from letters written by Heidegger to Boss during the postwar period. As it happens, the publication of *Zollikon Seminars* coincided with the appearance of a collection of essays titled *Heidegger and Psychology*, edited (or re-edited) as a special issue of the *Review of Existential Psychology and Psychiatry*. Almost simultaneously, Jacques Derrida published a book called *De l'esprit: Heidegger et la question* in which much attention is given to Heidegger's notions of "spirit," "psyche" and "soul" – notions which are further explored in the massive companion volume entitled *Psyché: Inventions de l'autre.*[2]

Jointly this battery of writings has placed Heidegger's relation to psychology high on the intellectual agenda. As it seems to me, the importance of the theme is underscored or rendered acute by the theoretical quandaries besetting contemporary psychology and psychoanalysis. As is well known, modern scientific psychology arose as a countermove to the traditional mind–body bifurcation, more specifically as an effort to extend the canons of physics or natural science to the study of the human mind or psyche (a domain hitherto reserved for self-reflection). Despite differences of emphasis, Freudian psychoanalysis followed a similar path. However, while behavioral psychology focused on overt manifestations of psychic life, Freudian theory – at least in its scientific ambitions – sought to grasp the depth structure of the psyche by construing it as a nexus of instinctual (or else psycho-physiological) impulses. In proceeding along these lines, Freud virtually reversed the Cartesian distinction between *res cogitans* and *res extensa*, by projecting the operation of the *res extensa* – a synonym for the Newtonian view of nature (as a causal mechanism) – into the human psyche and particularly into the libidinal "unconscious" seen as "inner" human nature. At least in classical or orthodox psychoanalysis, libidinal drives are treated as the motor of psychic life amenable to causal explanation, while "ego" and "superego" components function as subsidiary agencies designed to adjust instincts to "external" constraints (imposed by society or reason). The accents are shifted in revisionary schools of psychoanalysis, particularly in ego and superego psychology – but only at the price of rendering the status of the ego and social norms elusive if not mysterious (from a scientific standpoint). The quandaries produced by these theoretical premises are pervasive and have frequently been noted. For how can inner, libidinal nature at all be adjusted to external social norms without provoking "denaturation" or psychic catastrophe? On the other hand, if confidence is placed in ego and superego components (along modified Cartesian or Kantian lines), how can normative demands be at all transferred to the domain of "phenomenal" nature (here inner libidinal nature)?

These dilemmas help to silhouette Heidegger's thought at least in a preliminary fashion. As is widely recognized, a central aim of Heidegger's thinking has been to erode or dismantle the Cartesian mind–body or subject–object bifurcation – though not by collapsing one pole into the other. A prominent expression of this effort is his formulation of human existence as being-in-the-world, with its stress on concrete engagement or "in-being" (in contrast to traditional inner–outer dichotomies). A corollary of this emphasis is Heidegger's long-standing critique of the "objectification" or reification of nature and the world – a reification which is the trademark of modern science in its application both to external nature and to psychic phenomena (or "inner" nature). Regarding the latter, one must recall Husserl's fervent indictment of "psychologism" as a reductive congealment of mental life – an indictment indelibly imprinted on later phenomenological inquiry. Heidegger's own opposition to psychologism emerged already quite clearly in passages of *Being and Time*, and it gathered momentum in subsequent writings, including the "Letter on Humanism";[3] however, the contours of his alternative conception remained relatively opaque until the recent publication of *Zollikon Seminars*. Apart from their general philosophical import, these *Seminars* are instructive for a number of reasons. Addressed as they are to medical psychiatrists, the seminar transcripts highlight Heidegger's pedagogical skills – his patient endeavor to communicate complex insights to non-philosophical specialists. In addition, the transcripts help to debunk the thesis of "two Heideggers," that is, of the radical gulf separating the later from the early opus. Throughout the *Seminars*, Heidegger freely invokes arguments taken from *Being and Time* regarding the ontological structure of *Dasein* and its existential modalities; he also explicitly embraces "phenomenology" (as an inquiry into the being of phenomena). In the following I shall first give a condensed synopsis of some key themes articulated in *Zollikon Seminars*. Next, I shall examine some leading commentaries on Heidegger's psychological conception as found in *Heidegger and Psychology*; a main issue at this point will be Heidegger's relation to Freud and his attitude to the unconscious. By way of conclusion I shall explore the broader implications of these discussions for our understanding of psyche, consciousness, and nature (including human nature).

I

Readers of *Being and Time* may recall this pithy phrase : "The existential analytics of *Dasein* is prior to any psychology, anthropology, and (above all) biology." The priority or primacy of existential analytics, Heidegger affirmed at the time, was due to the "ontological" character of its inquiry, that is, its focus on the being of man (*quid sit homo*) in contrast to the "ontic" investigations of empirical psychology and other human sciences.[4] The same primacy was reasserted eloquently in the opening seminar or lecture of September 1959, held in the psychiatric clinic of Zurich. The main emphasis of the lecture was on the differentiation between human being and empirical-ontic givenness or between *Dasein* and *Vorhandensein*. Human existence, Heidegger stated, "is in essence never a mere object existing somewhere, and particularly not a self-enclosed or encapsulated entity." Among self-enclosed entities wrongly substituted for *Dasein* the lecture included the notions of the "ego," of subjectivity and inner "psyche" familiar from traditional metaphysics and psychology: "All those objectifying capsule-conceptions customary up to now in psychology and psychopathology – conceptions of a psyche, a subject, person, ego, or consciousness – have to be abandoned in favor of a completely different view grounded in the analytics of *Dasein*." What was implied though not clearly explicated in this statement was the complementarity and mutal presupposition of subject and object, mind (psyche) and body (soma) in traditional thought. The different view of human existence propounded in the lecture was the conception of *Da-sein* seen as "being-in-the-world." In this formula, *Dasein* did not merely signify "being-there" in the sense of being located in physical space; rather, it denoted the openness of existence to being and its meaning, that is, to the being and meaning of all encountered phenomena. To exist as *Dasein*, we read, means "to keep open a dimension allowing possible access to the significance of phenomena"; boldly put: human *Dasein* "is" an arena of meaning-disclosure, but "not and under no circumstances something to be objectified."[5]

As recorded in the volume, the interval between the first session and the next seminar–conducted in Boss's home in Zollikon – was a period of five years. In some measure, the interval is bridged by a series of discussions held between Boss and Heidegger at various places and on a number of pertinent topics (of which I select a few). Heidegger's critical attitude toward psychology and psychoanalysis is underscored on several occasions. "Modern psychology, anthropology and psychopathology," he observed at one point, "view 'man' as an object in a broad sense, as a being-at-hand [*Vorhandenes*], that is, as an ontic domain, as the totality of empirically ascertainable human traits." What is neglected in this approach is the question of the "humanity" of man, particularly the aspect that humans in principle are able to "relate" to other beings and to themselves – which, in turn, is possible because of an ontological quality: the openness of being. Humanity (*humanitas*) in this context means the "free relation of humans to whatever they encounter" and also the willingness to "let oneself be claimed" by encounters and relationships. This conception of human existence, Heidegger added, stands in contrast to the objectifying thrust of modern science whose canons have come to dominate empirical psychology as well as other human sciences. In the modern scientific worldview, inaugurated by Galileo and Newton, "nature" denotes a "spatio-temporal nexus of extended points or particles in motion" – a construal which radically eliminates all qualitative features as well as ontological considerations. The basic aim of Newtonian science is to measure or quantitatively calculate space–time movements, for the sake of providing causal explanations and predictions.

Contemporary "behavioral sciences," including psychology and sociology, basically subscribe to the Galilean-Newtonian definition of nature and its concomitant conceptual framework; as a result, the human being is likewise seen as a "spatio-temporal point in motion." Needless to say, this approach is far removed not only from existential analytics but also from the outlook of the Greeks whose thinking was oriented ontologically toward "the being of humans and their world."[6]

Heidegger's objections or reservations extended to Freudian psychoanalysis (at least in its orthodox self-understanding). In tracing human behavior to underlying libidinal impulses operating in the "unconscious," Heidegger noted, Freud sought to uncover the causal nexus governing human life in a quasi-naturalistic manner; in doing so, he obeyed the Newtonian demands for causal explanation and prediction – demands radically at odds with the quality of human phenomena. "In the entire construct of Freud's libido theory," Heidegger asked sharply, "is there even any room for 'man' (or human existence)?" A negative response was suggested by science's objectifying bent. "Instinct [*Trieb*]," we read, "is always an attempt at explanation. However, the primary issue is never to provide an explanation, but rather to remain attentive to the *phenomenon* one seeks to explain – to what it is and how it is." For Heidegger, attempts to explain human phenomena out of instincts or libidinal impulses have the methodological character of a science – but a science "whose subject matter is not man but rather mechanics" (or nature mechanistically construed). These comments are particularly noteworthy in view of the accusation of a "regressive" or archaic naturalism frequently leveled at Heidegger's thought. *Zollikon Seminars* distances itself emphatically from such regression. What guides or directs human life, Heidegger insisted, is not a "mythological libido," not an instinct or impulse which "somehow impels or compels me from behind," but it is rather "something which is impending, a task in which I am involved, or something which lays claim to me." The expression or formulation "something impels me" (in a compulsive sense) is actually already a misconstrual and objectification of what is happening or what is really at stake. From the perspective of an existential analytics, that which urges or propels (*der Drang, das Drängende*) is rooted in *Dasein*; urgency marks "being-in-the-world" itself. By contrast, Freudian psychoanalysis grasps only a deficient mode of urgency, namely, the lapsing of *Dasein* into compulsive urges or impulses: "This lapse is treated as the distinctively human characteristic, while urgency is reified into instinctual behavior [*Triebhaftigkeit*]."[7]

In addition to critiquing libido theory as a general framework, Heidegger in discussion also attacked various assumptions or theses commonly associated with Freudian psychoanalysis. A prominent case in point is the theory of "repression" (*Verdrängung*) postulating the dispatching or exiling of psychic experiences into the unconscious. In Heidegger's view, repression so construed involved merely a spatial removal of items from conscious knowledge to a hiding place screened from awareness. In lieu of this construal with its sharp consciousness–unconsciousness dichotomy, Heidegger invoked the complex interlacing or intertwining of concealment and unconcealment, of clearing and veiling. "Freud's notion of repression," we read, "has to do with the hiding or stashing away of an idea or representation [*Vorstellung*]." By contrast, concealment (*Verbergung*) is "not the antithesis to consciousness, but rather belongs to the clearing – a clearing which Freud did not grasp." Just as concealment was not simply an unconscious or counter-conscious domain, so clearing was not synonymous with consciousness in Freud's sense – although clearing could give rise to, and was indeed the precondition of, conscious reflection. Properly understood, clearing was never pure light or reason but rather always "clearing of self-concealment" – where the latter phrase means that "what is inaccessible discloses itself as inaccessible." Corollaries of the Freudian repression were notions like "introjection," "projection" and "transference." As Heidegger indicated, all such notions were artificial constructions, predicated on subject–object relations neglectful of the primary experience of being-in-the-world. Thus, introjection suggests the subjective internalization of another's behavior – a view contradicted by mother–child relations. In imitating the mother, we read, the child blends with the mother's behavior or shares "the mother's being-in-the-world" – which is the opposite of introjecting the mother inside the child. A similar neglect is operative in projection or the ascription of inner feelings to others. According to Heidegger, the psychological theories of projection and empathy are "pointless" because they presuppose, but abstract from, the "co-being [*Mitsein*] with others" which is a crucial feature of being-in-the-world. Likewise, transference is parasitical on a primary "mood" or "tuning" (*Gestimmtheit*) which pervades *Dasein* and co-being prior to subject–object or ego–alter relations.[8]

In opposing Freud's libido theory, one should note that Heidegger did not simply opt for a version of ego psychology – where consciousness and the ego are privileged over unconscious impulses. From the perspective of existential analytics, *Dasein* could never be reduced to a "self-contained subject," but rather meant a mode of being-in-the-world caringly related to things, to utensils, and especially to fellow human beings (on the level of co-being). Moreover, *Dasein* meant sojourning or being placed in the clearing (of being) with its intricate balance of concealment and unconcealment. Against this background, ego psychology and the entire approach starting from consciousness or an "inner-psychic" domain was bound to appear as artificial, as a "construction devoid of evidence." In Heidegger's words: "In customary psychological conceptions of the ego the world-relation is lacking; for this reason the notion of 'ego cogito' remains abstract." In existential terms, the ego was only a narrow crystallization of being-in-the-world, valid for limited purposes and in restricted contexts. By limiting itself to finite boundaries, we read, "the human being becomes an ego – but not through an act of self-expansion whereby the self-conscious ego erects itself into the center and yardstick of everything knowable." One way to correct traditional ego-conceptions was by focusing on human embodiment – provided a careful distinction was made between the physical body (*Körper*) and the "lived body" (*Leib*). The phenomenon of the human body, Heidegger insisted, could never be grasped on the basis of the traditional mind–body division deriving from Descartes, where the body (as *res extensa*) is assumed to be somehow moved or animated by psychic impulses originating in the mind (or *res cogitans*). The human body, he stated, "does *not* initially exist by itself and is subsequently animated by a psychic current, moving for example through the hand. Rather, the body is the necessary, though not sufficient condition for relations (to the world)." For physicians and medically trained psychiatrists embodiment was difficult, perhaps impossible to comprehend, because of their tendency to misconstrue the lived body as a physical entity or reduce it to a causal nexus. Against this tendency it was important to accept and preserve the bodily phenomenon (*Leib-phänomen*) in its integrity, that is, as something "unique and irreducible, especially irreducible to (causal) mechanisms."[9]

By the time the recorded seminar sessions were resumed in 1964 (from now on in Zollikon), Heidegger had decided to provide a broader philosophical background for his audience, chiefly in an effort to lure participants away from a dogmatically accepted scientism or positivism (extolling the canons of natural science). A central theme at this point was the "ontic–ontological difference," that is, the distinction between empirically ascertainable entities or traits and the meaning or "being" of such entities. As Heidegger noted – summarizing arguments familiar from earlier writings – there are two kinds of phenomena or rather two levels or dimensions of phenomena: namely, an "ontic" or empirically observable level and an "ontological" level not amenable to sense perception. In this differentiation, ontological strata have necessarily disclosed themselves "antecedently" prior to the perception of ontic features; for, "before we can perceive the presence of this or that table, we must already have become attentive to the possibility of presence as such." Hence, Heidegger stated, ontological phenomena are "primary in rank and status, but secondary in perception and reflection." Differently phrased: ontically observable entities are antecedently disclosed or rendered accessible by the ontological clearing of being, but being and clearing are commonly not considered or reflected upon. In this respect, the difference of being from beings was "the most fundamental and also the most difficult" distinction. The difficulty was compounded in our time by the predominance of natural science with its focus on observable entities and their causal connections. "Today the belief holds sway," we read, "that science alone yields objective truth. Science in fact is *the* new religion – in comparison with which an attempt to 'think being' appears arbitrary and 'mystical'." From an existential vantage, however, the latter attempt was by no means arbitrary and not even optional; for, as human beings "we can exist only on the ground of this (ontic–ontological) difference." To be sure, exploration of this ground required a special readiness and attentiveness – which was a distinctive and pre-eminent aptitude of humans, one involving a genuine "transformation" of ordinary existence. As Heidegger added, exploring the difference did not denote so much an abandonment of science as rather an effort "to enter into a reflective relation to science and to ponder seriously the latter's boundaries."[10]

Over long stretches, subsequent discussions were devoted precisely to such a pondering of science's boundaries and underlying presuppositions. In Heidegger's presentation, modern science approached nature (seen as *res extensa*) from a specific angle: namely, that of the "lawfulness" (*Gesetzmässigkeit*) and calculability of phenomena – an angle predicated on deeper, ontological premises. In the framework inaugurated by Galileo and Newton, science examines the laws or rules governing the movement of extended points in space and time; according to the later Kantian formulation, nature as such means the "lawfulness of phenomena in space and time" or the existence of things "as determined by general laws." These formulas were not themselves derived from scientific observations but rather dependent on theoretical "suppositions" or presuppositions which in turn relied on taken-for-granted assumptions or an unquestioned "acceptance" of the structure of the world. In Heidegger's words: "The presupposition of a 'nature' as specified by science implies simultaneously an *acceptio*: what is taken for granted in this presupposition are the modalities of space, movement, causality, and time." Special attention in *Zollikon Seminars* is given to the modalities of space and time – which modern science construes as rule-governed, homogeneous categories. Regarding space, the Galilean-Newtonian framework postulates something like an external container indiscriminately embracing things or empirical objects – which is a far cry from premodern, especially early Greek conceptions of space. In early Greek thought, we read, "all bodies have their own location (or *topos*) in accordance with their distinctive nature – which means that heavy bodies are below, lighter ones above. Different spatial locations thus are qualitatively distinguished . . . Galileo cancels all these qualitative locations, thereby cancelling the distinction between above and below." In seeking to recover a non-quantitative, non-homogeneous conception, Heidegger radically distanced himself from the view of space as external container or else as a general category under which things can be subsumed, relying instead on the notion of a "clearing" disclosing and "making room" for the appearance of phenomena. In the case of human *Dasein*, in particular, space denotes an "opening" or open context for the encounter of other beings – which is a requisite quality of being-in-the-world.[11]

Even more extensive than the treatment of space is the discussion of time in *Zollikon Seminars*. From a scientific perspective, time signifies basically homogeneous clock-time, that is, the linear succession of temporal moments; in modern physics, this linear succession is simply added as a further dimension to the three dimensions of space. As Heidegger counters, however, scientific clock-time – with its focus on the succession of "nows" – neglects the retention of the past and the impending character of the future by regarding past and future simply as modes of non-being (as "no-longer" or "not-yet"). Taking up thoughts developed in *Being and Time*, he reasserts the temporality of being itself: "The notion of being in the sense of presence is insufficient for grasping time, because presence is defined as present or now; thus, the question arises whether being (as presence) should not rather be construed in terms of temporality and as sustained by the latter." According to Heidegger, temporality is a pre-eminent characteristic of human *Dasein*, given its special attentiveness to the meaning of being – a characteristic which should not be mistaken for a purely "inner" quality or for a mode of consciousness or subjective experience (as suggested by Bergson and Husserl). From an existential vantage, there is an intimate nexus or connection between time and *Dasein*, a nexus missed or bypassed in notions like "*Zeitsinn*" or "*Zeitbewusstsein*" (sense or consciousness of time). Seeking to elucidate existential temporality, *Zollikon Seminars* highlights the aspects of significance (that one has time "for something"), of datability (or non-randomness), of duration, and of "publicity" (or the publicly shared character of time). Regarding the first aspect, that of significance, it is crucial not to confuse the "having" of time with a possessive relationship whereby a human subject would own or appropriate time as an object. In Heidegger's words: "The 'having' in having time does not denote an indifferent dealing with time as an object. Rather, it is temporality itself which engenders and temporalizes *Dasein's* sojourn" or being-in-the-world. The manner in which *Dasein* is temporalized is threefold, being oriented toward the past, the present, and the future. Thus, "the time I have I have in the mode of anticipation [*gewärtigend*], re-presentation [*gegenwärtigend*], and retention (*behaltend*). This three-fold having . . . is genuine temporality."[12]

As constitutive features of human *Dasein*, spatiality and temporality are intimately connected with embodiment, that is, with *Dasein's* concrete insertion in the world. Accordingly, subsequent seminar discussions revolved repeatedly around the "lived body" (*Leib*) and around the general issue of "psychosomatics," that is, the relation between body and psyche. Although widely used in medical circles, Heidegger noted, psychosomatics is a dubious and deeply problematical conception, because it refers to the correlation or interdependence of body and psyche where only the former is assumed to be scientifically measurable (while the latter is relegated to intuition). Challenging the traditional mind–body bifurcation and by implication psychosomatics as a scientific approach he asked: "Are the relations between psyche and soma something psychic (or psychological), or are they somatic, or are they neither the one nor the other?" To illustrate his preference for the last alternative, Heidegger gave the examples of crying and blushing: "On which side do tears belong? Are they something somatic or something psychic? Neither the one nor the other." In the case of blushing, although redness can as such be measured, blushing from shame resists measurement. Thus, "is blushing something somatic or something psychic? Neither the one nor the other." To undercut the mind–body or psyche–soma division it was necessary to adopt the perspective of the lived body in contradistinction from the anatomical body (*Körper*). From the vantage of lived embodiment, human conduct is not merely externally observable or measurable behavior; nor is it an internal or inner-directed phenomenon where the body would serve as the conduit of psychic impulses or of subjective intentionality. A case in point is the movement of the human hand. "How should this movement be characterized? As an expressive movement?" Heidegger queried. Even if it were granted that the movement brought something internal to the fore or to expression, this statement would miss the character of the movement itself – namely, its specific quality as a "gesture" (*Gebärde*) or as a manifestation of *Dasein* and its being-in-the-world. "Expression" was already an interpretation or rather misinterpretation by pointing to something "behind" the movement or to its inner cause, thus bypassing the gesture itself as bodily movement. In analogy to the term *Gebirge* (as a gathering of mountains), *Gebärde* had to be seen as a "gathering comportment": "In philosophy we must not limit the term *Gebärde* to the domain of 'expression', but must apply it rather to every human comportment seen as embodied being-in-the-world."[13]

In *Zollikon Seminars*, Heidegger's critique of "expressivism" and its reliance on an inner–outer schema extended to prevalent types of existential psychology and psychoanalysis, in particular to Ludwig Binswanger's *Daseinsanalyse*. While appreciating the latter's departure from scientism, Heidegger remonstrated against Binswanger's pervasive subjectivism (or mentalism) as well as his confusion of ontic-empirical and ontological levels of analysis. Commenting on the use of "existential analytics" (*Daseinsanalytik*) in *Being and Time*, Heidegger insisted that the goal of such analytics was not to establish ontic (and certainly not causal) relations among elements, but rather to uncover a "systematic nexus," namely, the unity of ontological conditions governing *Dasein* and its relation to being. In this sense, *Being and Time* inquired into the "ontological-existential constitution" of *Dasein*, an inquiry going beyond the description of ontic phenomena. In Heidegger's words: "The decisive construal of human being as *Dasein* in the sense of ek-stasis (toward being) is an ontological construal which transcends the conception of existence as 'subjectivity of consciousness.' This construal reveals as the basic structure of *Dasein* the understanding of being." Despite widespread misreadings, the point of *Being and Time* and its existential analytics was not to propound an empirical anthropology but rather (and exclusively) to renew the question of the "meaning of being." Instead of focusing – like much of traditional philosophy and metaphysics – on the essence of beings, *Being and Time* sought to explore "being as such," that is, the meaning of being and its possible disclosure or revealment. Against this background, the notion of "analytics" as used in that work was radically distinct from rival usages of the term, including Freud's causal psychodynamics and Husserl's analysis of consciousness. In *Daseinsanalytik* we read, the intent is not "to reduce symptoms to (causal) elements as in Freud's theory; rather, the attempt is made to analyze the features characterizing *Dasein* in its relation to being." On the other hand, "the distinction from Husserl and his phenomenology consists *not* in the presumed stress on ontic structures of *Dasein* but rather in the construal of human being as *Da-sein* – in explicit contrast to the treatment of 'man' as subjectivity or as transcendental ego-consciousness."[14]

The preceding comments served as backdrop to the critical assessment of Binswanger's approach. A major defect of his "existentialism" was its egocentrism, that is, its continued (though slightly modified) reliance on the philosophy of consciousness. As Heidegger stated: "When Binswanger portrays *Being and Time* as an extremely consistent elaboration of the teachings of Kant and Husserl, he is as wrong as he can possibly be. For the question posed in *Being and Time* was raised neither by Husserl nor by Kant; in fact, it was never previously raised in philosophy." Thus, in Binswanger's case, the continued reverberation of Husserl's phenomenology prevented a clear grasp of the "phenomenological hermeneutics of *Dasein*." To the extent that Binswanger amplified Husserl's legacy through a recourse to concrete "existential" phenomena, his approach remained limited to the ontic domain, thus missing the ontological turn propounded in *Being and Time*. An illustrative example is the treatment of "care" (*Sorge*) as one psychological disposition among others, and moreover as a particularly somber and self-centered disposition – a treatment which prompted Binswanger to supplement care with the more cheerful and outgoing disposition of "love." As Heidegger countered, this supplementation derived basically from a conflation of philosophy and ontic description – specifically from the failure to perceive the ontological-existential status of care. *Zollikon Seminars* at this point distinguished between different meanings of the terms *Daseinsanalytik* and *Daseinsanalyse*, mainly three: first, *Daseinsanalytik* as the analysis of the ontological structure of *Dasein* (as attempted in *Being and Time*); secondly, a concrete illustration or exemplification of this ontological structure (quasi-ontological *Daseinsanalyse*); and finally, *Daseinsanalyse* as the description of concrete existential experiences on the level of an ontic anthropology. The last type could in turn be subdivided into an existential anthropology of "normalcy" and an existential psychopathology and psychotherapy. On this level, a merely abstract analysis and general classification of phenomena was insufficient; rather, *Daseinsanalyse* here had to be focused "on the concrete historical existence of contemporary 'man', that is, of human beings living in contemporary industrial society." Properly understood, Binswanger's approach was located on that level – although he misconstrued his endeavors as an implementation of the analytics of *Being and Time*. As Heidegger observed in a discussion with Boss (held roughly at the same time): Binswanger's work selected from *Being and Time* the notion of "being-in-the-world," but mistook it in an empirical-contextual sense; in so doing, he bypassed the existential structure which is crucial for a fundamental ontology: namely, the "understanding of being" (*Seinsverständnis*). Yet, "an existential analysis which omits the relation to being operative in *Seinsverständnis* is not an analysis of *Dasein*" (as seen in *Being and Time*).[15]

In the concluding seminar sessions Heidegger turned to the status of psychoanalysis and psychotherapy, in an effort to elucidate his own view of an existentially informed *Daseinsanalyse*. As he pointed out, the theme of psychiatry and psychotherapy is human existence or *Dasein*, and particularly the agonies and possible deformations afflicting *Dasein*. Given this focus, psychiatry could not possibly emulate the canons of natural science with their emphasis on measurement and calculation; emulation of these canons would result not in a properly "human science" (*Wissenschaft vom Menschen*) but in the "technical construction of a human machine." In attempting to outline some parameters of an existential psychiatry, Heidegger drew attention to a psychiatric report dealing with the issue of "stress." Commenting on the report, he immediately extricated the topic from a narrow behaviorism which sees stress merely as an external, causally effective stimulus. In existential terms, he noted, stress has the character of a demand made on human life, in the sense that something addresses and "lays claim" to *Dasein's* care (*Beanspruchung*). Such an address or claim is not intelligible on stimulus-response premises but only on the basis of human being-in-the-world, that is, of *Dasein's* insertion in the world and its attendant exposure to things, fellow humans, and being itself. "As long as 'man' is conceived as a world-less ego," we read, "the inescapability of demands cannot be understood; stress seen as demand belongs, however, to the basic constitution of ek-sisting *Dasein*." In the language of *Being and Time*, demands are a corollary of *Dasein's* exposure or "thrownness" in the world, together with the endeavor to make sense of encounters through language: "Only on the basis of the correlation of thrownness and understanding via language can *Dasein* be addressed by beings; the possibility of such an address, in turn, is the condition of possibility of a demand or claim – whether this claim takes the form of stress or of relief from stress." Even the latter type of relief involves or exerts a claim; far from signifying a simple negation or cessation of demands, relief is a mode of existence as it is steadily addressed by world and beings.[16]

II

Even though necessarily condensed, the preceding synopsis of *Zollikon Seminars* should provide a glimpse of the volume's rich texture of themes and arguments. In view of widespread assertions of the abandonment of phenomenology in Heidegger's later work, a striking feature of the seminars is the continued invocation of phenomenological inquiry (as inquiry into the "appearance" of being) – and this during the heyday of structuralism and cybernetic systems theory. Repeatedly the seminars speak of the need to distinguish the phenomenological mode of seeing and interpreting from the prevalent behaviorist or natural-science methodology. The basic rule of such seeing, we read at one point, is the endeavor to "let every phenomenon show itself in its distinctive qualities." Thus, phenomenology "neither draws (logical) conclusions nor engages in dialectical mediations"; rather, it seeks to "keep the thinking gaze open for the phenomenon" – and nothing else. With respect to the seeing and interpreting of phenomena all proofs or forms of scientific demonstration always come "too late," since they necessarily rely on extrinsic elements. At another point, Heidegger defines the central characteristic of phenomenology as a concrete "engagement" (*Sicheinlassen*), namely, an engagement with everything encountered in the course of our being-in-the-world. If there is an element of will in phenomenology, it is the determination "not to shield oneself against this engagement." Differentiating phenomenological engagement from both conceptual logic and emotivism, a later passage observes: "There is something else, prior to all conceptualization and emotive experience. This other domain – prior to conceiving and emoting – is that of phenomenology. But we must properly comprehend the distinguishing mark of phenomenology and guard against misconstruing it as just one among other 'approaches' and schools in philosophy."[17]

Another, still more prominent theme of the seminars is the juxtaposition of Heidegger's thought and Freudian psychoanalysis – a topic which previously had often remained on the level of speculation. Commentators addressing the topic in the past have tended to be split into two camps: those defending and those rejecting the compatibility of Heideggerian ontology and Freudianism (in either its orthodox or a suitably revised form); a central issue in these debates has been the status of the Freudian notion of the "unconscious" and, by implication, the underlying conception of human existence or human "nature." The volume *Heidegger and Psychology* contains essays written by leading representatives of the two camps, namely, Joseph Kockelmans and William Richardson – whose arguments I shall briefly recapitulate here. In his essay titled "Daseinsanalysis and Freud's Unconscious", Kockelmans sharply differentiates *Daseinsanalyse* – construed as a "regional ontology" inspired by Heidegger's *Being and Time* – from both Freudian psychoanalysis and scientific or behavioral psychology. As he notes, the models governing the latter types of inquiry were taken from the natural sciences, that is, physics, chemistry, and biology; even when a narrow physicalism is avoided, orthodox Freudianism continues to speak of "forces, functions, psychisms, energy sources, drives" and the like. In its cruder form, Freudian psychoanalysis seeks to trace symptoms of psychic illness causally to a "malfunctioning" of the human body, the brain or the nervous system. Yet, Kockelmans counters, "it will be obvious that such an 'explanation', however important within certain limits, is totally irrelevant to the question of precisely how certain emotions and feelings, ideas, illusions, or hallucinations are to be related to these organic disturbances." By contrast, *Daseinsanalyse* has effectively resisted and combatted every type of scientific reductionism; while not questioning the legitimacy of research in biology, physiology or neurology, its adepts insist that human existence and mental illness cannot be "understood" or rendered intelligible on this basis. Inaugurated by Binswanger and continued by Medard Boss and others, *Daseinsanalyse* has produced an overall theoretical framework which is "totally different" from Freud's psychoanalytic theory – one which "does not make a machine out of a human being, but lets man show himself as human"; on a practical level, it has developed a therapy which can be employed with people "who could not be helped otherwise."[18]

A particularly dubious or problematical ingredient of Freudian psychoanalysis, in Kockelmans' view, is the notion of the unconscious and its relation to libidinal drives. As he points out, Freud's theory originally aimed at a more or less rigorous physiological reduction of mental phenomena. At that point, mental phenomena were seen as processes occurring in an entity called "psyche" which in turn was conceived as a complex reflex mechanism of external stimuli, a mechanism propelled by libidinal "energy" derived from the excitations of bodily organs. The relation between body and mind was construed as a causal nexus, with mental processes basically effecting a "motor discharge of energy" designed to reduce an excess of bodily excitation. However, starting with *The Interpretation of Dreams* (1900), Freud faced the problem of relating his causal "energetics" with the task of interpreting meanings and symbols, a task for which physiological explanation seemed only partially helpful. In an effort to render the connection more plausible, Freud at this point introduced a division within the psyche or psychic structure, by distinguishing between consciousness and the unconscious, between consciously intended meanings and unintended and cognitively unintelligible or opaque meanings. In making this distinction, his theory endorsed a split between the purposiveness of human life and resistances to purposive goals, between teleology (of meaning) and counter-teleology. While initially introduced as simply a margin of consciousness, the unconscious soon became stabilized and localized as part of a complex psychic system. In his later writings, Freud tended to reassert the preeminence of energetics or physical forces over mental phenomena; in the end, the characteristics attributed to the unconscious were assigned to the libidinal *id* which in turn was energized by bodily excitations. Although acknowledging his departure from standard behaviorism, Freud throughout maintained the legitimacy of an inquiry transgressing overtly observable phenomena: "A gain in meaning is a perfectly justifiable ground for going beyond the limits of direct experience."[19]

Relying on the chief spokesmen of *Daseinsanalyse*, Kockelmans challenges and rejects the Freudian unconscious as an untenable assumption. In one of his clinical case studies, Binswanger had termed it unacceptable to construe "behind" consciousness a second, recessed layer of the mind, or "behind" the conscious personality an unconscious second person. Although admitting that Freud's notion pointed obliquely to a concrete dimension of human life, he denounced the libidinal *id* – conflated with the unconscious – as a natural-scientific construct which objectified human existence by reducing it to a "reservoir of instinctual energy." The only way to make sense of the unconscious, for Binswanger, was to recast it in light of Heidegger's conception of *Dasein*, and particularly in terms of the existential categories of thrownness and facticity: "We can say of the psyche as well as of the organism that they belong to the hidden, but *as hidden* 'disclosed' ontological character of the facticity of thrownness of the being we call 'man' in his thereness [*Da*]." In a similar spirit, Medard Boss advanced several arguments to undermine and defeat Freud's notion. One difficulty was the dependence of the unconscious on the legacy of subjectivity and the philosophy of consciousness – a legacy which Heidegger had called into question in his critique of modern thought from Descartes to Kant and beyond. Given that Freud had failed to articulate a coherent theory of consciousness, his companion notion of the unconscious was likewise defective and incoherent. Another problem was the attempted derivation of consciousness from unconscious mental processes and ultimately from bodily excitations. In Boss's view, it was "completely incomprehensible" how consciousness could arise out of such an enigmatic causal connection. Finally, the trouble with the unconscious was that it was basically a needless or superfluous hypothesis – once relevant phenomena were approached from the vantage of existential analysis or *Daseinsanalyse*. According to Boss, we read, "if one carefully examines all the phenomena on which Freud founded his conception of the unconscious, he finds time and again that Freud makes assumptions which are unjustifiable and that a legitimate explanation of these phenomena is possible without any appeal to the unconscious in the sense of Freud."[20]

Apart from invoking the testimony of Binswanger and Boss, Kockelmans also takes to task a leading spokesman of the opposing view – Richardson – who in a paper of 1965 had tried to locate "the place of the unconscious in Heidegger." In that paper, Richardson had first compared the unconscious with Husserl's notion of "non-thetic" or non-thematic intentionality but then had shifted the accent resolutely to

Heidegger's *Being and Time* and his conception of *Dasein* as a non-subjective or "pre-subjective" self, suggesting in the end that "the place where unconscious processes may be situated in Heidegger's thought seems to be in the existential-ontological dimensions of this *onto-conscious self.*"[21] For Kockelmans, expressions like non-subjective or pre-subjective are dubious as characterizations of human *Dasein*, while there is simply "no textual foundation" in *Being and Time* for the phrase "onto-conscious self." In his own view, Heideggerian ontology and Freudian psychoanalysis are incompatible and mutually exclusive on a theoretical plane. "It seems to me meaningless," he writes, "to try to 'build' Freudian ideas into Heidegger's fundamental ontology or Heideggerian ideas into Freud's psychoanalysis. Personally, I reject Freud's philosophical ideas on the ground that they rest on assumptions which in my opinion cannot possibly be justified philosophically." From a Heideggerian vantage, Freud's theory suffers from two main defects: first, he construed "empirical" entities (like organism, psyche, the unconscious) which were phenomenologically unwarranted; secondly, he failed to correlate his physiological energetics with the dimension of meaning. In both respects, *Daseinsanalyse* is said to be superior. Above all, the latter has "no room and no need" for an unconscious, just as little as it has room or need for a "theory of consciousness" (in the Cartesian and Kantian vein). "Thus, in my opinion," Kockelmans concludes, "Richardson was wrong in trying to find a Daseinsanalytic parallel to Freud's unconscious within the perspective of fundamental ontology."[22]

In *Heidegger and Psychology* Kockelman's view does not go unchallenged. Together with reproducing (in an Appendix) Richardson's paper of 1965, the volume contains a more recent essay by the same author entitled "The Mirror Inside: The Problem of the Self". The essay boldly seeks to establish a linkage between Heideggerian ontology and Freudian psychoanalysis as reinterpreted in the work of Jacques Lacan. In Richardson's own words, the question he tries to address is "whether a Heideggerian concept of the structure of man might offer a philosophical context within which to think Lacan's psychological/metapsychological/structuralist distinction between self and ego." In Lacan's complex theoretical framework, the essay focuses chiefly on the formative "mirror stage" of early infancy and the subsequent entrance of the child into the "symbolic order" of discursive language. According to Lacan, the child – after an initial phase of amorphous existence – first discovers some kind of "self" or unity of self by experiencing some reflection of itself, primarily through self-reflection in a mirror. By identifying with the reflected image of itself, the child acquires a sense of the "I" or ego which undergirds and informs its further development. As should be noted, however, the reflected image is in some sense external to or other than the infant; thus, the mirror stage produces simultaneously the initial identification as well as the primordial alienation or self-estrangement of the child. Although internally divided and unstable, emerging ego-identity provides a protective shield or a defense mechanism against a possible relapse into the earlier amorphous chaos; in Lacan's words, the process involves the "assumption of the armor of an alienating identity, which will mark with its rigid structure the subject's entire mental development." The process of identification-*cum*-alienation is intensified with the child's entry into language, that is, into the discursive structures of the adult social world. At this point, Lacan's central modification or rethinking of orthodox Freudianism comes into view: namely, his "linguistic turn" or his rethinking of both ego-consciousness and the unconscious in terms of linguistic structures. Basically, by entering adult discourse the child acquires a clearly particularized ego-identity vastly more nuanced than the earlier dyadic mirror-relation; at the same time, however, all dimensions of experience not subsumable under the ego are exiled into a netherworld of the unconscious which itself has the character of a "transindividual" language not amenable to conscious control.[23]

Elaborating on Lacan's linguistic turn, Richardson discusses in detail numerous features of recent (structural) linguistics – not all of which are germane in the present context. As he indicates, Lacan adopted from Roman Jacobson the notion of two "fundamental axes" of language: namely, the axis of combination and the axis of selection or substitution – which, in rhetorics, correspond to metonymy and metaphor respectively. The relevance of these categories for psychoanalysis was evident particularly in reference to the theory of "dream work" which, in Freud's account, involved the two processes of "condensation" and "displacement." Following Jacobson's suggestion, Richardson comments, Lacan "claims that condensation is a form of substitution" and "hence to be located linguistically along the axis of selection" (or metaphor), while displacement "functions by reason of contiguity, hence is to be located linguistically along the axis of combination" (or metonymy). Returning to the issue of identity formation, the essay presents the child's entry into adult language as the initiation into the "symbolic order" of culture or civil society, where both mature language and society obey rigidly enforced civil norms. In Lacan's formulation, both discursive language and society represent the "law" or the "name of the father," the latter standing as the symbol and guardian of the social or symbolic order; in his words, "the law of man (society) has been the law of language" (seen as socially controlled discourse). Initiation into culture, however, is not a painless or smooth process of integration. The name

(*nom*) of the father is also the "no" of the latter's authority, whereby
unregulated or pre-discursive layers of self are banished into unconscious
or "transindividual" language – which Lacan also calls "the other scene"
or simply "the Other." In transplanting the earlier dyadic relation with
the reflected image (typically the mother), the symbolic order ruptures
an ontological, quasi-symbiotic linkage – thus producing a loss or "lack
of being" which, in turn, engenders a life-long yearning or "desire." As
Richardson states: "The basic dynamic of the human subject for Lacan
is not libido, as it is for Freud, but desire, as it is for Hegel"; this longing
or desire "erupts in the infant with the rupture of the dyadic, quasi-
symbiotic relation with the mother by which the infant experiences in
its separation from her the negation of itself, hence its *manque à être* – its
own lack of (or better, want of) being, out of which its wanting (its desire)
is born." In subsequent life, "the child's desire – its endless quest for a
lost paradise – must be tunnelled like an underground river through the
subterranean passageways of the symbolic order."[24]

Taking up the question raised in its opening pages, the essay in its
conclusion suggests possible ways of relating Lacan's framework with
Heideggerian thought. One, and perhaps the primary, linkage consists
in the ontological conception of *Dasein* as transcending ontic identity.
In Heideggerian terms, Richardson comments, *Dasein* is an ek-static or
"ex-centric" self insofar as its own being resides in the exposure or "openness to the being of all beings." Given its ek-static quality, *Dasein* is
"more than a conscious ego" or a name for self-identity; by virtue of its
constant transcendence of other beings and itself (in the direction of
being), *Dasein* can be called a "genuinely de-centered, ex-centric self."
This description, however, corresponds closely to Lacan's view of the
divided subject or of "the self's radical ex-centricity to itself." The parallel
carries over into the notion of ontological exposure – which Lacan picks
up when he speaks of the "dimension of being: *Kern unseres Wesens* are
Freud's own terms." For Lacan, relatedness to being is both the ground
of *Dasein*'s well-being and also the source of possible illness or pathology;
as he says, "a neurosis is a question which being poses for a subject 'from
the place where it was before the subject came into the world' (Freud's
phrase which he used in explaining the Oedipal complex to Little Hans)."
Another way of establishing a linkage between Lacan and Heidegger is
by resorting to the domain of language. In elucidating this connection,
Richardson turns both to Heidegger's discussion of "speech" in *Being and
Time* and (more centrally) to his later reflections on language as "*logos*"
in which being is gathered. In early Greek thought, we read, "being was
experienced as a gathering process that collected all beings together
within themselves and in relationship to one another"; in Heidegger's

retrieval of being as *logos*, what "gathers the many unto themselves and lets them relate to one another, is an experience of language, of aboriginal language." This notion of *logos* as aboriginal language, in Richardson's assessment, is not far removed from Lacan's linguistic turn and especially his linguistic reformulation of the Freudian unconscious: "If Jacobson and his colleagues in their researches discover the laws of phonemes or the two great axes of language that Lacan then sees to be structuring the unconscious as it permeates man, then these are historical modalities, discernible by scientific scrutiny, of the primordial *logos* as such."[25]

III

The discussions or debates reported above clearly give rise to a host of difficult and complex issues. To some extent, the publication of *Zollikon Seminars* contributes to a clarification of these issues – or at least serves to underscore their ambivalent, perhaps irresoluble character. A prominent case in point is the status of the Freudian unconscious and its relation to ego consciousness. On repeated occasions – both in seminar sessions and discussions with Boss – Heidegger remonstrates against the notion of the unconscious, which he construes as a part of psychodynamics and thus of the reduction of human experience to a causal-explanatory scheme. Treated as a motive of behavior, he observes at one point, the unconscious is "unintelligible" because a motive cannot be conflated with causal impulses. At the same time, *Zollikon Seminars* critiques ego consciousness and the entire tradition of the "philosophy of consciousness," to the extent that it assigns a foundational role to the subject (or *res cogitans*). From Heidegger's vantage, *Dasein* is an intricately structured being-in-the-world which cannot be reduced to a subject–object relation – without on this count collapsing into a causal nexus (of drives). Consciousness and self-consciousness, against this background, are at best an emergent property of *Dasein* – a property which does not cancel *Dasein's* primary ontological exposure.[26] To the extent that Lacan – or Richardson as his interpreter – still invokes the Freudian terminology of the unconscious, he implicitly pays tribute to modern metaphysics and to the consciousness–unconsciousness doublet challenged by Heidegger. Some reservations probably should also be voiced regarding the parallel constructed by Richardson between Lacan's linguistic turn and Heidegger's "aboriginal language." Although both thinkers share a strong concern with language, the sense or direction of their preoccupation probably does not coincide. In the case of Lacan, one should not ignore his indebtedness to post-Saussurean, structuralist linguistics with its stress on the purely arbitrary character of signifiers – a stress which banishes the "Real" or the "Other" to an extra-linguistic domain in a manner hardly congruent with Heidegger's ontological conception of language (highlighting its disclosure of being).

These observations do not necessarily vindicate Kockelmans' radically anti-Freudian stance. Given Heidegger's repeated self-distantiation from Binswanger and his lingering subjectivism (along Husserlian lines), it seems hardly warranted to assign Heidegger unmistakably to *Daseinsanalyse* or to erect an unbridgeable gulf between Heideggerian ontology and Freudian psychoanalysis (at least in its non-orthodox versions). In light of *Zollikon Seminars*, Richardson's notions of a pre- or non-subjective self and even of the "onto-conscious" character of *Dasein* do not strike me as entirely far-fetched; nor does the correlation of onto-logical ek-stasis and Lacanian "ex-centricity" seem implausible. Particularly congenial with Heidegger's perspective, in my view, is Lacan's conception of psychotherapy and of the rootedness of illness in a "lack of being." Several passages in *Zollikon Seminars* link human pathology with an ontological lack or "privation." "If we negate something not by simply excluding it but rather by retaining it as a lack or want," Heidegger says at one point, "then we call such negation a *privation*". The endeavors of the medical profession, he continues addressing his psychiatric audience, occur "in the domain of negation understood as a privation" – because they revolve around human illness or pathology. In the case of illness, well-being or being-in-the-world is not simply absent or eliminated but disturbed. In this sense, illness is not a "mere" negation of *Dasein*'s situatedness, but a phenomenon of privation; every privation, however, implies a relatedness to being or to the condition which is wanting or of which one is in want. Thus, "to the extent that you deal with illness you actually deal with well-being in the sense of a lack of well-being which is to be restored."[27]

Heidegger's affinities with a non-orthodox Freudianism are underscored in *Zollikon Seminars* by frequent protestations against idealism and mentalism (which, it is true, do not fully cancel certain culturalist overtones). In my own view, the path to a viable connection of existential ontology and psychoanalysis was traced some time ago by Merleau-Ponty in his essay "Phenomenology and Psychoanalysis". In this essay, Merleau-Ponty sided with those who, separating psychoanalysis from a "scientific or objectivist ideology," treat the Freudian unconscious rather as "an archaic or primordial consciousness" and the repressed as "a zone of experience that we have not integrated". This construal, in his view, did not vindicate a mentalist approach nor the integration of psychoanalysis into the "philosophy of consciousness" (along Husserlian lines). As he observed, drawing his inspiration more from Heidegger than Husserl: "All consciousness is consciousness of something or of the world, but this *something*, this world, is no longer . . . an object that is what it is, exactly adjusted to acts of consciousness. Consciousness is now the 'soul of Heraclitus' and being, which is around it rather than in front of it, is a being of dreams, by definition hidden." According to Merleau-Ponty, it was important to attend more to Freud's concrete investigations than to his terminology or his theoretical constructs. Freud's genius, he noted, was not that of philosophical or theoretical formulation; instead, it resided in "his contact with things, his polymorphous perception of work, of acts, of dreams, of their flux and reflux"; thus, his thought was sovereign "in his listening to the confused noises of a life." The task of both contemporary psychoanalysis and existential philosophy or ontology was to listen to these baffling sounds. From this perspective, the relation between existential phenomenology and Freudianism was not one of super- and sub-ordination, nor one of simple convergence: The accord between the two perspectives should not be seen to consist "in phenomenology's saying clearly what psychoanalysis had said obscurely"; rather, it is by what the former "implies or unveils at its limits – by its *latent content* or its *unconscious* – that it is in consonance with psychoanalysis." In his theoretical endeavors, Freud pointed to the domains of the *id* and the superego; likewise, Husserl in his last writings spoke of "historical life as a *Tiefenleben*" (a point, one might add, deepened by Heidegger's stress on historicity). What results from these notions is not a parallelism or coincidence of the two modes of inquiry but the fact that both are "aiming toward the same *latency*."[28]

It is not clear that Heidegger would have concurred with these comments (written roughly at the time of the first seminar session in Zurich). Throughout *Zollikon Seminars*, Heidegger is intensively and almost exclusively preoccupied with differentiating his thought from a narrow naturalism or physicalism, that is, from the reduction of existential analytics to causal-empirical processes. Though warranted in part by the concrete context – the scientistic outlook of most seminar participants – the emphasis effectively militated against any accommodation or rapprochement with the Freudian legacy. Heidegger's attacks in many seminar sessions on scientism – always carefully distinguished from science as such – are eloquent and occasionally vehement and iconoclastic. "The more powerful are today the effects and utility of science," he observes at one point, "the weaker is the ability and willingness to reflect on science insofar as it claims to represent *the* truth of reality." Yet, he asks, what results from a scientism left to its own devices? Nothing less than "the self-destruction of man" – which is a paradoxical outcome given modern science's reliance on subjectivity and human mastery (over nature). Another passage speaks of the "idolatry" organized by mass media around modern science and technology, an idolatry in comparison with which "the supposed superstition of primitive peoples seems like child's play." In the goal of human mastery promoted by modern science Heidegger in a later context perceives an imperialistic "dictatorship of the spirit" in which spirit itself is reduced to a mere instrument of calculation and control. At the same time, mankind's relentless assault on nature – guided by the Cartesian motto to become "maître et possesseur de la nature" – has destructive and self-destructive consequences for the agent of domination. "If scientism governs the conception of human *Dasein*," he adds, "and if the latter is viewed as a feedback mechanism (as is done in cybernetics), then the destruction of human existence is complete. Thus I do not react against science as such but against scientism or the absolutization of natural science."[29]

While outspoken or blunt in denouncing technology's assault on nature, *Zollikon Seminars* is relatively subdued or reticent regarding an alternative relationship of *Dasein* to nature – including "internal" human nature. In this respect, Merleau-Ponty's view seems again pertinent when he stated that phenomenology has perhaps "succeeded too well," that today "biologism and objectivism reign no longer" (at least not uncontested), and that "idealist" formulations are an inadequate counterpoint to scientism. What is clear in *Zollikon Seminars* is that human nature cannot be construed in terms of a naturalist psychodynamics stressing causal drives, impulses or instincts. At the same time, human nature cannot be equated with a rational ego distancing nature from itself in the mode of a subject–object relation. Following the lead of *Being and Time*, *Zollikon Seminars* presents *Dasein* as a mode of existence concerned with and exposed to being – a portrayal whose "humanist" overtones are in danger of eclipsing human inherence in nature as part of being-in-the-world.[30] Only occasionally in the seminars does Heidegger allude to a notion of nature which is not identical with the object of natural-scientific analysis. Thus, commenting on the modern stress on objectivity and objectification, he states: "Something present, however, can also be encountered in such a manner that it is seen as showing itself forth and arising on its own. This is *physis* in the Greek sense." The Greek way of seeing, he adds, was dedicated to "preserving and 'saving' the phenomena as they show themselves in an untouched or inviolate state" – which stands in sharp contrast to the methods of modern science. This view of nature as self-disclosing or self-unfolding being is a prominent theme in Heidegger's postwar writings. Thus, his essay on "The

Question Concerning Technology" distinguishes the Greek conception of nature or *physis* from other modes of showing or bringing forth, including craftwork and poetic or artistic production. "Arising or unfolding on its own," we read, "*physis* too is a *poiesis* or a bringing forth; it is even the highest type of such *poiesis*. For, what is present in terms of *physis* carries the origin or source of its disclosure in itself, as is shown by the blossoming-forth of blossoms."[31]

In my own view, this alternative conception of nature – though undeveloped in *Zollikon Seminars* – may well be one of the most significant insights in Heidegger's later writings; it also makes an important contribution to the theoretical conundrums of traditional psychoanalysis and psychotherapy. In Freudian and post-Freudian literature, the task of psychotherapy is frequently seen in the liberation of libidinal drives or impulses – construed as "inner" human nature – from social constraints and the "discontents" of civilization; conversely, opponents of *id*-psychology define the therapeutic goal as the exit from blind impulses and the reintegration of the patient into social life and the norms of "communicative rationality." With a distinct political edge (against capitalist discontents), the first outlook has been emphatically advocated by Herbert Marcuse, as part of a quasi-Marxist strategy of human emancipation; liberation in his formulation meant basically the dismantling of "excess" social regulations and the freeing of libidinal strivings in the service of the "pleasure principle" and the "eroticization" of human life. In light of Heidegger's critique of psychodynamics, however, this libidinal strategy may well be inadequate or counterproductive; in fact, its naturalist premises appear as an integral part of modern metaphysics with its focus on causal explanation and its division of inner-psychic processes from external social bonds. In large measure, Heidegger's arguments in *Zollikon Seminars* and his later writings can be seen as an effort to extricate *Dasein* both from libidinal compulsion and an abstract-rationalist normativism – thus clearing the path to the disclosure and innocent-poetic self-unfolding of nature (as *physis*). This effort is recognized at least implicitly in Derrida's *De l'esprit* which records Heidegger's cautious, sometimes halting move beyond physicalism and a *Geist*-centered ontology. With specific reference to Freud's legacy, the basic gist of such a move has been eloquently stated by Merleau-Ponty in these words:

The psychoanalysis that we accept and like is not the (reductive) one that we refused. We refused, as we always will, to grant to the phallus which is part of the objective body, the organ of micturition and copulation, such power of causality over so many forms of behavior. What we have learned from all the material drawn from dreams, fantasies, and behaviors, and finally even in our own dreaming about the body, was to discern an imaginary phallus, a symbolic phallus, oneiric and poetic. It is not the useful, functional, prosaic body which explains man; on the contrary, it is the human body which rediscovers its symbolic or poetic weight.[32]

NOTES

1   Martin Heidegger, *Zollikoner Seminare*: *Protokolle-Gespräche-Briefe*, ed. Medard Boss (Frankfurt-Main: Klostermann, 1987).
2   See Keith Hoeller, ed., *Heidegger and Psychology*, Special Issue of *Review of Existential Psychology and Psychiatry* (1988); most of the essays in this volume had previously appeared in vol. 16 (1978–9) of the same *Review*. See also Jacques Derrida, *De l'esprit*: *Heidegger et la question* (Paris: Editions Galileé, 1987), and *Psyché*: *Inventions de l'autre* (Paris: Editions Galileé, 1987), esp. pp. 395–451.
3   Heidegger's opposition to psychologism can actually be traced back to his doctoral dissertation of 1914 (on *The Doctrine of Judgment in Psychologism*). Regarding the fervor of this opposition compare Boss's comments: "Even before our first encounter, I had heard of Heidegger's abysmal aversion to all modern scientific psychology. To me, too, he made no secret of his opposition to it. His repugnance mounted considerably after I had induced him with much guile and cunning to delve directly for the first time into Freud's own writings . . . He simply did not want to have to accept that such a highly intelligent and gifted man as Freud could produce such artifical, inhuman, indeed absurd and purely fictitious constructions about homo sapiens." See Medard Boss, "Martin Heidegger's Zollikon Seminars", in *Heidegger and Psychology*. p. 9.
4   Heidegger, *Sein und Zeit* (11th edn; Tübingen: Niemeyer, 1967), par. 9 and 10, p. 45.
5   *Zollikoner Seminare*, pp. 3–4. The above citations are paraphrases due to the absence of a verbatim protocol.
6   *Zollikoner Seminare*, pp. 197–9. An aggravated case of reductive scientism, in Heidegger's view, is the resort to physiological or chemical explanations of behavior (p. 200): "From the fact that chemical interventions in the human organism (itself chemically construed) produce certain effects one concludes that chemical physiology is the ground and cause of human psychic life. But this is a fallacy."
7   *Zollikoner Seminare*, pp. 217–19.
8   *Zollikoner Seminare*, pp. 207–10, 228–9.
9   *Zollikoner Seminare*, pp. 204, 207, 220, 232–3, 235. Compare also the comment (p. 215): "The lived human body can in principle never be regarded as a mere being-at-hand [*Vorhandenes*], if one wishes to treat it properly; if I regard it in this manner, I have already destroyed it as a lived body."
10 *Zollikoner Seminare*, pp. 7–8, 20–21.

11 *Zollikoner Seminare*, pp. 14–16, 30–32, 35–7, 40.

12 *Zollikoner Seminare*, pp. 42–4, 47–8, 54–5, 60–61, 77, 84–5. In this context, Heidegger offered a detailed phenomenological analysis of representation (*Vergegenwärtigung*) seen as an existential "being-with" (*Sein bei*) things in the world (pp. 86–96).

13 *Zollikoner Seminare*, pp. 102–4, 106, 115–16, 118. Heidegger applied this notion of gesture also to the phenomenon of blushing. Rather than simply expressing an inner condition, he stated (p. 118), blushing too "is a gesture insofar as the blushing person relates to fellow humans . . . I emphasize this so much in order to lure you away from the misconstrual as expression. The French psychologists also misconstrue everything as an expression of inner-psychic states – instead of seeing the body-phenomenon in its inter-human relatedness." Regarding psychosomatics compare also these comments in a discussion with Boss (pp. 248–9): "The term 'psychosomatic medicine' attempts to synthesize two entities which do not exist . . . Soma and psyche are related to *Dasein not* in the way that red and green relate to color, because psyche and soma are not two types of the genus 'man'."

14 *Zollikoner Seminare*, pp. 150–51, 155–6.

15 *Zollikoner Seminare*, pp. 151–2, 157, 163–4, 236. In the same discussion. Heidegger complained about Binswanger's "inadequate interpretation" of being-in-the-world and transcendence (p. 237): "Although these phenomena are termed basic, they are ascribed to a *Dasein* which is treated in isolated fashion and seen anthropologically as *subject*. Thus, psychiatric *Daseinsanalyse* relies on a truncated *Dasein* whose basic trait has been surgically removed." Simultaneously, Heidegger objected to the opposition of "care" and "love": "Properly understood, namely in a fundamental-ontological sense, *care* can never be differentiated from 'love'; rather, it is the name for the ekstatic-temporal structure of *Dasein's* basic trait, its *Seinsverständnis*. Love is founded on this *Seinsverständnis* just as solidly as is care." The same discussion contains fascinating comments on transcendence, selfhood, difference, and *Ereignis* (pp. 240–42).

16 *Zollikoner Seminare*, pp. 180–85, 187.

17 *Zollikoner Seminare*, pp. 82, 89, 143, 172.

18 Joseph J. Kockelmans, "Daseinsanalysis and Freud's Unconscious", in Hoeller, ed., *Heidegger and Psychology*, pp. 22, 24–6. Among relevant literature, Kockelmans refers primarily to Ludwig Binswanger, "Heidegger's Analytic of Existence and its Meaning for Psychiatry", in Joseph Needleman, ed., *Being-in-the-World: Selected Papers of Ludwig Binswanger* (New York: Basic Books, 1963), pp. 206–21; and Medard Boss, *Psychoanalysis and Daseinsanalysis* (New York: Basic Books, 1963).

19 Kockelmans, "Daseinsanalysis and Freud's Unconscious", pp. 28–31. The last citation is from Sigmund Freud, "The Unconscious" (1915), in *Standard Edition* (London: Hogarth Press, 1953), vol. 14, pp. 166–7.

20 Kockelmans, "Daseinsanalysis and Freud's Unconscious", pp. 32, 34–5. Compare Boss, *Psychoanalysis and Daseinsanalysis*, pp. 90–93.

21   William J. Richardson, "The Place of the Unconscious in Heidegger", in Hoeller, ed., *Heidegger and Psychology*, *p. 187*; the article appeared first in *Review of Existential Psychology and Psychiatry*, vol. 5 (1965), pp. 265–90.

22   Kockelmans, "Daseinsanalysis and Freud's Unconscious", pp. 32–4, 37–9.

23   William J. Richardson, "The Mirror Inside: The Problem of the Self", in *Heidegger and Psychology*, pp. 96, 98–9. Compare also Jacques Lacan, *Écrits: A Selection*, tr. Alan Sheridan (New York: Norton, 1977), p. 4.

24   Richardson, "The Mirror Inside", pp. 101–7; see also Lacan, *Écrits: A Selection*, pp. 61, 66.

25   Richardson, "The Mirror Inside", pp. 107–10; see also Lacan, *Écrits: A Selection*, pp. 166, 168, 171.

26   *Zollikoner Seminare*, pp. 189–91, 233.

27   *Zollikoner Seminare*, pp. 58–9. At a later point (p. 63) Heidegger characterizes our present age of technological "progress" as an age of privation.

28   Maurice Merleau-Ponty, "Phenomenology and Psychoanalysis: Preface to Hesnard's *L'Oeuvre de Freud*" (1960), in Alden L. Fischer, ed., *The Essential Writings of Merleau-Ponty* (New York: Harcourt, Brace & World, 1961), pp. 81, 84–7. Regarding exegesis; the essay (p. 86) recommends that we "learn to read Freud the way we read a classic, that is, by understanding his words and theoretical concepts, not in their lexical and common meaning, but in the meaning they acquire from within the experience which they announce and of which we have behind our backs much more than a suspicion. Since our philosophy has given us no better way to express the *intemporal*, that *indestructible* element in us which, says Freud, is the unconscious itself, perhaps we should continue calling it the unconscious – so long as we do not forget that the word is the index of an enigma – because the term retains, like the algae or the stone one drags up, something of the sea from which it was taken." The essay also contains a reference to "Doctor Lacan," applauding him for going "beyond the limits of a philosophy of consciousness" and for thus "retracing the steps of a phenomenology which is deepening itself."

29   *Zollikoner Seminare*, pp. 123, 133, 139, 160.

30   Merleau-Ponty, "Phenomenology and Psychoanalysis", p. 85. The paucity of references to "nature" in *Being and Time* has been duly noted by Graham Parkes who finds it "indeed disappointing that Heidegger failed to elaborate" on the notion in that work; see his "Thoughts on the Way: *Being and Time* via Lao-Chuang", in Parkes, ed., *Heidegger and Asian Thought* (Honolulu: University of Hawaii Press, 1987), p. 116. Parkes cites a "rather cryptic footnote" contained in an essay of 1929 which differentiates nature both from beings-at-hand and beings-to-hand: "The decisive thing is that nature lets itself be encountered neither in the surroundings of the environment (*Umwelt*) nor primarily as something to which we relate. Nature is originally manifest in *Dasein* insofar as the latter exists as disposed-attuned

(*befindlich-gestimmt*) in the midst of what-is." See Heidegger, "Vom Wesen des Grundes", in *Wegmarken* (Frankfurt-Main: Klostermann, 1967), pp. 51–2, note 55; tr. by Terrence Malik as *The Essence of Reasons* (Evanston: Northwestern University Press, 1969), pp. 80–83, note 55.

31 *Zollikoner Seminare*, pp. 129, 143; also Heidegger, "The Question Concerning Technology", in David F. Krell, ed., *Martin Heidegger: Basic Writings* (New York: Harper & Row, 1977) p. 293. Regarding the status of nature in Heidegger's work see the instructive essay by Manfred Riedel, "Naturhermeneutik und Ethik im Denken Heideggers", *Heidegger Studies*, vol. 5 (1989), pp. 153–72.

32 Merleau-Ponty, "Phenomenology and Psychoanalysis", p. 83.

Index